ROBERT F. KANABY, Publisher
Mary E. Struckhoff, Editor
NFHS Publications

To maintain the sound traditions of this sport, encourage sportsmanship and
minimize the inherent risk of injury, the National Federation of State High
School Associations writes playing rules for varsity competition among student-
athletes of high school age. High school coaches, officials and administrators
who have knowledge and experience regarding this particular sport and age
group volunteer their time to serve on the rules committee. Member associations
of the NFHS independently make decisions regarding compliance with or
modification of these playing rules for the student-athletes in their respective
states.

NFHS rules are used by education-based and non-education-based organizations
serving children of varying skill levels who are of high school age and younger. In
order to make NFHS rules skill-level and age-level appropriate, the rules may be
modified by any organization that chooses to use them. Except as may be
specifically noted in this rules book, the NFHS makes no recommendation about
the nature or extent of the modifications that may be appropriate for children who
are younger or less skilled than high school varsity athletes.

Every individual using these rules is responsible for prudent judgment with
respect to each contest, athlete and facility, and each athlete is responsible for
exercising caution and good sportsmanship. These rules should be interpreted
and applied so as to make reasonable accommodations for disabled athletes,
coaches and officials.

2009-10 High School Basketball Rules by Topic

Published jointly by the National Federation of State High School
Associations, Referee Enterprises, Inc., and the National Association of
Sports Officials.

NATIONAL FEDERATION OF
STATE HIGH SCHOOL
ASSOCIATIONS
P.O. Box 690
Indianapolis, IN 46206
Phone: 317-972-6900
Fax: 317-822-5700
www.nfhs.org

REI/NASO
P.O. Box 161
Franksville, WI 53126
Phone: 262-632-8855
Fax: 262-632-5460
www.referee.com
www.naso.org

ISBN-13: 978-1-58208-117-5

Printed in the United States of America

Table of Contents

Introduction

Rules by Topic is a collection of information like no other.

Combining numerous NFHS educational elements into one collective resource will improve rules understanding and retention.

Included in the book:

Rules — Official NFHS rules book language and references are linked, combining related items by topic. That way, all related items are found in one location, from definitions to penalties.

Case plays — Taken right from the NFHS case book, related case plays are imbedded within the topic for easy reference.

Rationales — The reasons behind the rules are included, used from previous years' Comments on the Rules and rule change summaries. You not only see the rule, you learn the reason behind it.

Fundamentals — Related rules book fundamentals are connected to the specific topic.

In Simple Terms — Summary statements that take complex rules and make them easier to understand are found throughout the book.

Did You Know? — Historical tidbits provide basis for the rules as written today.

Signals — Thumbnail images of the correct signals are connected to penalties for easy reference.

Rules by Topic is designed to complement the official NFHS publications. While not replacing the rules book and case book, *Rules by Topic* offers a different way to learn the rules. Some rules and case plays are repeated because they apply to more than one topic.

Rules by Topic will change the way you look at rules and will greatly enhance your rules knowledge.

Topic 1

Court and Equipment

Key Terms

The playing court shall be a rectangular surface free from obstructions and dimensions not greater than 94 feet in length by 50 feet in width (1-1).

The frontcourt of a team consists of that part of the court between its end line and the nearer edge of the division line, including its basket and the inbounds part of the backboard (4-13-1). The backcourt of a team consists of the rest of the court, including the entire division line and the opponent's basket and inbounds part of the opponent's backboard (4-13-2).

A team's own basket is the one into which players try to throw or tap the ball (4-5-1).

Boundary lines of the court consist of end lines and sidelines (4-9-1). The inside edges of these lines define the inbounds and out-of-bounds areas (4-9-2).

Topic:
The Playing Court

The playing court shall be a rectangular surface free from obstructions and with dimensions not greater than 94 feet in length by 50 feet in width. IDEAL MEASUREMENTS ARE: High School Age – 84 by 50 feet. These are the dimensions for the playing court only (1-1).

Topic:
Lines

Sidelines and End Lines

The playing court shall be marked with sidelines, end lines and other lines. There shall be at least 3 feet (and preferably 10 feet) of unobstructed space outside boundaries. The sidelines and end lines shall be a minimum of 2 inches in width (1-2-1).

If, on an unofficial court, there is less than 3 feet of unobstructed space outside any sideline or end line, a narrow broken line shall be marked on the court parallel with and 3 feet inside that boundary. This restraining line becomes the boundary line during a throw-in on that side or end. It continues to be the boundary until the ball crosses the line (1-2-2).

Center Restraining Circle and Dividing Line

A 2-inch wide restraining circle shall be drawn at the center of the court with a radius of 6 feet measured to the outside edge. Spaces for nonjumpers around the center restraining circle are 36 inches deep (1-3-1).

A division line 2 inches wide, shall divide the court into two equal parts. If the court is less than 74 feet long, it should be divided by two lines, each parallel to and 40 feet from the farther end line (1-3-2).

COMMENT: Border lines that are the natural color of the court are permissible. The area within these lines need not be one color, but the continuous 2-inch wide outline must be clearly visible to the officials. If the floor has a logo in the center of the court, that logo should not distract from the visibility of the center line or center circle.

Dividing Line: Caseplay

1.3.2 SITUATION: A team mascot logo is painted in the center restraining circle. The host school used multi-colored paint for the continuous lines over the team mascot logo in the center restraining circle. **RULING:** The area within these lines need not be of one color, but the continuous line must be clearly visible.

In Simple Terms

A solid or shadow-bordered 2-inch wide line is permissible. A shadow line is a line that designates the required 2-inch width by use of border or outline lines at least 1/4 inch wide. It shows where the line actually is.

Three-Point Line

A three-point field-goal line, 2 inches wide in the form of a semicircle, shall be drawn at each end of the court as shown on the appended court diagram. The semicircle has a radius of 19 feet 9 inches from a point in the middle of the free-throw lane directly below the center of the basket to the outside edge of the line. The semicircle shall be extended with a 2-inch wide line perpendicular to the end line, the length of which shall be 63 inches from the inside edge of the end line (1-4-1). The three-point field-goal line shall be the same color as the free-throw lane boundary lines and free-throw semicircle (1-4-2).

Free-Throw Lane

A free-throw lane, 12 feet wide measured to the outside of each lane boundary, and the semicircle with the free-throw line as a diameter, shall be marked at each end of the court with dimensions and markings as shown on the appended court diagram. All lines designating the free-throw lane, but not lane-space marks and neutral-zone marks, are part of the lane (1-5-1).

The lane-space marks (2 inches by 8 inches) and neutral-zone marks (12 inches by 8 inches) identify areas which extend 36 inches from the outer edge of the lane lines toward the sidelines. There are four lane spaces on each lane boundary line (1-5-2).

Free-Throw Line

A free-throw line, 2 inches wide, shall be drawn across both circles, which have an outside radius of 6 feet as shown on the appended court diagram. It shall be parallel to the end line and shall have its farthest edge 15 feet from the plane of the face of the backboard (1-6-1).

Topic:
Court Equipment

Backboards

The backboards shall be the same size at both ends of the court. The backboard shall be one of three types: (1) a rectangle 6 feet horizontally and 4 feet vertically; or (2) a rectangle 6 feet horizontally and 3 1/2 feet vertically; or (3) a fan-shaped backboard, 54-inches wide and with dimensions as shown on the diagram (1-7-1).

Each of the backboards shall be of any rigid material. The front surface shall be flat and, unless it is transparent, it shall be white. Tinted glass backboards are prohibited beginning with those manufactured after January 1, 1995 (1-7-2).

If the backboard is transparent, it shall be marked as follows: A rectangle shall be centered behind the ring and marked by a 2-inch white

---

In Simple Terms

It is not legal to paint a fan-shaped board on a rectangular backboard.

---

line. The rectangle shall have outside dimensions of 24 inches horizontally and 18 inches vertically. For the rectangular backboard, the top edge of the baseline shall be level with the ring. For the fan-shaped backboard, the baseline shall be omitted, and the two vertical lines shall be extended to the bottom of the backboard. The rectangular target in a bright orange or black color may be used on a nontransparent backboard. The border of the backboard shall be marked with a white line. The border shall be 3 inches or less in width (1-7-3).

Either type backboard may be transparent or nontransparent. No logo, marking, lettering, etc., is permitted on the backboard, backboard padding, or basket (1-7-4).

Each backboard shall be midway between the sidelines, with the plane of its front face perpendicular to the floor, parallel to the end line, and 4 feet from it (1-8-1). The upper edge of the backboard shall be 13 feet above the floor for the rectangular, and 12 feet 8 inches for the fan-shaped. The backboard shall be protected from spectators to a distance of at least 3 feet at each end (1-8-2).

Backboard Padding and Support Systems

The bottom and each side of the all-rectangular backboards shall be padded with a poly high-carb vinyl-type material that meets the Bashor resilience test with a range of 20-30. The padding must cover the bottom surface of the board and the side surface to a distance of 15 inches up from the bottom. The front and back surfaces must be covered to a minimum distance of 3/4 inch from the bottom of the backboard. The padding shall be 1 inch thick from the front and back surfaces of the backboard. The material shall be 2 inches from the bottom edge of the backboard. It is recommended that the padding be mounted on the backboard by adhesive or material such as Velcro, channel, etc. The padding shall be a single, solid color and shall be the same color on both backboards (1-9-1).

Any backboard support behind the backboard and at a height of less than 9 feet above the floor shall be padded on the bottom surface to a distance of 2 feet from the face of the backboard. All portable backstops must have the bases padded to a height of 7 feet on the court-side surface (1-9-2).

As below and behind backboards, all support systems should be at least 8 feet behind the plane of the backboard face and at a height of 7 feet or more above the floor (1-9-3).

Any backboard support, all of which is not directly behind the backboard, should be at least 6 inches behind it if the support extends above the top and at least 2 feet behind it if the support extends beyond the side. Any overhead backboard support structure which must be forward-braced due to space limitations, architectural or structural restraints, shall meet the following requirements: A front, diagonal-brace system must be located above a line extending upward and into the playing court at a maximum 45-degree angle from a point on a vertical line located a minimum of 6 inches behind the front side of the backboard at a minimum height of 4 feet 6 inches above the basket ring (1-9-4).

Backboard Padding and Support Systems: Caseplay

1.9.1 SITUATION: What are the rule requirements for padding on rectangular backboards? RULING: The rule provides that all rectangular backboards shall be padded with material at least 2 inches thick on the bottom and side edges and extend a distance of 15 inches up the sides from the bottom. The edges of the board on front and back must be padded on the bottom and 15 inches up the sides with at least 1-inch-thick padding that extends ? inch up or in from the edge. The padding may be any single, solid color, but shall be the same color on both backboards.

Topic:
Basket

Basket Size and Net

Each basket shall consist of a single metal ring, 18 inches in inside diameter, its flange and braces, and a white-cord 12-mesh net, 15 to 18 inches in length, suspended from beneath the ring (1-10-1).

Each ring shall not be more than 5/8 inch in diameter, with the possible addition of small-gauge loops on the bottom edge for attaching a 12-mesh net. The ring and its attaching flange and braces shall be bright orange in color (1-10-2).

The cord of the net shall be not less than 120-thread nor more than 144-thread twine, or plastic material of comparable dimensions with no additional extensions. It shall be constructed to momentarily check the ball as it passes through (1-10-3).

Basket Direction

Each team's basket for practice before the game and for the first half shall be the one farther from its team bench (4-5-2). The teams shall change baskets for the second half (4-5-3).

If by mistake the officials permit a team to go the wrong direction, when discovered all points scored, fouls committed, and time consumed shall count as if each team had gone the proper direction. Play shall resume with each team going the proper direction based on bench location (4-5-4).

Basket Ring

Each basket ring shall be securely attached to the backboard/support system with a ring-restraining device. Such a device shall ensure that the basket stays attached in the event a glass backboard breaks. Each basket ring shall have its upper edge 10 feet above and parallel to the floor and shall be equidistant from the vertical edges of the backboard. The nearest point of the inside edge of the ring shall be 6 inches from the plane of the face of the backboard (1-11-1).

Movable and nonmovable rings are legal. Movable basket rings shall have rebound characteristics similar to those of nonmovable rings. The pressure-release mechanism should ensure these characteristics, as well as protect both the ring and backboard. The design of the ring and its construction should ensure player safety (1-11-2).

For those rings with a lock/release mechanism, the pressure-release mechanism must not disengage until a static load of 230 pounds has been applied to the top of the ring at the most distant point from the backboard. The pressure-release mechanism must be preset by the manufacturer at the required static-load setting and may be sealed or field adjustable. When released, the ring shall not rotate more than 30 degrees below the original horizontal position. After release and with the load no longer applied, the ring shall return automatically and instantaneously to the original position (1-11-3).

Topic:
The Ball

The ball shall have its color be the approved orange shade or natural color (1-12-1a). It shall be spherical (1-12-1b). It shall have a deeply-pebbled cover with horizontally shaped panels bonded tightly to the rubber carcass (1-12-1c).

The circumference shall be within a minimum of 291/2 inches to a maximum of 30 inches for high school boys' competition or within a minimum of 281/2 inches to a maximum of 29 inches for high school girls' competition (1-12-1d 1&2).

The weight shall be within a minimum of 20 ounces to a maximum of 22 ounces for high school boys' competition or within a minimum of 18 ounces to a maximum of 20 ounces for high school girls' competition (1-12-1e 1&2).

The black rubber rib separating the panels shall not exceed 1/4 inch in width (1-12-1f). The ball shall include the NFHS Authenticating Mark (1-12-1g).

The ball shall be inflated to an air pressure such that when it is dropped to the playing surface from a height of 6 feet, measured to the bottom of the ball, it shall rebound to a height, measured to the top of the ball, of not less than 49 inches when it strikes on its least resilient spot, nor more than 54 inches when it strikes on its most resilient spot (1-12-2).

The home team shall provide a ball which meets the specifications. The referee shall be the sole judge of the legality of the ball and may select a ball provided by the visiting team (1-12-3).

The Ball: Caseplay

1.12.3 SITUATION: The game ball supplied by the home team does not have the NFHS Authenticating Mark. The visiting team does have a ball with the NFHS Authenticating Mark. Must the referee accept the visitor's approved ball for game use? **RULING:** Yes, the home team shall provide a ball that meets specifications in order for it to be used. The referee shall be the sole judge of the legality of the ball and may select a ball provided by the visiting team. A current list of NFHS Authenticating Mark balls can be found on the NFHS Web site.

Topic:

Team Bench Locations and Coaching Box

The location of each team's bench shall be designated by game management. It is recommended that the benches for team members and coaches of both teams be placed along that side of the court on which the scorer's and timer's table is located (1-13-1).

The coaching box shall be outlined outside the side of the court on which the scorer's and timer's table and team benches are located. The area shall be bounded by a line 28 feet from the end line, the sideline, a line no more than 14 feet from the 28-foot line toward the end line, and the team bench. These lines shall be located off the court, be 2 inches wide (1-13-2).

 Rationale

The coaching box was put in as a way for coaches to further communicate with their players. It is designed to assist coaches in communicating with players on the court.

 COMMENT: State associations may alter the length and placement of the 14-foot (maximum) coaching box.

The time-out area shall be the area inside an imaginary rectangle formed by the boundaries of the sideline (including the bench), end line, and an imaginary line extended from the free-throw lane line nearest the bench meeting an imaginary line extended from the coaching-box line (1-13-3).

Team Bench Locations and Coaching Box: Caseplays:

1.13.1 SITUATION: Upon arrival on the court, the visiting team is advised its team bench is located on the right side of the scorer's and timer's table. This location means the visiting team's substitutes will have to go considerably further than the home team to reach the reporting area. The visiting coach complains to the referee. **RULING:** The referee has no authority to move the location of either bench, unless it involves player safety. Game or home management is responsible for designating the location of the team benches. The visiting coach must accept this designation, unless player safety is involved. Obviously, it is intended that the benches be on the floor-level seats or bleachers and that the team benches be approximately the same distance from the table whenever possible. The referee should report the unusual bench location to the state association office.

1.13.2 SITUATION: Fire marshall regulations prevent the adopted 14-foot coaching box from being located at the prescribed location due to bleacher stairs. May the coaching box be located: (a) 40 by 26 feet from the end line; or (b) 22 by 8 feet from the end line? **RULING:** In (a), no. It is recommended the coaching box be 28 feet by 14 feet from the end line unless state association approval is given for an alternate location. Because of possible interference with the scorer's table, this location should not be approved. In (b), with state association approval, the coaching box may be located at a spot different from the prescribed 28 feet by 14 feet from the end line. The 22 feet by 8 feet from end line is permitted if approved by the state association.

Topic:
Other Court Equipment

Red/LED Light, Audible Signal

A red light behind each backboard or an LED light on each backboard is permitted to signal that time has expired for a quarter or extra period. In facilities without a red light behind or an LED light on each backboard, the audible timer's signal shall indicate that time has expired (1-14).

Rationale

The change permits equipment currently found in some facilities to be utilized rather than ignored. All other end-of-period rules remain intact. During their pregame responsibilities, game officials should determine if red/LED lights are present in order to adjudicate end-of-period situations properly.

Red/LED Light, Audible Signal: Caseplay

*5.6.2 SITUATION: During the pregame warm-up, the officials observe that the facility has functioning LED lights on each backboard. A1 begins the act of shooting just prior to the expiration of time in the first quarter. The covering official observes the attempt in A1's hands when the LED light is activated, but the ball appears to be out of the hands when the horn is sounded. The ball goes in the basket. RULING: No goal; the quarter expired prior to the release of the try.

 COMMENT: Red/LED lights provide a visual reference for officials to determine when a period has ended. The red/LED lights and the horn are expected to be synchronized, but since light travels faster than sound, it may appear that one follows the other. The red/LED lights give a more precise indication that a period has expired (1-14; 6-7-6).

Clock and Scoreboard

A visible game clock and scoreboard are mandatory. An alternate timing device and scoring information system shall be available in the event of malfunction (1-15).

Possession Arrow

A visible display shall be located at the scorer's and timer's table to indicate team possession for the alternating-possession procedure (1-16).

"X" Locates Scorer

An "X" 12 inches long and 2 inches wide shall be placed on the floor out of bounds directly in front of the official scorer to help substitutes with the proper location (1-17).

Music/Sound Effects/Artificial Noisemakers

The playing of music/sound effects shall only be permitted during pregame, time-outs, intermission and post-game. The use of artificial noisemakers shall be prohibited (1-18).

Music/Sound Effects/Artificial Noisemakers: Caseplay

1.18 SITUATION: In (a) the band from the home team is playing during a live ball; (b) the electronic scoreboard is playing broken-glass sound effects just after an opponent's missed field-goal attempt; or (c) fans from the visiting team are using artificial noisemakers during an opponent's attempted free throw. **RULING:** All situations are prohibited by rule. The officials should notify game management in (a) to instruct the band to only play during the permitted times; in (b) to instruct the scoreboard operator to cease the prohibited acts; and in (c) to have a public-address announcement made stating that the use of any artificial noisemakers is prohibited at all times. In all situations, if the problem continues it may result in a technical foul being assessed to the team supporter(s).

Topic:
Uniforms

Team jerseys shall include the team member's number, which shall be at least 6 inches high on the back and at least 4 inches high on the front and not less than 3/4 inch in width excluding the border (3-4-3a).

The number shall be centered vertically and horizontally (3-4-3b). The number(s) on the front and back of the team jersey shall be the same color and style (3-4-3c). Each team member shall be numbered on the front and back of the team jersey with plain Arabic numerals. The following numbers are legal: 0, 1, 2, 3, 4, 5, 00, 10, 11, 12, 13, 14, 15, 20, 21, 22, 23, 24, 25, 30, 31, 32, 33, 34, 35, 40, 41, 42, 43, 44, 45, 50, 51, 52, 53, 54, 55. A team member list shall not have both numbers 0 and 00 (3-4-3d).

No more than three colors may be used on the number. The style of the number must be clearly visible and conform to one of the following.

• A solid contrasting color with no more than two solid color 1/4-inch borders around the entire number. If the team jersey color is used as a border, it must be counted as one of the allowed colors (3-4-3e-1).

• The team jersey color itself when bordered with not more than two 1/4-inch solid border(s) contrasting with the team jersey color (3-4-3e-2).

• A solid contrasting color with a "shadow" trim of a contrasting color on part of the number not to exceed 1/2 inch in width and may be used with one 1/4-inch border(s) (3-4-3e-3).

The torso of the team jersey shall be the same single solid color for all team members (3-4-1a). The torso is the portion of the jersey from an imaginary line at the base of the neckline extending to each armhole, down to the bottom hem of the jersey and from side seam/insert to side seam/insert. The imaginary line at the base of the neckline shall not extend beyond 1? inches from the lowest point of the neckline apex/opening (3-4-1-b). The torso color shall be white for the home team and a contrasting dark color for the visiting team (3-1-4-c). There are no color/design restrictions in the area of the team jersey from the imaginary line at the base of the neckline to the shoulder seam and in the corresponding area on the back of the jersey (3-1-4-d). Side inserts, including trim/piping/accent color(s), shall be no more than 4 inches in width (2 inches on each side of seam) of any color(s) or design, centered vertically below the armpit. Side inserts for all team jerseys shall be the same width (3-1-4-e). Trim, piping or an accent color differing from the torso color shall not exceed 1 inch around the arm openings.

> ## In Simple Terms
>
> The home team shall wear white jerseys and the visiting team shall wear dark jerseys.

There are no restrictions in the area of the team jersey from the base of the neckline to the shoulder seam. (If a back panel is used, it must be of the same size and color as the corresponding front area) (3-4-7).

If used, lettering with team names and/or abbreviations or team member's names must be placed horizontally on the jersey (3-4-4-a). The lettering above a number may be arched, but the first and last letters must be on the same horizontal plane, such plane shall not be below a plane extending through the top of the number(s) (3-4-4-b). Lettering below a number must have the first and last letters on the same horizontal plane and said plane shall not be above a plane extending through the bottom of the numbers(s) (3-4-4-c). Any point on any letter shall not be closer than one inch to any point on any number(s) (3-4-4-d).

Any form of decorative accent (e.g., paw, halo, crown, star) on an identifying name or abbreviation is only permitted if the name or abbreviation is located above the number (3-4-4-e)). If a tail is used in the lettering of an identifying name or abbreviation, the name or abbreviation must be located below the number (3-4-4-f).

One commemorative/memorial patch may be worn on the jersey. The patch shall not exceed 4 square inches, shall not be a number and must be located above the neckline or in the side insert (3-4-2-c). An institutional or conference logo/mascot may be located at the apex/opening of the neckline (3-4-2-d).

Only one manufacturer's logo/trademark/reference is permitted on the uniform pants/skirt (3-4-5-a).

Undershirts shall be similar in color to the torso of the shirt and shall not have frayed or ragged edges. If the undershirt has sleeves, they shall be the same length. A visible manufacturer's logo/trademark/reference is not permitted on the undershirt (3-5-5).

Compression shorts/tights shall be a single solid color similar to the predominant color of the pants/skirt; the length shall be above the knee. Undergarments shall not extend below the pants/skirt (3-5-6).

Uniforms: Caseplays

3.4.2 SITUATION: Team B is wearing jerseys which have: (a) a small basketball patch with a No. 12 on it attached to the upper right front; or (b) a black 2-inch wide band attached around the shoulder strap. Both items are in memory of an injured teammate. **RULING:** The shirts in (a) are illegal. The penalty is a technical foul charged directly to the head coach. The shirts in (b) are legal (10-5-4).

3.4.3 SITUATION: Team A team members are wearing white jerseys. The numbers are: (a) solid red with a 1/4-inch border of green and another of blue; (b) solid blue with a 1/4-inch border of white and another of red; or (c) solid blue with a 1/4-inch border of yellow and another of blue. **RULING:** The color combinations are all legal. It is permissible to use three colors — a solid color in contrast with the shirt color and two different solid-color borders. In (b), the white border is legal and must be counted as one of the two allowable borders. The color/style of the numbers must be the same on front and back.

3.4.4 SITUATION: Team A is wearing jerseys which have: (a) the school name below the numbers with the lettering starting in the front and continuing around the side to the back; or (b) the school name above the number and the mascot name below the number. **RULING:** The shirts in (a) are illegal and the penalty is a technical foul charged directly to the head coach. Two identifying names on the front of the shirt are legal in (b) (10-5-4).

3.4.5 SITUATION: Prior to the jump ball to start the game, the officials observe that the five Team B starters are all wearing pants which have (a) a manufacturer's logo and a school's mascot which meets the proper dimension limitations; or (b) a manufacturer's logo that exceeds the limitation of 2? square inches by 2? square inches in any one dimension.

RULING: Legal uniforms in (a). In (b), illegal pants. The Team B head coach is charged directly with a technical foul. (3-6-2; 10-5-4)

Topic:
Team Member's Equipment and Other Apparel

The referee shall not permit any team member to wear equipment or apparel which, in his/her judgment, is dangerous or confusing to other players or is not appropriate (3-5-1).

Equipment which is unnatural and designed to increase a player's height or reach or to gain an advantage shall not be permitted. Equipment and apparel shall not be modified from the original manufactured state and shall be worn in the manner the manufacturer intended it to be worn (3-5-4).

Undershirts shall be similar in color to the torso of the jersey and shall be hemmed and not have frayed or ragged edges. If the undershirt has sleeves, they shall be the same length (3-5-5).

Undergarment or tights shall not extend below the pants/skirt (3-5-6). Compression shorts may be worn if the length is above the knee and they are of a single color similar to the predominant color of the pants/skirt.

Jewelry is prohibited. Religious and medical-alert medals are not considered jewelry. A religious medal must be taped and worn under the uniform. A medical-alert medal must be taped and may be visible (3-5-7).

A player not wearing the pants/skirt properly and above the hips and/or a player not tucking in a game jersey (front and back) designed to be worn inside the pants/skirt, shall be directed to leave the game (3-3-5).

The referee shall not permit any team member to participate if in his/her judgment, any item constitutes a safety concern, such as, but not limited to, a player's fingernails or hairstyle (3-7).

Team Member's Equipment and Other Apparel: Caseplays

3.3.5 SITUATION: B1 fouls A1. Just before A1 goes to the line for a one-and-one, the official observes: (a) A1 pull the shirt out of his/her pants; or (b) A1's pants being worn below the hips. **RULING:** In both (a) and (b), A1 will be directed to put the shirt in the pants or pull up the pants, and must leave the game immediately following his/her last free throw(s). The lane is cleared for the free throw and Team B is awarded the ball for a throw-in, whether or not the last free throw is successful.

3.5 SITUATION A: What are the standards which the referee must use in determining whether a team member will be permitted to wear certain equipment? **RULING:** There are three criteria which determine the legality of equipment. First, any equipment which, in the judgment of the referee, is dangerous to others. In this respect, elbow, wrist, hand, finger or forearm guard, cast or brace made of hard and unyielding leather, plaster, pliable (soft) plastic, metal or any other hard substance shall always be declared illegal "even though covered with soft padding." Thus, the rule does not permit that this provision be set aside. The prohibition of the use of hard substance material does not apply to the upper arm, or shoulder if the hard material is appropriately padded so that in the judgment of the referee it is not hazardous to others. Knee and ankle braces are permitted, but all exposed hinges must be covered. Equipment which could cut or cause an opponent to have an abrasion is also always illegal and, therefore, is prohibited.

It will be noted that the listing of equipment which is always illegal is not inclusive. It cannot identify every item which is not permitted. The generalization is required since the referee's judgment is necessary. The second standard provides that "any equipment which is unnatural and designed to increase the player's height or reach, or to gain an advantage, shall not be used." The referee is given no leeway here and judgment is not required. The third criterion provides that equipment used must be appropriate for basketball and not be confusing. In this sense, gloves, football face masks and helmets are not acceptable. A protector for a broken nose, even though made of hard material, is permissible if it does not extend so as to endanger others, if it is not sharp and if it has no cutting edges. Eyeglass protectors are considered appropriate equipment for basketball provided they meet the qualifications for legal equipment, including the third criterion.

Religious and medical-alert medals are not considered jewelry and may be worn provided: 1) religious medals are taped and worn under the uniform, necklaces/bracelets must be removed or also taped and completely under the uniform; and 2) medical-alert medals are taped to the body (portions may be visible to show medical information), necklaces/bracelets must be removed or also completely taped. An artificial limb may not be worn unless it has been specifically approved by the state association and such authorization statement is available to the referee.

The referee must rule on the legality of any piece of equipment which is worn to protect an injury. Protective equipment must be individually inspected and approved using the criteria outlined. In the case of headwear for medical, cosmetic or religious reasons, the state association may approve upon proper documentation.

3.5 SITUATION B: The officials are on the court prior to the game observing the team warm-ups. One official notices that a member of Team A is wearing a decorative necklace. **RULING:** The official should inform the team member to remove the jewelry immediately. Upon compliance, the team member may continue to warm up with his or her teammates and may start the game without penalty.

3.5 SITUATION C: May a team member wear: (a) shoes which have a light mechanism or have lights which are activated by heel contact with the floor; or (b) gloves? **RULING:** No, in both (a) and (b). In (a), the shoes may be worn if the lights are deactivated. In (b), gloves are not needed to play the game and are not considered to be appropriate.

*3.5.5 SITUATION: Prior to the opening jump, an official notices A1 is wearing an undershirt with sleeves cut off and hemmed at the shoulders. A2 and A3 are both wearing undershirts with normal length sleeves. All undershirts are similar in color to the game jersey. **RULING:** All players are wearing legal apparel. The rule does not require all players to wear the same length sleeves on their undershirts, but each individual player must have sleeves the same length on his/her undershirt when worn.

3.5.6 SITUATION A: Substitute A6 is beckoned and enters the court to replace A1. A6 is wearing: (a) compression shorts below the game pants which extend below the knees; (b) cut-off jeans extending below the game pants; or (c) jewelry. **RULING:** The items in (a), (b) and (c) are illegal and A6 will not be allowed to participate while wearing the items. No penalty is involved. A6 simply cannot participate until the illegal items are removed (3-5-6).

3.5.6 SITUATION B: A player, for religious reasons, may not wear shorts. Would he/she be able to wear tights under the basketball uniform shorts, warm-ups or a skirt instead of shorts? **RULING:** NFHS basketball uniform rules do not require that the uniform pants be "shorts." However, undergarments or tights may not be worn which extend below the pants, therefore wearing tights "below the uniform shorts" would be illegal. The player could wear long pants or a skirt as the uniform "bottom" and be in compliance (3-4).

Guards, Casts, Braces and Compression Sleeves

Guards, casts, braces and compression sleeves must meet the following guidelines:

- A guard, cast or brace made of hard and unyielding leather, plaster, pliable (soft) plastic, metal or any other hard substance may not be worn on the elbow, hand, finger/thumb, wrist or forearm; even though covered with soft padding (3-5-2a).

- Hard and unyielding items (guards, casts, braces, etc.) on the upper arm or shoulder must be padded (3-5-2b).

- Knee and ankle braces are permitted but all exposed hinges must be covered. Most over-sleeves recommended by manufacturers are acceptable. These braces may be padded or unpadded (3-5-2c).

- Guards, casts braces or compression sleeves must be worn for medical reasons (3-5-2d).

 COMMENT: Each state association may authorize the use of artificial limbs which in its opinion are no more dangerous to players than the corresponding human limb and do not place an opponent at a disadvantage.

Sweatbands, Headwear and Head Decorations

Sweatbands, headwear and head decorations must meet the following guidelines:

- Headbands and sweatbands must be white, black, beige or a single solid color similar to the torso of the jersey and must be the same color for each item and all participants (3-5-3a).

- A headband is any item that goes around the entire head. If worn, only one headband is permitted, it must be worn on the forehead/crown, it must be nonabrasive and unadorned and it must be a maximum of 2 inches (3-5-3b).

- If worn, only one sweatband is permitted on each wrist, each must be worn on the arm below the elbow, each must be each must be moisture-absorbing, nonabrasive and unadorned, and each must be a maximum of 4 inches (3-5-3c).

- Rubber, cloth or elastic bands may be used to control hair. Hard items, including, but not limited to, beads, barrettes and bobby pins, are prohibited (3-5-3d).

• Head decorations and headwear, except those specified above, are prohibited (3-5-3e).

 COMMENT: State associations may on an individual basis permit a player to participate while wearing a head covering if it meets the following criteria:

• For medical or cosmetic reasons – In the event a participant is required by a licensed medical physician to cover his/her head with a covering or wrap, the physician's statement is required before the state association can approve a covering or wrap which is not abrasive, hard or dangerous to any other player and which is attached in such a way it is highly unlikely that it will come off during play (3-5-3 exception a).

• For religious reasons – In the event there is documented evidence provided to the state association that a participant may not expose his/her uncovered head, the state association may approve a covering or wrap which is not abrasive, hard or dangerous to any other player and which is attached in such a way it is highly unlikely it will come off during play (3-5-3 exception b).

Sweatbands, Headwear and Head Decorations: Caseplays

*3.5.3 SITUATION A: The predominate color of the Team A jerseys are red. Prior to the game, an official notices that A1 is wearing (a) a black headband and black wristbands; (b) beige pre-wrap around the entire head; and (c) beige pre-wrap around the entire head and red wristbands. **RULING:** Legal in (a) and (b). Illegal equipment in (c); the headband color does not match the wristband color. The official shall inform the player and the head coach that these items are illegal and may not be worn during the game.

*3.5.3 SITUATION B: The predominate color of the Team A jerseys are white. Prior to the game, an official notices that A1 is wearing a multi-colored hair-control device that does not go entirely around the head and A2 is wearing a black "scrunchie" to control the hair and beige pre-wrap around the entire head. **RULING:** Legal equipment provided all Team A members are wearing beige-colored headbands and wristbands.

*3.5.3 SITUATION C: The predominate color of the Team A jerseys are royal blue. Substitute A6 is beckoned onto the court to replace A1. A6 attempts to enter (a) wearing red pre-wrap as a pony-tail holder and royal blue wristbands; (b) wearing red pre-wrap around the entire head and royal blue wristbands. **RULING:** Legal in (a); red pre-wrap used to control the hair that does not go around the entire head is permissible. Illegal in (b); pre-wrap that goes around the entire head must be white, black, beige or the predominate color of the team jersey.

Topic:
Logos and Trademarks

One visible manufacturer's logo/trademark/reference or school logo/mascot is permitted on the sweatbands, headbands and compression shorts (3-6-1). The size shall be limited to 2 1/4 square inches and shall not exceed 2 1/4 inches in any dimension on each item (3-6-2).

Logos and Trademarks: Caseplays

3.6.1 SITUATION: A6 enters the game with an excessive manufacturer's logo/trade-mark on his/her: (a) socks; or (b) wristbands. **RULING:** Legal in (a). In (b), A6 may not participate and is directed to return to the bench until legally equipped.

 COMMENT: The restriction on visible manufacturer's logo size is in effect on pants/skirts, compression shorts, wristbands and headbands. The shoes and socks are not considered part of the uniform for purpose of visible logo size.

Topic 2

Players, Substitutes and Coaches

Key Terms

A player is one of five team members who are legally on the court at any given time, except intermission (4-34-1).

A substitute becomes a player when he/she legally enters the court. If entry is not legal, the substitute becomes a player when the ball becomes live. A player becomes bench personnel after his/her substitute becomes a player or after notification of the coach following his/her disqualification (3-3-3; 4-34-3).

Topic:
Starters

A team must begin the game with five players, but if it has no substitutes to replace disqualified or injured players, it must continue with fewer than five. When there is only one player participating for a team, the team shall forfeit the game, unless the referee believes that team has an opportunity to win the game (3-1-1 Note).

At least 10 minutes before the scheduled starting time, each team shall supply the official scorer with the name and number of each team member and designate the five starting players. Failure to comply results in a technical foul (3-2-1; 10-1-1 Penalty).

After the 10-minute time limit specified, a team is charged with a maximum of one technical foul regardless of how many times it changes a designated starter, unless necessitated by illness, injury, illegal equipment or apparel, etc., or to attempt a technical-foul free throw (3-2-2; 10-1-2 Penalty).

After the 10-minute time limit specified, a team is charged with a maximum of one technical foul regardless of how many times it adds a name to the team member list; requires the scorer to change a team member's or player's number in the scorebook; requires a player to change to the number in the scorebook; or it has identical numbers on team members and/or players (3-2-2a through e; 10-1-2 Penalty).

> ### In Simple Terms
> The official scorebook shall remain at the table throughout the game and during halftime to eliminate the appearance of any improprieties.

Scorer Duties
The scorer shall keep a record of the names and numbers of players who are to start the game and of all substitutes who enter the game (2-

11-1) and notify the nearer official when there is an infraction of the rules pertaining to submission of the roster, substitutions or numbers of players (2-11-2).

It is recommended the team member's numbers be entered into the scorebook in numerical order (2-11-1 Note).

Starters: Caseplays

3.1.1 SITUATION: After six players have been disqualified, Team A has only four who are eligible to continue in the game as players. In a gesture of fair play, the coach of Team B indicates a desire to withdraw a player so that each team will have four players on the court. **RULING:** This is not permissible. Team B must have five players participating as long as it has that number available. If no substitute is available, a team must continue with fewer than five players. When only one player remains to participate, that team shall forfeit the game unless the referee believes this team still has an opportunity to win the game.

3.2 SITUATION A: Seven minutes before the scheduled starting time for the game, Team A presents its team roster and its starting lineup to the scorer and then, at six minutes prior to the game starting time, Team A presents two additional names to the scorer for the team list. **RULING:** Team A is assessed one technical foul for the violation of not presenting its team member list nor designating its starting lineup at least 10 minutes prior to the scheduled game starting time. Team A is also assessed one technical foul for the two names which were added to its team roster six minutes prior to game starting time (10-1-1, 2).

3.2 SITUATION B: A1, who is designated as a starter 10 minutes prior to the scheduled starting time of the game, becomes ill or is injured before the game starts. **RULING:** A1 may be replaced without penalty as illness or injury is considered to be an extenuating and unavoidable situation which permits a substitution. A1 would be permitted to enter the game later (10-1-2a).

3.2.2 SITUATION A: Team A properly submits its team member list and designates its five starters. However, the number for each team member is erroneously indicated. The error is not detected until after the game has started. **RULING:** Only one team technical foul is charged regardless of the number of players and substitutes not wearing the number indicated in the scorebook. Each player must wear the number indicated in the scorebook or change the scorebook number to that which he/she is wearing. Any substitutes who become players and require the changing of the number indicated for them in the scorebook will not result in a penalty as the one maximum technical has already been charged to the team for an administrative infraction (10-1-1 Penalty).

3.2.2 SITUATION B: Three minutes before the game starts, it is discovered: (a) two Team B members have wrong numbers in the scorebook; or (b) two Team B team members are wearing the same number. **RULING:** In (a), if either or both team member's number is changed in the scorebook, one technical foul is charged to Team B. If there is no request for change or if neither becomes a player, thus avoiding the change, there is no penalty. In (b), a technical foul is charged to Team B upon discovery of the identical numbers. Only one team member may wear a given number; the other must change to a number not already in use before participating (10-1-2).

*3.2.2 SITUATION C: Team A substitute No. 25 reports to the table for the first time with approximately one minute remaining in the second quarter and is beckoned onto the court. In (a), the ball is put in play by a throw-in from A1 to A2. The horn sounds and the scorer informs the officials that No. 25 is not listed in the scorebook. In (b), No. 25 plays the remainder of the second quarter. During halftime intermission, the official scorer realizes No. 25 is not listed in the scorebook and informs the officials when they return to the court before the start of the third quarter. **RULING:** In (a), No. 25 is currently in the game and became a player when he/she legally entered the court. Since his or her name and number must now be entered into the scorebook, a technical foul is charged to Team A. In (b), no penalty is assessed since No. 25 is not currently in the game. If No. 25 attempts to enter the game in the second half, his or her name and number will be added to the scorebook and a technical foul charged to Team A (3-2-2b; 10-1-2b).

3.2.2 SITUATION D: It is discovered that all Team A members are wearing different shirt numbers than those entered in the scorebook. This discovery is made: (a) three minutes prior to the scheduled starting time; or (b) as the teams take positions prior to the jump to start the game. Is there a penalty? **RULING:** In both (a) and (b), a maximum of one technical foul is charged to Team A, regardless of how many players or squad members are involved. The correct numbers will be entered in the scorebook (10-1-2c Penalty).

3.2.2 SITUATION E: Team A properly submits its team member list and designates the five starters as required at least 10 minutes before the scheduled start of the game. Anytime thereafter, either before the game starts or during the game, the coach asks the scorer to change a number in the scorebook: (a) so it corresponds to what the team member is wearing; (b) because a player's shirt has excessive blood on it; or (c) because a player's shirt is torn. **RULING:** In (a), a technical foul is charged to Team A. In (b) and (c), the shirt is changed and the number change made in the scorebook without any penalty.

*3.2.2 SITUATION F: Team A designates No. 32 as a starter by the 10-minute time frame prior to the game. In (a), as the teams take the floor for the opening jump ball, the scorer recognizes that No. 34 is on court instead of No. 32 for Team A and notifies the officials. In (b), following about two minutes of play in the first quarter, a time-out is called. The scorer notifies the officials that although Team A No. 32 was a designated starter, No. 34 started instead and is still in the game. **RULING:** In (a), if Team A's coach replaces No. 34 for the correct designated starter, No. 32, no penalty is assessed. If Team A's coach elects to start the game with No. 34 instead of No. 32, a technical foul is assessed to Team A for changing a designated starter. In (b), no penalty is assessed. The infraction had to be discovered and penalized before the ball became live to start the game. Once the ball became live, it was too late to penalize for this specific infraction (3-2-2a; 10-1-2a Penalty).

10.1.2 SITUATION: (a) Three minutes prior to the start of the game; or (b) during a time-out in the second quarter of play, the Team B coach requests the scorer to add a name to the team list or change a team member's number in the scorebook. When is the penalty invoked for this administrative infraction? **RULING:** The infraction occurs when the scorer is advised to add to or change the scorebook. The technical foul must be charged when it occurs and enforced when the ball next becomes live. Once the ball has become live, it is too late to penalize.

Topic:
Bench Personnel/Team Members

Bench personnel are all individuals who are part of or affiliated with a team, including, but not limited to: substitutes, coaches, manager(s) and statistician(s). During an intermission, all team members are bench personnel (4-34-2).

A team member is a member of bench personnel who is in uniform and is eligible to become a player (4-34-4). A player becomes bench personnel after his/her substitute becomes a player or after notification of the coach following his/her disqualification (3-3-3; 4-34-3).

Bench Personnel/Team Members: Caseplays

3.3.1 SITUATION E: Substitutes A6, A7 and A8 report only their own numbers to the scorer for entry. The substitutes are beckoned into the game by an official and enter the court. Before their replacements leave the court, a fight breaks out with five (of the eight on-court) players from Team A and three players from Team B involved. **RULING:** Substitutes become players when they legally enter the court; in this case, when the official beckoned them onto the court. The players being replaced by A6, A7 and A8 were not known at the time of the fight to determine what players would be classified as "bench personnel." The officials and scorer shall make an effort to determine who substitutes A6, A7 and A8 were replacing when the fight broke out. If the players being replaced by the substitutes cannot be determined, the only recourse the officials have to determine what penalties to assess the head coach for the involvement of bench personnel is to assess the maximum penalty. Of the five Team A players involved, assume three were bench personnel and assess three indirect technical fouls to the head coach, which results in ejection. Team B would also be awarded four free throws (two for each additional player involved in the fight). All participants are disqualified for flagrant fouls. Play would be resumed with a Team B throw-in from the division line opposite the scorer's table (10-3-9 Penalty; 10-4-1h Penalty; 2-3).

> ## In Simple Terms
>
> In all technical foul situations involving bench personnel, the head coach is also charged indirectly. For states utilizing the coaching box, an indirect technical foul means the coach loses the opportunity to stand.

3.4.15 SITUATION A: After the horn sounds to end the first half, A1 removes his/her jersey near the team bench. **RULING:** A technical foul is charged to A1 and an indirect technical foul is charged to the head coach; A1 is considered bench personnel in this situation (10-3-7).

4.34.1 SITUATION: Team A calls a time-out; at the conclusion of the time-out as the teams are returning to the court, A1 curses at the game officials. **RULING:** A1 is assessed a technical foul. The foul will count as one of A1's fouls toward disqualification and toward the team foul count.

 COMMENT: During a time-out, A1 is considered a player and not bench personnel.

4.34.2 SITUATION: The third quarter ends and as the teams are heading to their respective benches, team members A1 and B1 verbally taunt one another. **RULING:** Double technical foul charged to A1 and B1. During the intermission between quarters, all team members are bench personnel. Both head coaches are indirectly charged with technical fouls and lose their coaching box privileges. Play will resume at the point of interruption, which is an alternating-possession arrow throw-in, to begin the fourth quarter. (10-4-1c Penalty; 10-5 Note 1)

4.34.3 SITUATION: Substitute A6 reports to the scorer to replace player A1 and awaits entry to the game. The U2 beckons A6 onto the court, and (a) A6 enters the court to participate; (b) A6 enters the court and commits an unsporting, non-contact foul; or (c) A1 swears at the official while heading to the bench. **RULING:** A6 became a player upon being beckoned by the official and entering the court. Legal in (a). In (b) A6, now a player, is penalized with a technical foul which is added to the team foul total. In (c) A1, now bench personnel, is penalized with a technical foul, which is added to the team foul total and also charged as an indirect technical foul to the head coach.

10.3.3 SITUATION E: Only a few seconds remain in the second quarter. Team A is advancing the ball from backcourt to frontcourt. A1 is driving toward his/her basket and is about to dunk the ball when the signal indicates the end of the first half. Shortly after the signal, A1 dunks the ball and hangs on to the rim. **RULING:** A1 is assessed a technical foul for dunking a dead ball. The foul is also charged indirectly to the head coach since A1 is considered bench personnel. The third quarter begins with Team B being awarded two free throws and the ball at the division line. The alternating-possession arrow is not affected and remains unchanged (4-34-2; 5-6-2 Exception 4).

10.4.1 SITUATION B: At halftime, as the teams, coaches, and officials are making their way through a hallway to the dressing room, a Team A member verbally abuses one of the officials. **RULING:** A technical foul is charged to the team member and is also charged indirectly to the head coach. During intermission all team members are bench personnel and are penalized accordingly. If the conduct is flagrant, the team member shall be disqualified.

10.4.1 SITUATION C: After the signal sounds to end the first half, A1 removes his/her jersey near the team bench. **RULING:** A technical foul is charged to A1 and an indirect technical foul is charged to the head coach; A1 is considered bench personnel in this situation.

Topic:
Captains

Each team consists of five players, one of whom is the captain (3-1-1). The captain is the representative of his/her team and may address an official on matters of interpretation or to obtain essential information, if it is done in a courteous manner. Any player may address an official to request a time-out or permission to leave the court (3-1-2).

The officials shall notify the captains when play is about to begin at the start of the game (2-7-1).

A captain may request a defensive match-up if three or more substitutes from the same team enter during an opportunity to substitute (3-3-1e).

Topic:
Unconscious/Injured/Bleeding Player

A player who has been injured to the extent that the coach or any other bench personnel is beckoned and/or comes onto the court shall be directed to leave the game, unless a time-out is requested by, and granted to, his/her team and the situation can be corrected by the end of the time-out (3-3-6).

A player who is bleeding, has an open wound, has any amount of blood on his/her uniform, or has blood on his/her person, shall be directed to leave the game until the bleeding is stopped, the wound is covered, the uniform and/or body is appropriately cleaned, and/or the uniform is changed before returning to competition unless a time-out is requested by, and granted to, his/her team and the situation can be corrected by the end of the time-out (3-3-7).

If players from both teams are directed to leave the game because of injury/blood, both teams must request and be granted a time-out in order to keep each player in the game (3-3-6; 3-3-7 Note).

A player who has been determined by the official to be apparently unconscious shall not return to play in the game without written authorization from a physician (MD/DO) (2-8-5; 3-3-8).

The referee shall not permit any team member to participate if in his/her judgment, any item, such as, but not limited to, a player's fingernails or hair style constitutes a safety concern (3-7).

Rationale

While it is acknowledged that removing a player with blood could result in some unfair situations — the problem has nothing to do with fairness, but everything to do with minimizing risk.

Unconscious/Injured/Bleeding Player: Caseplays

2.8.5 SITUATION: A1 and B1 hit heads in diving for a loose ball and both are injured. In the opinion of the officials, A1 was unconscious for a short period of time. (a) The coach or trainer questions the officials' determination; or (b) the officials allow A1 to return later without a physician's authorization. **RULING:** In (a), even though they may disagree, A1 may not continue or return without a physician's written authorization. In (b), the rules do not allow A1 to return without a physician's authorization once it has been determined that A1 was apparently unconscious.

In Simple Terms

A team may call a time-out to keep a player in the game that has been injured or attended to. If players from both teams are injured, both teams must use time-outs in order to keep their respective players in the game.

3.3.6 SITUATION A: A1 is injured and play is stopped to permit the trainer or physician to administer aid (a) A1 is removed from the court and replaced within less than one minute; or (b) the injury is such that the physician will not allow A1 to be removed from the court until being certain it is prudent to do so. After approximately five minutes, A1 is moved from the court. **RULING:** No time-out is charged in either (a) or (b), regardless of the amount of time involved. The intent of the rule is to require an injured player to be removed without charging a team with a 60-second time-out, regardless of how much time is consumed prior to removal. A team may call a time-out if they wish to keep the player (if able) in the game (5-8-2a).

3.3.6 SITUATION B: A1 appears to be injured and an official properly halts play and the Team A coach rushes onto the court to check A1. However, A1 is OK and seems ready to play within a few seconds. **RULING:** A1 must be removed as the coach came onto the court. A1 may remain in the game if the coach does not come on the court and A1 is ready to play immediately. If the coach or other bench personnel have come onto the court, the player must be replaced. There is no set amount of time as to what is "immediately," but it should not involve more than a few seconds and it must be without the coach, trainer or doctor being beckoned and/or entering the court. The coach may also call a time-out to keep the player in the game (10-4-2).

3.3.7 SITUATION A: B1 is directed to leave the game because of excessive blood on his/her uniform shirt. Team B's manager has failed to pack any extra shirts. (a) The coach asks one of the substitutes to give his/her shirt to B1; or (b) Team A is able to find a shirt which B1 can wear even though it is not exactly the same color or style of the Team B shirts. The shirt will however, clearly identify B1 as a member of Team B and will not be confusing to either team or the officials. **RULING:** Acceptable procedure in both (a) and (b). In both situations the scorer will make necessary changes in the scorebook without penalty.

 # Rationale

The spirit and intent of the rule is to do everything possible to allow the player to use a different shirt and return without penalty. However, identical numbers shall not be allowed on the same team.

3.3.7 SITUATION B: A1 discovers she is bleeding and intentionally wipes blood on the arm of the both B4 and B5. In (a) neither the referee or umpire observes the bleeding or the action of A1; (b) U1 observes that A1 is bleeding from a cut on her arm; (c) U1 observes B4 and B5 with blood on their arm; or (d) U1 observes A1 bleeding, and observes A1's action of wiping blood on the arm of B4 and B5. **RULING:** In (a), A1 must leave the game when the bleeding is discovered; (b) A1 must leave the game when bleeding is observed; (c) B4 and B5 must leave the game when blood is observed on their person; (d) A1, B4 and B5 must leave the game and, A1 is charged with a technical foul for an unsporting act. If in the judgment of U1 the actions of A1 were flagrant, A1 would be disqualified from further competition. Any player or legally entering substitute may attempt the two free throws, after which B will have the ball for a division line throw-in. In all situations, a team may call a time-out to keep a player in the game.

3.3.7 SITUATION C: Officials discover blood on players A1 and B1 simultaneously and direct both players to leave the game. After notification by the officials, Team A chooses to call a time-out to keep A1 in the game, while Team B elects to substitute B6 for B1. **RULING:** B6 must enter the game prior to the official granting the time-out for Team A. A1 must be ready to play by the end of the time-out. B1 may not re-enter the game until the next opportunity to substitute after time has run off the clock.

*10.5.3 SITUATION A: A1 has been injured and has received extensive medical attention on the court. The coach: (a) helps assist the injured player to the bench; or (b) remains at the bench area while A1 is treated and helped to the bench. How much time does the coach have to replace A1? **RULING:** In both (a) and (b), the coach will have 20 seconds to replace the injured player. In (a), the 20 seconds should start after the coach can turn his/her attention from the injured athlete to the duty of making a replacement. In (b), the 20 seconds would begin as soon as A1 has been returned to the bench. In both cases, the timer should be instructed by the official when to start timing the 20 seconds, sound a warning horn at 5 seconds and to notify the official when the allowed time has elapsed.

Topic:
Substitutions

A substitute who desires to enter shall report to the scorer, giving his/her number (3-3-1).

The officials shall beckon substitutes to enter the court (2-7-7).

A captain may request a defensive match-up if three or more substitutes from the same team enter during an opportunity to substitute (3-3-1e).

Between quarters, at halftime and during a time-out, the substitute must report or be in position to report to the scorer, prior to the warning signal which is sounded 15 seconds before the end of the intermission or the time-out (3-3-1a).

 Rationale

In an effort to ensure clear communication between game and bench officials, and to minimize time taken for substitutions, limitations on when substitutes could enter during free throws were developed.

Substitutions between halves may be made by the substitute or a team representative (3-3-1b).

During multiple free throws resulting from personal fouls, substitutions may be made only before the final attempt in the sequence and after the final attempt has been converted (3-3-1c).

The substitute shall remain outside the boundary until an official beckons, whereupon he/she shall enter immediately. If the ball is about to become live, the beckoning signal should be withheld (3-3-2).

When a player is required by rule to be replaced prior to administering the free throw(s), then all other substitutes who have legally reported may also enter the game (3-3-1c Exception).

If entry is at any time other than between quarters, and a substitute who is entitled and ready to enter reports to the scorer, the scorer shall use a sounding device or game horn, if, or as soon as, the ball is dead and the clock is stopped (3-3-1d).

Substitutions: Caseplays

3.3.1 SITUATION A: During a 30-second time-out, A6 goes to the scorer to substitute for A1: (a) before the 15-second warning signal; (b) after the 15-second warning but before the time-out is over; or (c) as the players break the huddle and take their positions on the court just prior to the signal ending the time-out. **RULING:** The substitution will be allowed in (a), but denied in (b) and (c). As with a 60-second time-out, substitutions must be made before the warning signal is given.

3.3.1 SITUATION B: A time-out is granted to Team A with play to resume by administration of a free throw. A6 reports to enter after the timer's warning signal has sounded. Since A6 has reported too late to enter, could he/she enter if: (a) either team is granted a time-out; (b) the resumption of play is delayed because a player is injured getting into position for the free throw; or (c) Team A is willing to "buy" A6's way into the game with a technical foul? **RULING:** Permissible in (a) and (b), but not in (c).

> ## In Simple Terms
>
> A substitute may enter the game to replace a player any time the ball is dead and the clock is stopped.

3.3.1 SITUATION C: Substitute A6 reports to the scorer just after the warning signal is sounded during a time-out. The scorer advises A6 that he/she will not be allowed to enter until the next opportunity for substitution. The Team A coach beckons A6 to return to the bench. **RULING:** This is permissible. The substitute is not obligated to remain at the table. However, A6 would have to report again before being allowed to enter the court. If A6 remains at the table, he/she may actually replace any player.

10.2.1 SITUATION A: Substitute A1 enters the court without reporting to the scorer. The infraction is discovered: (a) before the ball becomes live; or (b) after the ball becomes live. **RULING:** In (a), a technical foul is charged to A1. In (b), it is too late to penalize A1.

10.2.1 SITUATION B: Team A substitute No. 24: (a) reports to the scorer, but enters the court without being beckoned; or (b) goes directly from the bench and onto the court without being beckoned. **RULING:** One technical foul is charged to No. 24 in (a) and (b). In (b), even though No. 24 failed to comply with both requirements, only one foul is charged.

10.2.2 SITUATION: During a live ball and with the clock running, substitute A6 enters the court. **RULING:** A technical foul is charged if recognized by an official before the ball becomes live following the first dead ball.

*10.3.3 SITUATION B: After a lengthy substitution process involving multiple substitutions for both Team A and Team B, A5 goes to the bench and remains there, believing he/she has been replaced. The ball is put in play even though Team A has only four players on the court. Team A is bringing the ball into A's frontcourt when the coach of Team A realizes they have only four players. The coach yells for A5 to return and he/she sprints directly onto the court and catches up with the play. **RULING:** No technical foul is charged to A5. A5's return to the court was not deceitful, nor did it provide A5 an unfair positioning advantage on the court.

*10.5.3 SITUATION B: A1 has been disqualified from the game for committing his/her fifth foul or a flagrant foul. The coach of Team A is notified and then the official instructs the timer to begin the replacement period. The player is then notified of the disqualification. The coach of Team A rises from the bench and: (a) talks until the sounding of the 5-second warning horn with the four remaining players who have gathered near the boundary; (b) immediately sends A6 to the table to report in. The coach then wishes to gather the players at the sideline for a conference; or (c) sends A6 toward the table but the timer indicates the 20 seconds have expired before A6 gets there.

RULING: Legal in (a), as long as a substitute reports in during the next 15 seconds. In (b), play will resume as soon as A6 has reported to the scorer. In (c), a technical foul is charged directly to the coach.

In Simple Terms

Time must run off the clock before a player who has been replaced can re-enter the game.

Re-entry

A player who has been replaced, or directed to leave the game shall not re-enter before the next opportunity to substitute after the clock has been started properly following his/her replacement (3-3-4).

Who May Be Substituted

The entering substitute shall not replace a designated jumper or a free thrower except, if a player awarded a free throw must withdraw because of an injury or disqualification, his/her substitute shall attempt the throw(s) or to attempt the free throw(s) for a technical foul (3-3-2; 8-2; 8-3).

If the substitute enters to replace a player who must jump or attempt a free throw, he/she shall withdraw until the next opportunity to substitute (3-3-2).

The thrower of a throw-in shall not be replaced by a teammate after the ball is at the thrower's disposal (9-2-9).

Who May Be Substituted: Caseplays

3.3.1 SITUATION D: B6 has properly reported to the scorer to enter the game. A1 is then fouled in the act of a three-point try. Prior to the first attempt, A1 is discovered to be bleeding: (a) B6 and A6, who is replacing bleeding A1, enter prior to the first free-throw attempt; (b) substitutes A7 and A8 report to the scorer's table after B6 and A6 enter the game; or (c) all substitutes in (a) and (b) enter the game when time-out is called by B3. **RULING:** In (a), A6 must replace bleeding-player A1 before the free throw is administered, B6 may also enter because he/she had legally reported to the table and another player had been directed to leave the game by the official. In (b), A7 and A8 must wait until prior to the last remaining free throw to enter the game. In (c), the time-out by B3 cannot be honored until the substitute for A1 has properly reported and entered. Once the time-out is granted, all substitutes may enter. A1 may remain in the game if Team A requests and is granted a time-out.

3.3.3 SITUATION A: A1 is injured during a play in which A1 has been fouled. As a result, A1 cannot attempt the free throw awarded to him/her. Substitute A6 replaces A1 and attempts the free throw which is successful. Substitute A7 replaces A6 before the clock starts. **RULING:** The substitution is legal (8-2).

3.3.3 SITUATION B: Team B is charged with a technical foul for an excess time-out. During this stopped-clock interval, A1 is replaced by A6. A1 then returns to the game and attempts the two free throws which are: (a) both successful; (b) both unsuccessful; or (c) one is successful and one is not. **RULING:** Once A1 re-entered, even illegally, and the ball became live, A1 was a legal player at that point. The resulting action in (a), (b) and (c) stands. The situation does not come under the provisions of the correctable-error rule, nor is there any provision for penalizing either Team A or A1 (3-3-4; 8-3).

10.5.4 SITUATION: A5 has just received his/her fifth foul of the game. A5 (a) is erroneously permitted to remain in the game for another two minutes before the scorer realizes the mistake; or (b) leaves the game after the coach is notified of the disqualification. At the intermission between the third and fourth quarter, A5 reports as a substitute and subsequently enters the game. **RULING:** In (a), as soon as the error is discovered, the player is removed from the game, no penalties are assessed. In (b), A5 will not actually "participate" until the ball becomes live. If detected prior to the ball becoming live, A5 would be directed to the bench and no penalty assessed unless the official deemed it was a deliberate attempt to circumvent the rules. If detected after the ball becomes live, it is a technical foul charged directly to the head coach. The player is immediately removed from the game and Team B is awarded two free throws and the ball (2-11-5 Note 2).

Topic:
Disqualified Player

A disqualified player is one who is barred from further participation in the game because of having committed his/her fifth foul (personal and technical), two technical fouls or a flagrant foul (4-14-1).

A player is officially disqualified and becomes bench personnel when the coach is notified by an official (4-14-2).

◻ Rationale

Disqualified players when ejected are to remain on the bench under the supervision of the head coach. By mandating the player to the bench, the ejected offender continues to remain under the jurisdiction of the officials should further problems occur. Any additional technical fouls issued now impact the coach accordingly.

Disqualified Player: Caseplays

4.14.1 SITUATION A: A1 is fouled by B1 while Team A is in the bonus. The covering official is at the table reporting the foul when A1 is charged with a technical foul by the official who is observing the players. The foul on A1 is his/her fifth. **RULING:** A1 is disqualified as both personal and technical fouls are counted. Because A1 has been disqualified he/she will not be allowed to attempt the free throw(s) resulting from B1's foul. The substitute for A1 will shoot the free throw(s) (8-2).

4.14.1 SITUATION B: A1 is charged with his/her fourth personal foul and reacts by using profanity. The covering official charges A1 with a technical foul. **RULING:** A1 is disqualified. The technical foul brings

A1's total fouls to five, which results in automatic disqualification. This technical is not charged indirectly to the head coach, as A1 was not "bench personnel" when the technical foul was charged (10-3-6b; 4-14-2).

4.14.1 SITUATION C: A1 is fouled by B2 and is awarded two free throws. The foul is B2's fifth foul. The new trail official reports the fifth foul to Team B's coach. Before a substitute is made, the lead official incorrectly permits A1 to attempt the first free throw. The officials realize the error and huddle to discuss the situation. **RULING:** The result of the first attempt shall stand. Team B's head coach shall be notified of B2's disqualification. Once B2 has been replaced, A1 shall attempt the second free throw.

 COMMENT: This is an official's error and not a correctable error situation according to Rule 2-10 (6-1-2c; 10-5-2; 2-8-3).

5.4.1 SITUATION A: A1 commits his/her fifth personal foul. Both the head coach and player are properly notified. Team A has substitutes available but the head coach from Team A does not send a substitute to the table within the 20-second time limit. The Team A head coach is assessed a technical foul. The head coach still does not send a substitute to the table. **RULING:** The official should forfeit the contest to the opposing team for the head coach delaying the contest and attempting to make a travesty of the game.

 COMMENT: The referee may forfeit a game if any player, team member, bench personnel or coach fails to comply with any technical foul penalty.

10.4.1 SITUATION D: A1 commits his/her fifth foul and is disqualified. On the way to the team bench, A1 removes his/her shirt or pulls it over their face: (a) before the coach is notified; or (b) after the coach is notified. **RULING:** In (a) and (b), a technical foul is charged to A1. In (b), an indirect technical foul is also charged to the head coach as A1 is considered to be bench personnel.

Topic:
Head Coaches' Rule

The head coach shall remain seated on the team bench, except:

• By state association adoption, the head coach may stand within the designated coaching box. The first technical foul charged directly or indirectly to the head coach results in loss of coaching-box privileges and the head coach must remain seated for the remainder of the game, except as stated below (10-5-1a).

• The head coach may stand within the coaching box to request a time-out or signal his/her players to request a time-out (10-5-1b).

• The head coach may stand and/or leave the coaching box to confer with personnel at the scorer's table to request a time-out as in 5-8-4 (10-1-5c).

• The head coach may stand within the coaching box to replace or remove a disqualified/injured player or player directed to leave the game (10-1-5d).

• The head coach may stand during a time-out, in the intermission between quarters and extra periods or to spontaneously react to an outstanding play a team member or to acknowledge a replaced player(s), but must immediately return to his/her seat (10-1-5e).

The head coach shall replace or remove a disqualified/injured player, or player directed to leave the game, within 20 seconds when a substitute is available (10-5-2). The head coach shall not permit a team member to participate after being removed from the game for disqualification (10-5-3).

The head coach shall not permit a team member to participate while wearing an illegal uniform (10-5-4).

Penalty

Two free throws plus ball for division-line throw-in. The foul is charged directly to the head coach (10-5 Penalty). The penalty for wearing an illegal uniform is penalized when discovered. Only one technical foul is charged regardless of the number of offenders (10-5-4 Penalty).

A single flagrant foul, the second direct technical foul or the third technical (any combination of direct or indirect) charged to the head coach results in disqualification and ejection. Ejected adult bench personnel shall leave the vicinity (out of sight and sound) of the playing area immediately and are prohibited from any further contact (direct or indirect) with the team during the remainder of the game. Failure to comply with the rules of ejection may result in the game being forfeited (10-5 note 1).

Head Coach: Caseplays

10.5 SITUATION: (a) The head coach is charged (directly or indirectly)

with a third technical foul, or a second direct technical. **RULING:** In (a), the coach shall leave the vicinity or the playing area and have no further contact with the team. The official has no option and may not set aside the provision which requires removal. This also applies to all adult bench personnel who receive two technical fouls (10-5 Note).

10.5.1 SITUATION A: With the clock running, the Team A coach is off the bench and: (a) applauds a good play by A1, but then is immediately seated; (b) stands at the end of the bench area to give instructions to players in the far end of the court; or (c) shakes hands with a replaced player. **RULING:** Legal in (a) and (c), but a direct technical foul in (b). The action in (b) is not one of the listed situations which allow a coach to be off the bench unless the coach is within the optional coaching box as adopted by the state association (10-4-4).

10.5.1 SITUATION B: The official has just bounced A1 the ball for a free-throw attempt. The official notices that A2 is near A's bench area and the coach of Team A is standing and having a conference with A2. **RULING:** Unless the coach is in the optional coaching box the official should sound the whistle and assess the technical foul directly to the coach. In those states which are not using the optional coaching box as part of bench rule, the coach is not allowed to be off the bench in this situation. The lane is cleared for A1's attempt and is followed by administration of the technical foul.

10.5.1 SITUATION C: The coach of Team A leaves the bench area and goes to the table to seek information other than a correctable error: (a) during a time-out; or (b) during the intermission between the first and second quarters. **RULING:** A technical foul is charged directly to the coach in both (a) and (b). If this information is required, it must be secured by a manager or statistician, etc., when the clock is stopped and the ball is dead. A coach is not permitted at the table for this purpose. To allow exceptions would open the door for exploitation and would result in situations which could not be enforced consistently.

10.5.1 SITUATION D: The coach of Team B rises and accompanies B6 to the table to make sure the substitute reports properly. **RULING:** This is a technical foul charged directly to the coach. The coach is not allowed to be off the bench or out of the optional coaching box for this purpose.

10.5.1 SITUATION E: The coach of Team B sits on the opposite end of the bench from where the optional coaching box is located. The coach rises only when permitted by rule. **RULING:** Legal. The coach is not required to use the optional coaching box even though it has been adopted by the state association. However, if the coach begins the game by sitting somewhere other than where the box is located, he/she may not use the box privileges any time during the game. The coach must begin the game in a position within the box if he/she wishes to stand when permitted under the optional coaching-box provisions.

10.5.1 SITUATION F: A team member of Team B is charged with a technical foul for dunking during warm-ups. The infraction occurs in a game played in a state which utilizes the optional coaching box. **RULING:** The team member is charged with a technical foul and the head coach is charged indirectly. Whenever the coach has been charged (directly or indirectly) with a technical foul, he/she shall be informed that the privilege of using the coaching box has been lost for the entire game. The rule is in effect any time the coach personally commits the infraction directly or when it is charged indirectly because of illegal acts or unsporting conduct by bench personnel (10-5 Note 1).

10.5.2 SITUATION A: A1 has been injured and has received extensive medical attention on the court. The coach: (a) helps assist the injured player to the bench; or (b) remains at the bench area while A1 is treated and helped to the bench. How much time does the coach have to replace A1? **RULING:** In both (a) and (b), the coach will have 20 seconds to replace the injured player. In (a), the 20 seconds should start after the coach can turn his/her attention from the injured athlete to the duty of making a replacement. In (b), the 20 seconds would begin as soon as A1 has been returned to the bench. In both cases, the timer should be instructed by the official when to start timing the 20 seconds, sound a warning horn at 5 seconds and to notify the official when the allowed time has elapsed.

10.5.2 SITUATION B: A1 has been disqualified from the game for committing his/her fifth foul or a flagrant foul. The coach of Team A is notified and then the official instructs the timer to begin the replacement period. The player is then notified of the disqualification. The coach of Team A rises from the bench and: (a) talks until the sounding of the 5-second warning horn with the four remaining players who have gathered near the boundary; (b) immediately sends A6 to the table to report in. The coach then wishes to gather the players at the sideline for a conference; or (c) sends A6 toward the table but the timer indicates the 20 seconds have expired before A6 gets there. **RULING:** Legal in (a), as long as a substitute reports in during the next 15 seconds. In (b), play will resume as soon as A6 has reported to the scorer. In (c), a technical foul is charged directly to the coach.

10.5.3 SITUATION: A5 has just received his/her fifth foul of the game. A5 (a) is erroneously permitted to remain in the game for another two minutes before the scorer realizes the mistake; or (b) leaves the game after the coach is notified of the disqualification. At the intermission between the third and fourth quarter, A5 reports as a substitute and subsequently enters the game. **RULING:** In (a), as soon as the error is discovered, the player is removed from the game, no penalties are assessed. In (b), A5 will not actually "participate" until the ball becomes live. If detected prior to the ball becoming live, A5 would be directed to the bench and no penalty assessed unless the official deemed it was a deliberate attempt to circumvent the rules. If detected after the ball becomes live, it is a technical foul charged directly to the head coach. The player is immediately removed from the game and Team B is awarded two free throws and the ball (2-11-5 Note 2).

*10.5.4 SITUATION A: Prior to the start of the game, the officials notice that the home team is wearing orange jerseys and the visiting team is wearing red jerseys. **RULING:** The referee shall direct the home team to wear the required white jerseys. If they are unable to comply, a technical foul shall be charged directly to the head coach. The visiting team is awarded two free throws followed by a division-line throw-in opposite the table. The alternating-possession arrow is set toward the home team when the ball is at the disposal of the thrower-in. The home team's head coach has lost his/her coaching-box privileges for the remainder of the game in states utilizing the optional coaching box (3-4-1c).

*10.5.4 SITUATION B: Team A is wearing jerseys that have a visible manufacturer's logo above the neckline. Team B's coach informs the official of the logos just as the ball is about to be inbounded to begin the second quarter. **RULING:** Illegal jerseys. A technical foul is charged directly to Team A's head coach when the infraction is discovered. Team B is awarded two free throws followed by a division-line throw-in opposite the table. Team A's head coach has lost his/her coaching-box privileges for the remainder of the game in states utilizing the optional coaching box (3-4-2a).

In 1994, the rules committee revised the head coaches rule so that two direct technical fouls charged directly to the coach results in ejection. Previously, a coach was allowed any combination of three technical fouls which meant a coach could have received three direct technical fouls before ejection.

Did You Know?

Topic 3

Scoring

PlayPic™

Key Terms

A goal is made when a live ball enters the basket from above and remains in or passes through. No goal is scored if an untouched throw-in goes through the basket (5-1).

The act of shooting begins simultaneously with the start of the try or tap and ends when the ball is clearly in flight, and includes the airborne shooter (4-41-1). An airborne shooter is a player who has released the ball on a try for a goal or has tapped the ball and has not returned to the floor (4-1-1).

A try for field goal is an attempt by a player to score two or three points by throwing the ball into a team's own basket (4-41-2). The try starts when the player begins the motion which habitually precedes the release of the ball (4-41-3). The try ends when the throw is successful, when it is certain the throw is unsuccessful, when the thrown ball touches the floor or when the ball becomes dead (4-41-4).

A tap for goal is the contacting of the ball with any part of a player's hand(s) in an attempt to direct the ball into his/her basket (4-41-5). The tap starts when the player's hand(s) touches the ball (4-41-7). The tap ends in exactly the same manner as a try (4-41-8).

A free throw is the opportunity given a player to score one point by an unhindered try for goal from within the free-throw semicircle and behind the free-throw line (4-20-1).

Topic:
Goal

A goal is made when a live ball enters the basket from above and remains in or passes through. No goal is scored if an untouched throw-in goes through the basket (5-1-1). Whether the clock is running or stopped has no influence on the counting of a goal. If a player-control foul occurs before or after a goal, the goal is canceled (5-1-2).

After a goal is made, the ball becomes dead, or remains dead (6-7-1).

> ## Fundamental #3
>
> If a live ball enters the thrower's basket from above and remains in or goes through, the goal counts unless cancelled by a throw-in violation or a player-control foul.

Goal: Caseplays

5.1.1 SITUATION: A pass, a tap or a try for field goal by A1 comes down several feet in front of the basket. The ball strikes the floor without touching any player and bounces into the basket. Are two points counted for A: (a) if not complicated by expiration of time for a quarter or extra period or by a foul occurring while the ball is in flight; or (b) if time expires while the ball is in flight or a foul occurs while the ball is in flight? **RULING:** In (a), two points are scored. The tap or the try for field goal by A1 ends when the ball touches the floor but a field goal is sometimes scored when it is not the result of a tap or a try. In the case cited, credit the two points to A1. In (b), since a pass is not a try, the ball becomes dead immediately. However, a try or tap by A1 towards A's basket does not become dead until the try or tap ends, which it does when it touches the floor (4-41-2, 4, 5).

5.2.3 SITUATION: A1 completes the throw-in to A2 to begin the second half. A2 is confused and dribbles toward the basket Team A used during the first half and dunks the ball into the basket of Team B. **RULING:** Legal goal. Two points are awarded to Team B. The ball is bounced to a player of Team A out of bounds at the basket of Team B. Team A may put the ball in play from anywhere along the end line as after any score by B (earned or awarded) (5-2-1; 7-5-7).

Topic:
Try

A try for field goal is an attempt by a player to score two or three points by throwing the ball into a team's own basket (4-41-2). A team's own basket is the one into which its players try to throw or tap the ball (4-5-1).

The try starts when the player begins the motion which habitually precedes the release of the ball (4-41-3). The try ends when the throw is successful, when it is certain the throw is unsuccessful, when the thrown ball touches the floor or when the ball becomes dead (4-41-4).

Try: Caseplays
4.41.1 SITUATION: B1 commits a common foul by holding A1 during a field-goal try, but after A1 has completed the act of shooting. The foul occurs before the bonus rule applies. The attempt is: (a) successful; or (b) unsuccessful. **RULING:** A personal foul is charged to B1 in both (a) and (b), but no free throw is awarded to A1 in either case. In both (a) and (b), the ball is awarded to Team A at the spot out of bounds nearest where the foul occurred (7-5-4a).

4.41.2 SITUATION: A1 becomes confused and throws the ball at the wrong basket. A1 is fouled by B1 and the ball goes into the basket. Is this a successful basket? If A1 missed, would A1 be awarded two free throws for the foul by B1? **RULING:** No goal. The ball became dead when the foul occurred. When a player throws at the opponent's basket, it is not a try. If the team is in the bonus when B1 fouled A1, A1 is given either a one-and-one attempt or two free throws at Team A's basket. If Team A was not in the bonus, then the ball is awarded to Team A for a throw-in at the out-of-bounds spot nearest the foul (7-5-5).

4.41.4 SITUATION A: While the ball is in flight on a try for goal by A1: (a) B1 touches the ball and then time expires; or (b) time expires and then B1 touches the ball. The ball continues in flight and enters Team A's basket. **RULING:** The goal is scored in both (a) and (b), as B1's touching did not cause the try to end. However, in both (a) and (b), if B1's touching is either goaltending or basket interference, the ball becomes dead and two points will be awarded (6-7 Exception a; 9-11, 12).

4.41.4 SITUATION B: A1's three-point try is short and below ring level when it hits the shoulder of: (a) A2; or (b) B1 and rebounds to the backboard and through the basket. **RULING:** The three-point try ended when it was obviously short and below the ring. However, since a live ball went through the basket, two points are scored in both (a) and (b) (5-1).

Airborne Shooter

An airborne shooter is a player who has released the ball on a try for a goal or has tapped the ball and has not returned to the floor (4-1-1). The airborne shooter is considered to be in the act of shooting (4-1-2).

Airborne Shooter: Caseplays

4.1.1 SITUATION: A1 is high in the air on a jump shot in the lane. A1 releases the ball on a try and is then fouled by B1 who has also jumped in an unsuccessful attempt to block the shot. A1's try is: (a) successful; or (b) unsuccessful. **RULING:** A1 is an airborne shooter when the ball is

Prior to 1961, the visiting team could "warm-up" before the game at a basket of its choice and then switch to start the game. Visiting teams hoped to gain a "psychological advantage" by making the home team practice at one basket before the game, but shoot at the other basket once the game started.

released until one foot returns to the floor. An airborne shooter is in the act of shooting. B1 has fouled A1 in the act of shooting. A1 is awarded one free throw in (a), and two in (b) (4-41-1).

Dunking

Dunking or stuffing is the driving, forcing, pushing or attempting to force a ball through the basket with the hand(s) (4-16-1).

Three-Point Goal

A successful try, tap or thrown ball from the field by a player who is located behind the team's own 19-foot, 9-inch arc counts three points (5-2-1).

 # Rationale

The three-point goal was added in 1987 as a way to add a positive feature to the game and reduce the congestion around the basket, while also allowing a team more of an opportunity to catch-up without fouling.

Three-Point Goal: Caseplays

5.2.1 SITUATION A: A1 attempts a three-point goal. B1 slaps the ball: (a) while it is in downward flight outside the cylinder, but above the ring level; or (b) while it is in the cylinder after bouncing off the ring. **RULING:** It is defensive goaltending in (a) and defensive basket interference in (b). Three points are awarded in both cases as a result of the violation (9-11, 12).

5.2.1 SITUATION B: With 2:45 left in the second quarter, B1 has the ball on the left wing in Team B's frontcourt, standing behind the three-point arc. B5 makes a backdoor cut toward the basket. B1 passes the ball toward the ring and B5 leaps for the potential "alley-oop" dunk. The ball, however, enters and passes through the goal directly from B1's pass and is not touched by B5. **RULING:** Score three points for Team B. A ball that is thrown into a team's own goal from behind the three-point arc scores three points, regardless of whether the thrown ball was an actual try for goal.

5.2.1 SITUATION C: A1 throws the ball from behind the three-point line. The ball is legally touched by: (a) B1 who is in the three-point area; (b) B1 who is in the two-point area; (c) A2 who is in the three-point area; or (d) A2 who is in the two-point area. The ball continues in flight and goes through A's basket. **RULING:** In (a) and (b), three points are scored since the legal touching was by the defense and the ball was thrown from behind the three-point line. In (c), score three points since the legal touch by a teammate occurred behind the three-point line. In (d), score two points since the legal touch by a teammate occurred in the two-point area.

Player Location

The location of a player or nonplayer is determined by where the player is touching the floor as far as being outside (behind/beyond) or inside the three-point field-goal line (4-35-1c).

When a player is touching the three-point line, the player is located inside the three-point line (4-35-2).

The location of an airborne player is the same as at the time such player was last in contact with the floor or an extension of the floor, such as a bleacher (4-35-3).

Player Location: Caseplay

4.35.1 SITUATION: A1 has both feet on the floor behind the three-point line. A1 jumps and releases the ball on a successful try and then lands inside the line. **RULING:** Three points are scored (5-2-1).

Topic:
Tap

A tap for goal is the contacting of the ball with any part of a player's hand(s) in an attempt to direct the ball into his/her basket (4-41-5). The tap starts when the player's hand(s) touches the ball (4-41-7). The tap ends in exactly the same manner as a try (4-41-8).

When play is resumed with a throw-in or free throw and three-tenths (.3) of a second or less remains on the clock, a player may not gain control of the ball and try for a field goal. In this situation only a tap could score (5-2-5). This rule does not apply if the clock does not display tenths of a second (5-2-5 Note).

Rationale

Results of studies confirm that players cannot catch the ball and release it on a try when three-tenths (.3) of a second or less show on the clock when the clock is started correctly.

Tap: Caseplays

5.2.5 SITUATION A: The game clock shows three-tenths of a second or less in the third quarter when A2: (a) taps the ball; or (b) grabs A1's missed free throw or throw-in pass and quickly shoots. In both cases the ball leaves A2's hand(s) before the end-of-period signal and goes through A's basket. **RULING:** Count the goal in (a), but not in (b).

5.2.5 SITUATION B: With three-tenths of a second or less left in the first half, Team B has been charged with only four team fouls. A1 is at the free throw line for one free throw. A1's shot hits the rim and bounds off. A2 legally taps the ball toward the basket and is fouled by B3. The ball had left A2's hand and the foul occurred before the end-of-period signal. The tap is unsuccessful. **RULING:** B3's foul is considered in the "act of tapping" and will result in two free throws for A2. The lane will be cleared and the period ends after A2's free throw attempts (4-41-1,5,6,7).

5.2.5 SITUATION C: With three-tenths of a second or less left in a tied game, each team is in the bonus. Team A has a throw-in on the end line near their basket. A1 throws the ball to A5 on the near block who catches the ball and quickly shoots. A5 is fouled by B3 just prior to the end-of-period signal. The ball goes through A's basket. **RULING:** Since A5 may not control the ball and attempt a try with three-tenths of a second or less, A5 cannot score a goal and is not considered in the act of shooting. However, B3's foul cannot be ignored and is considered a common foul. A5 is awarded a one-and-one bonus free-throw situation with the lane cleared. A5's free throw attempts will determine if the game is over or if an overtime period is necessary (4-41-6).

Fundamental #18

Whether the clock is running or is stopped has no influence on the counting of a goal.

Topic:
Scoring at End of Period

   Each quarter or extra period ends when the signal illuminates or sounds indicating time has expired, except that if the ball is in flight during a try or tap for field goal, the quarter or extra period ends when the try or tap ends (5-6-2 exception 1).

   If a foul occurs so near the expiration of time that the timer cannot get the clock stopped before time expires or after time expires, but while the ball is in flight during a try or tap for field goal. The quarter or extra period ends when the free throw(s) and all related activity have been completed. No penalty or part of a penalty carries over from one quarter or extra period to the next except when a correctable error is rectified. No free throw(s) shall be attempted after time has expired for the fourth quarter or any extra period, unless the point(s) would affect the outcome of the game (5-6-2 exception 3).

If a technical foul occurs after the ball has become dead to end a quarter or extra period, the next quarter or extra period is started by administering the free throws. This applies when the foul occurs after any quarter has ended, including the fourth quarter, provided there is to be an extra period. If there is no way to determine whether there will be an extra period until the free throws are administered, the free throws are attempted immediately, as if the foul had been part of the preceding quarter (5-6-2 exception 4).

 COMMENT: The expiration of time for a quarter or extra period does not always cause the ball to become dead nor end the quarter or extra period. The ending of a quarter or extra period often lags both the expiration of time and the ball becoming dead. If there is no foul, it ends at the time the ball becomes dead. If the ball is in flight following a try or tap, this coincides with the expiration of playing time. If the ball is in flight following a try or tap and there is no foul, the quarter or extra period ends when the ball becomes dead. If there is a foul after time expires and before the ball becomes dead, the quarter or extra period ends after the resulting free throw(s). The free throw(s) is a part of that quarter or extra period and, if a tie is involved, the result of the free throw(s) will determine whether additional play is required (5.6 Comment A).

5.6 SITUATION: A1 is fouled in the act of shooting by B1. A1's try or tap is successful to make the score with Team A leading 62-58. When the foul occurs, the clock is stopped with 0:00 showing, but no end-of-period signal (horn or light) has indicated. **RULING:** A1 will attempt the free throw with lane spaces occupied as required. The fourth period time has not expired until the period-ending signal.

5.6.2 SITUATION A: While the ball is in flight during a try by A1, time for the second quarter expires after which B1 touches the attempt on its upward flight toward the basket, however, the ball subsequently goes through the basket. **RULING:** The touching does not end the try. The goal is scored (4-41-4; 5-6-2 Exception 1).

5.6.2 SITUATION B: Time for the first quarter expires while the ball is in flight during a field-goal try by A1. B1 intentionally fouls A2 before the field-goal attempt has ended. After the ball has become dead following the last free throw by A2, A3 flagrantly fouls B1. **RULING:** A3 is disqualified for a flagrant technical foul. Because the foul by A3 was committed after the first quarter had ended. The second quarter will begin with the free-throw attempts by any Team B player. Team B is then awarded the ball at the division line opposite the table for a throw-in. This throw-in does not affect the possession arrow (7-5-4b; 10-3-7).

5.6.2 SITUATION C: The ball is in flight during a try by A1 when time for the fourth quarter or for any extra period expires. The try is successful to make the score: (a) A-60, B-60; or (b) A-61, B-60. Clearly after the ball becomes dead, A2 contacts B1. **RULING:** A technical foul is charged if contact during a dead ball is intentional or flagrant. If flagrant, it results in disqualification in addition to the free throws. In (a), an extra period is played and this extra period is started by administering the penalty for the technical foul. If this occurrence is after an extra period, the procedure is the same as after the fourth quarter. The next extra period starts with the penalty for the technical foul. In (b), the free throws are treated the same as if they were part of the preceding quarter or extra period. If only one free throw is successful, an extra period is played and the overtime period is started with a jump. If neither or if both free throws are successful, the game is ended (5-6-2 Exception 3, 4; 7-5-6a; 10-3-7).

5.6.2 SITUATION D: Team A trails 60-59 with just a few seconds remaining in the fourth quarter of play. A1 is fouled in the act of shooting by B1 but time expires before the ball is in flight. A1 is awarded two free throws. The coach of Team B is charged with a technical foul before A1's attempts. A1 makes: (a) neither throw; (b) one throw; or (c) both throws. When does Team A shoot the free throws resulting from the technical foul? **RULING:** In (a) and (b), the two free throws for the technical foul are attempted as part of the fourth quarter as the foul occurred before the fourth quarter had ended. In (a), the two free throws for the technical foul will determine if an extra period is necessary. In (b), the one successful free throw ties the game and if either free throw for the technical foul is successful, no extra period is required. In (c), the two successful free throws dictate there will be no extra period. The free throws for the technical foul are not administered as the outcome of the game has been determined. A quarter or extra period does not end until all free throws which could affect the outcome of the game have been attempted and related activity has been completed (4-41-1; 5-6-3 Exception; 6-7-7).

In Simple Terms

Free throws should not be shot if time has expired and the free throws won't affect the outcome of the game.

5.6.2 SITUATION E: A1 has been awarded two free throws after time has expired in the fourth quarter. Team B leads 62-60 and A1 misses the first free throw. **RULING:** The second free throw will not be attempted (5-6-2 Exception 3).

5.6.2 SITUATION F: Following the end-of-game signal which has Team A leading 62-60, the coach of Team A sprints after the game officials and shouts profanity at the referee who has just left the playing court outside the end line. **RULING:** The referee shall charge the coach with a flagrant technical foul and the results of the two free throws will determine whether an extra period will be necessary. The jurisdiction of the officials had not ended as the referee was still within the visual confines of the playing area (2-2-4).

 COMMENT: If a technical foul occurs after the ball has become dead to end a quarter, the next quarter is started by administering the free throws. This applies even when the foul occurs after the first half has ended. It also applies when the foul occurs after the second half has ended, provided the score is tied. If the score is not tied, the free throws are administered unless the outcome of the game will not be affected. If the outcome is not already decided, the free throws are attempted immediately as if the foul had been a part of the fourth quarter. In this case, if any overtime period is necessary, it will start with a jump ball. The division line throw-in following the technical foul cannot be carried over to the overtime as the fourth quarter ended with the last free throw (5-6-2).

5.6.2 SITUATION G: The score is tied when A1 is fouled in the act of shooting and the try is unsuccessful. Playing time for the fourth quarter expires while the ball is in flight. No players are allowed along the lane. A1's first free-throw attempt is successful. Immediately following the made free throw the occupants of the Team A bench rush onto the court and a mini celebration takes place. **RULING:** The second free throw is not required. No penalty unless the celebration or any act is unsporting and a foul is charged to Team A before the final score has been approved (5-6-2 Exception 3).

5.6.2 SITUATION H: Team A is leading 61-60. B1 fouls A1 in the act of shooting as time expires. As the officials approach the scorer's table, the Team A coach rushes the floor and begins screaming obscenities at the officials. **RULING:** A flagrant technical foul is assessed to the Team A coach. The foul at the expiration of time is no longer ignored. The flagrant technical foul on the Team A coach created a false double foul situation, which may affect the outcome of the game. The penalties are administered in the order in which they occurred. With the lane cleared, A1 shoots two free throws for being fouled in the act of shooting. If both are successful, the game is over. If one or both are missed, an eligible player from Team B shoots the two technical foul free throws. The free throws will determine the outcome of the game or an extra period will be played.

COMMENT: Jurisdiction of the officials is terminated when all officials leave the visual confines of the playing area. While the preferred action would be for all officials to immediately leave the playing area, such an observable action by the coach should be penalized as unsporting or flagrant (10-4-1c; 4-19-9; 5-6-2 Exception 3).

6.7 SITUATION A: The ball is in flight during a try or a tap for goal by A1 when time for the third quarter expires. After time expires, the ball is on the ring or in the basket or is touching the cylinder above the basket when it is touched by: (a) A2; or (b) B1. The ball then goes through the basket or does not go through. **RULING:** In (a) and (b), the ball became dead as the try ended with the violation. In (a), no points can be scored because of the offensive basket interference by A2. However, in (b), since the touching is defensive basket interference by B1, two points are awarded to A1. Whether or not the ball goes through the basket has no effect upon either ruling (4-6; 6-7 Note; 9-11).

Topic:
Other Ways to Score

Scoring via Free Throws

A free throw is the opportunity given a player to score one point by an unhindered try for goal from within the free-throw semicircle and behind the free-throw line (4-20-1).

A goal from a free throw counts one point for the free-thrower's team and is credited to the free thrower (5-2-2).

Scoring via Violation

Basket Interference

Basket interference occurs when a player touches the ball or any part of the basket (including the net) while the ball is on or within either basket (4-6-1) or touches the ball while any part of the ball is within the imaginary cylinder which has the basket ring as its lower base (4-6-2).

Dunking or stuffing is legal and is not basket interference (4-6 exception).

Basket interference at the opponent's basket is one of the only two infractions for which points are awarded (5-2-4).

Goaltending

Goaltending occurs when a player touches the ball during a field-goal try or tap while it is in its downward flight entirely above the basket ring level and has the possibility of entering the basket in flight, or an opponent of the free thrower touches the ball outside the cylinder during a free-throw attempt (4-22).

Goaltending by the defense is one of the only two infractions for which points are awarded (5-2-4).

Goaltending: Caseplay

7.5.7 SITUATION A: B1 goaltends on airborne shooter A1's try. A1 fouls B1 in returning to the floor. RULING: Since no free throws result from the player-control foul, B's throw-in is from anywhere along the end line because of the awarded goal for B1's goaltending violation (9-12 Penalty 1).

Fundamental #7

The only infractions for which points are awarded are goaltending by the defense or basket interference at the opponent's basket.

Scoring and Fouls: Continuous Motion

Continuous motion applies to a try or tap for field goals and free throws, but it has no significance unless there is a foul by any defensive player during the interval which begins when the habitual throwing movement starts a try or with the touching on a tap and ends when the ball is clearly in flight (4-11-1).

If an opponent fouls after a player has started a try for goal, he/she is permitted to complete the customary arm movement, and if pivoting or stepping when fouled, may complete the usual foot or body movement in any activity while holding the ball. These privileges are granted only when the usual throwing motion has started before the foul occurs and before the ball is in flight (4-11-2).

Continuous motion does not apply if a teammate fouls after a player has started a try for a goal and before the ball is in flight. The ball becomes dead immediately (4-11-3).

Topic:
Throw-in After Goal

After a goal, the team not credited with the score shall make the throw-in from the end of the court where the goal was made and from any point outside the end line. A team retains this privilege if the scoring team commits a violation or common foul (before the throw-in ends and before the bonus is in effect) and the ensuing throw-in spot would have been on the end line (7-5-7b). Any player of the team may make a direct throw-in or he/she may pass the ball along the end line to a teammate(s) outside the boundary line (7-5-7a).

 # Rationale

The team entitled to a non-designated spot throw-in should not be penalized by a foul or violation on the scoring team. That team shall retain the privilege to run the end line.

Throw-in After Goal: Caseplays

7.5.7 SITUATION B: Team A scores a field goal. B1 picks up the ball after the made basket, then proceeds out of bounds to start the throw-in process. B1 runs along the end line out of bounds while attempting to find an open teammate for the throw-in. Immediately after B1 releases the throw-in pass, (a) the ball is kicked by A2 near the end line; (b) the ball is kicked by A2 near the division line; or (c) the ball is deflected out of bounds across the end line off of A2. **RULING:** In (a) and (b), A2 has violated by kicking the ball. In (a), Team B will be awarded a throw-in and retain the right to run the end line on the ensuing throw-in. In (b), Team B will put the ball in play at a designated spot nearest the violation, which is the division line. In (c), A2 legally contacted the ball and subsequently hit it out of bounds, ending the throw-in. Team B is awarded a designated spot throw-in on the end line.

7.5.7 SITUATION C: Team B has scored a field goal and A1 has the ball along the end line for a throw-in. Team A is not in the bonus. Prior to the ball being thrown inbounds by A1: (a) B1 fouls A2 inbounds near A1; (b) B1 fouls A2 at the division line; (c) B1 fouls A2 beyond the division line; or (d) A2 requests a time-out. **RULING:** In (a) and (d), Team A may throw-in from anywhere out of bounds along the end line following the foul reporting and the time-out. In (b) and (c), the ball will be given to Team A for a throw-in from the spot out of bounds nearest to where the foul occurred.

7.5.7 SITUATION D: Team A scores a field goal. B1 picks up the ball and steps out of bounds at the end line to prepare for a throw-in. Before the throw-in is completed, A2 is called for an intentional (or flagrant) foul on B3 near the end line. **RULING:** B3 would shoot the two free throws for the intentional (or flagrant) foul with the lane cleared. Team B will then have a designated spot throw-in on the end line (7-5-4b).

7.5.7 SITUATION E: While A1's three-point field-goal attempt is in flight, A3 fouls B1 (B is not in the bonus) near the bottom block area. The three-point field-goal attempt is successful. **RULING:** Score the three-point goal for A1. Team B will be permitted to run the end line on the ensuing throw-in (5-7-7 Exception 2).

7.5.7 SITUATION F: A1 is fouled during an unsuccessful try and is awarded two free throws. While A1's successful first free throw is in flight, A2 fouls B1 along the lane. Team B is not in the bonus. The lane is cleared for A1's second attempt. A1 then violates by having a foot through the free-throw-line plane prematurely. **RULING:** The free-throw violation by A1 cancels the second attempt. Since Team B is not in the bonus, it results in a designated spot throw-in from the nearest spot out of bounds from where A2's foul occurred. Team B may not run the end line as the last free throw was unsuccessful (9-1-3e).

Topic 4

Control

Key Terms

A fumble is the accidental loss of player control when the ball unintentionally drops or slips from a player's grasp (4-21). A pass is movement of the ball caused by a player who throws, bats or rolls the ball to another player (4-31). A dribble is ball movement caused by a player in control who bats (intentionally strikes the ball with the hand(s)) or pushes the ball to the floor once or several times (4-15-1). An interrupted dribble occurs when the ball is loose after deflecting off the dribbler or after it momentarily gets away from the dribbler (4-15-5). Rebounding is an attempt by any player to secure possession of the ball following a try or tap for goal (4-37-1).

Topic:
Player Control

A player is in control of the ball when he/she is holding or dribbling a live ball inbounds (4-12-1; 4-15-5).

The player is not in control while slapping the ball during a jump, when a pass rebounds from his/her hand, when he/she fumbles; when he/she bats a rebound or pass away from other players who are attempting to get it; or during an interrupted dribble (4-15-4 Note 2; 4-15-5).

> ## Fundamental #1
>
> While the ball remains live, a loose ball always remains in control of the team whose player last had control, unless it is a try for a goal.

Neither team control nor player control exists during a dead ball, throw-in, a jump ball or when the ball is in flight during a try or tap for goal (4-12-6).

Topic:
Team Control

A team is in control of the ball when a player of the team is in control (4-12-2-a), while a live ball is being passed among teammates (4-12-2-b) and during an interrupted dribble (4-12-2-c).

Team control continues until the ball is in flight during a try or tap for goal; an opponent secures control; or the ball becomes dead (4-12-3a through c).

Fundamental #2

Neither a team nor any player is ever in control during a dead ball, jump ball or throw-in or when the ball is in flight during a try for a field goal.

While the ball remains live a loose ball always remains in control of the team whose player last had control, unless it is a try or tap for goal (4-12-4).

Team control does not exist during a jump ball or the touching of a rebound, but is re-established when a player secures control (4-12-5).

Neither team control nor player control exists during a dead ball, throw-in, a jump ball or when the ball is in flight during a try or tap for goal (4-12-6).

 COMMENT: A player is in control only when the player is holding or dribbling a live ball inbounds, but team control includes passing activity. When a team secures control, that team continues to be in control until the ball is in flight on a try or tap for goal, or an opponent has secured control or the ball has become dead. This has an influence on rules such as team-control fouls, three-seconds and frontcourt/backcourt. No team is in control while the ball is dead, during a throw-in or a jump, after the ball has left the hand on a try or tap for goal, nor during the period which follows any of these acts while the ball is slapped away from other players in an attempt to secure control.

Team Control: Caseplays

4.12.2 SITUATION: A1's missed try rebounds directly to A's backcourt where A2 gains control. Is this a violation? **RULING:** No. Both player and team control ended when A1 released the ball on a try. The rebound into A's backcourt was not in control of either team (9-9-1).

4.12.6 SITUATION: During a throw-in by A1 from the end line by A's basket: (a) A2 is in the restricted lane area; or (b) the throw-in is touched by A2 before it goes across the division line where it is recovered by A3. **RULING:** There is no three-second count in (a) or a backcourt rule in effect in (b) during a throw-in. The throw-in ends in (b) when A2 legally touches the ball, but the backcourt count does not start until A3 gains control (9-7, 8).

Topic 5

Jump Ball and Held Ball

Key Terms

A jump ball is a method of putting the ball into play to start the game and each extra period by tossing it up between two opponents in the center restraining circle, or if the ball is touched simultaneously and goes out of bounds before the alternating-possession procedure has been established (4-28-1). Team control does not exist during a jump ball but is established when a player secures control (4-12-5).

A held ball occurs when opponents have their hands so firmly on the ball that control cannot be obtained without undue roughness or when an opponent places his/her hand(s) on the ball and prevents an airborne player from throwing the ball or releasing it on a try (4-25-1, 2).

Alternating possession is the method of putting the ball in play by a throw-in other than the start of the game and the start of each extra period (6-4-1).

> ## Fundamental #4
>
> The jump ball, throw-in and the free throw are the only methods of getting a dead ball live.

Topic:
Jump Ball

To start the game and each extra period, the ball shall be put in play in the center restraining circle by a jump ball between any two opponents (6-2-2). In all other jump-ball situations the teams will alternate taking the ball out of bounds for a throw-in. (4-28-2).

The referee shall designate the official to toss the ball in the center restraining circle for all jump-ball situations (2-5-1). The ball becomes live when it leaves the referee's hand on the toss (6-1-2a).

> ## In Simple Terms
>
> On a jump ball, the ball becomes live when it leaves the referee's hand on the toss. However, the clock does not start until the ball is legally tapped.

The jump ball begins when the ball leaves the referee's hand(s) and ends when the touched ball contacts a nonjumper, the floor, a basket or backboard (4-28-3).

The clock shall be started when the tossed ball is legally touched (5-9-2).

Jump Ball: Caseplays

6.1.2 SITUATION A: Is the ball live before the tossed ball is legally tapped? **RULING:** Yes.

Topic:

Jump Ball Administration

For any jump ball, each jumper shall have both feet within that half of the center restraining circle which is farther from his/her basket (6-3-1).

When the referee is ready and until the ball is tossed, nonjumpers shall not move onto the center restraining circle or change position around the center restraining circle (6-3-2a, b).

Teammates may not occupy adjacent positions around the center restraining circle if an opponent indicates a desire for one of these positions before the referee is ready to toss the ball (6-3-3).

The referee shall then toss the ball upward between the jumpers in a plane at right angles to the sidelines. The toss shall be to a height greater than either of them can jump so that it will drop between them (6-3-4).

Until the tossed ball is touched by one or both jumpers, nonjumpers shall not have either foot break the plane of the center restraining circle cylinder or take a position in any occupied space (6-3-5a, b).

The tossed ball must be touched by one or both of the jumpers after it reaches its highest point. If the ball contacts the floor without being touched by at least one of the jumpers, the referee shall toss it again (6-3-6).

Neither jumper shall touch the tossed ball before it reaches its highest point, leave the center restraining circle until the ball has been touched, catch the jump ball or touch the ball more than twice (6-3-7a-d).

The jump ball and the restrictions end when the touched ball contacts one of the eight nonjumpers, an official, the floor, a basket or backboard. During a jump ball, a jumper is not required to face his/her own basket, provided he/she is in the proper half of the center restraining circle. The jumper is also not required to jump and attempt to touch the tossed ball. However, if neither jumper touches the ball it should be tossed again with both jumpers being ordered to jump and try to touch the ball (6-3-7 note).

Jump Ball Administration: Caseplays

6.3.2 SITUATION: The referee is ready to toss the ball to start the game. (a) A1 who was on the center restraining circle backs off; (b) B1 moves onto the restraining circle into an unoccupied spot; (c) B2 moves off the circle and goes behind A2 and is within 3 feet of the circle; or (d) B3 moves off the circle about 5 feet and moves around behind A3 and A4 who are occupying spaces on the circle. **RULING:** Legal in (a) and (d), but a violation in both (b) and (c). Moving off the restraining circle in (a), and around the circle when more than 3 feet away as in (d), is permissible. It is a violation to move onto the circle as in (b), until the ball leaves the official's hand, or into an occupied space as in (c), until the ball is touched. The violation by B results in a throw-in for Team A (4-3).

6.3.7 SITUATION: During a jump: (a) jumper A1 touches the ball simultaneously with both hands and then with one hand followed with one hand again; or (b) jumpers A1 and B1 do not touch the ball until one or both have returned to the floor. **RULING:** In (a), simultaneous touching counts as one, but the second separate touch causes a violation by A1 for touching the ball more than twice. In (b), it is legal; however, if the tossed ball contacts the floor without being touched, the referee shall toss it again.

Ball Last Touched Simultaneously

If the ball goes out of bounds and was last touched simultaneously by two opponents, both of whom are inbounds or out of bounds, or if the official is in doubt as to who last touched the ball or if the officials disagree, play shall be resumed by the team entitled to the alternating-possession throw-in at the spot out of bounds nearest to where the simultaneous violation occurred (7-3-1).

If the alternating-possession procedure has not been established, play shall be resumed by a jump ball between the two players involved in the center restraining circle (7-3-2).

 # Rationale

The two players who knocked the ball out are responsible for the ball being out of bounds even though no control was established. To be fair, those two players are required to jump the subsequent jump ball until control is established.

Ball Last Touched Simultaneously: Caseplay

6.4.1 SITUATION C: Following the jump between A1 and B1 to start the first quarter, the jump ball: (a) is touched by A2 and it then goes out of bounds; (b) is touched simultaneously by A2 and B2 and it then goes out of bounds; (c) is simultaneously controlled by A2 and B2; or (d) is caught by A1. **RULING:** In (a), Team B will have a throw-in. The alternating-possession procedure is established and the arrow is set toward A's basket when a player of Team B has the ball for the throw-in. Team A will have the first opportunity to throw-in when the procedure is used. In (b) and (c), A2 and B2 will jump in the center restraining circle regardless of where the ball went out or where the held ball occurred. In (d), Team B will have a throw-in because of the violation and the arrow for the alternating-possession will be pointed towards Team A's basket (4-12-1; 4-28-1).

Topic:
Held Ball

A held ball occurs when opponents have their hands so firmly on the ball that control cannot be obtained without undue roughness or when an opponent places his/her hand(s) on the ball and prevents an airborne player from throwing the ball or releasing it on a try (4-25-1, 2).

If a held ball or violation occurs so near the expiration of time that the clock is not stopped before time expires, the quarter or extra period ends with the held ball or violation (5-6-2 Exception 2).

Time-out occurs and the clock, if running, shall be stopped when an official signals a held ball (5-8-1b). When a held ball occurs, the ball shall become dead (6-7-3).

An alternating-possession throw-in shall result when a held ball occurs (6-4-3a, 7-4-7).

Held Ball: Caseplay

4.25.2 SITUATION: A1 jumps to try for goal or to pass the ball. B1 leaps or reaches and is able to put his/her hands on the ball and keep A1 from releasing it. A1: (a) returns to the floor with the ball; or (b) is unable to control the ball and it drops to the floor. RULING: A held ball results immediately in (a) and (b) when airborne A1 is prevented from releasing the ball to pass or try for goal.

Topic:
Alternating Possession

Alternating possession is the method of putting the ball in play by a throw-in other than the start of the game and the start of each extra period (6-4-1).

Rationale

Alternating possession was added to eliminate most jump ball situations which often took a long time to administer or were too often poorly administered.

Scorer's Duties

The scorer shall record the jump balls for the alternating-possession procedure and be responsible for the possession arrow (2-11-7).

The Arrow

The possession arrow is a device located at the scorer's table which is used to indicate the direction of a team's basket for the alternating-possession procedure (4-2-2).

Setting the Arrow

Alternating-possession control is established and the initial direction of the possession arrow is set toward the opponent's basket when a player secures control of the ball, as after the jump ball (4-3-1). The arrow can also be established when the ball is placed at the disposal of the free thrower after a common foul when the bonus free throw is in effect (4-3-2). The final way to establish the arrow is when the ball is placed at the disposal of the thrower after a violation during or following the jump before a player secures control, the free throws for a noncommon foul or a common foul before the bonus free throw is in effect (4-3-3).

In all jump-ball situations, other than the start of the game and each extra period, the teams will alternate taking the ball out of bounds for a throw-in. The team obtaining control from the jump ball establishes the alternating-possession procedure, and the arrow is set toward the opponent's basket. Control may also be established by the results of a violation or foul (6-4-1).

In Simple Terms

There are nine alternating possession situations:

1. Held ball.
2. Double personal foul.
3. Double technical foul.
4. Uncertainty as to who caused the ball to go out of bounds.
5. A simultaneous free-throw violation.
6. Ball lodges on a basket support.
7. Ball becomes dead with neither team in control and no goal is scored and no infraction or end of period is involved.
8. Opponents commit simultaneous personal or technical fouls.
9. Opponents commit simultaneous goaltending or basket-interference violations.

The direction of the possession arrow is reversed immediately after an alternating-possession throw-in ends. An alternating-possession throw-in ends when the throw-in ends or when the throw-in team violates (6-4-4).

The opportunity to make an alternating-possession throw-in is lost if the throw-in team violates. If either team fouls during an alternating-possession throw-in, it does not cause the throw-in team to lose the possession arrow (6-4-5).

Setting the Arrow: Caseplays

4.3.2 SITUATION: A1 is fouled by B1 just after the ball leaves the referee's hand(s) on the jump to start the first extra period of play. Both teams are in the bonus. How is the alternating-possession arrow established? **RULING:** When the bonus is in effect, the possession arrow is set toward the opponent's basket when the ball is placed at the disposal of the free thrower.

4.3.3 SITUATION: During the jump to start the game, A1 slaps the ball out of bounds. Before the ball is at B1's disposal for a throw-in, B2 is charged with a technical foul. **RULING:** Team A will attempt two free throws followed by a division-line throw-in opposite the table. When the ball is at the disposal of the thrower of Team A, the arrow will be set pointing toward Team B's basket.

6.4.1 SITUATION A: Twelve minutes before the game is scheduled to start, team member A1 dunks the ball and is charged with a technical foul. B1 is discovered to be wearing an illegal shirt, as the players prepare for the start of the game. **RULING:** The game will be started by awarding Team B two free throws for A1's technical foul. Team A will then be given two free throws and the ball for a division-line throw-in for B1's infraction. When the thrower of Team A has the ball for the throw-in, they have control for purposes of establishing the procedure and the arrow is immediately set toward B's basket. Team B will have the first opportunity for an alternating-possession throw-in (4-3).

6.4.1 SITUATION E: During the jump ball to start the game, after the ball is tossed: (a) B1 violates; (b) B1 fouls A1; or (c) A1 intentionally fouls B1. When is the possession arrow set? **RULING:** In (a) and (b), when the ball is in the possession of the thrower of Team A, Team A has gained control for purposes of establishing the procedure, and the arrow is immediately pointed in the direction of B's basket. In (c), the arrow is pointed in the direction of A's basket when a player of B has the ball or it is at the thrower's disposal for the throw-in following the free throws (4-3).

6.4.5 SITUATION A: Team A is awarded the ball for a throw-in under the alternating procedure. A1 commits a violation. **RULING:** B's ball for a throw-in because of the violation. In addition, the possession arrow is reversed and is pointed towards B's basket. Team B will have the next throw-in opportunity under the alternating procedure. Team A has lost its opportunity by virtue of the violation. A violation by Team A during an alternating-possession throw-in is the only way a team loses its turn under the procedure (6-4-4).

COMMENT: If a foul by either team occurs before an alternating-possession throw-in ends, the foul is penalized as required and play continues as it normally would, but the possession arrow is not reversed. The same team will still have the arrow for the next alternating-possession throw-in. The arrow is reversed when an alternating-possession throw-in ends.

6.4.5 SITUATION B: During an alternating-possession throw-in, thrower A1 holds the ball through the end-line plane and B1 grabs it, resulting in a held ball. **RULING:** Since the throw-in had not ended and no violation occurred, it is still A's ball for an alternating-possession throw-in (4-42-5).

Starting Quarters via Alternating Possession

The referee shall administer the alternating-possession throw-in to start the second, third and fourth quarters (2-5-2). The throw-in shall be from out of bounds at the division line opposite the scorer's and timer's table (6-4-2).

The referee shall confer with the official scorer at halftime to determine the possession arrow is pointed in the proper direction to begin play in the third quarter (2-5-6).

Starting Quarters via Alternating Possession: Caseplay

6.4.1 SITUATION B: A technical foul by B1 occurs during the dead ball which precedes the second quarter. **RULING:** Start the second quarter by administering the free throws. The last free throw is followed by a throw-in at the division line from the side opposite the table. The possession arrow is not reversed. The opportunity for a throw-in under the alternating-possession procedure is not affected by the foul (6-4-5; 8-5-2).

Throw-ins via Alternating Possession

Alternating-possession throw-ins shall be from the out-of-bounds spot nearest to where the ball was located. An alternating-possession throw-in shall result when a held ball occurs, the ball goes out of bounds and was last touched simultaneously by two opponents, simultaneous free-throw violations occur, or a live ball lodges between the backboard and ring or comes to rest on the flange, unless a free throw or throw-in follows.

In Simple Terms

The arrow is only reversed when an alternating-possession throw-in ends.

An alternating-possession throw-in also shall result when the ball becomes dead when neither team is in control and no goal, infraction nor end of a quarter/extra period is involved, opponents commit simultaneous goaltending or basket-interference violations or double personal, double technical or simultaneous fouls occur and the point of interruption is such that neither team is in control and no goal, infraction, nor end of quarter/extra period is involved (6-4-3 a-g).

Throw-ins via Alternating Possession: Caseplays

4.42.5 SITUATION: Team A is awarded an alternating-posession throw-in. A1's throw-in pass is illegally kicked by B2. **RULING:** As a result of B2's kicking violation, Team A is awarded a throw-in at the designated spot nearest to where the violation occurred. Since the throw-in was not contacted "legally," the throw-in had not ended. Therefore, the arrow remains with Team A for the next alternating-possession throw-in (6-4-4).

6.4.3 SITUATION C: A1 is fouled in the act of shooting by B1. A1's try lodges between the ring and the backboard. **RULING:** A1 is awarded two free throws and play continues as per any similar free-throw situation. Even though the ball lodged, alternating possession is not used as the ball is put in play with the free throws resulting from B1's foul. Alternating possession would have been used to resume play in this situation if no foul had been committed.

*6.4.1 SITUATION D: It is Team B's turn for the next throw-in under the alternating-possession procedure. By mistake, Team A is given that throw-in. Team A (a) commits a throw-in violation, or (b) releases the ball on the alternating-possession throw-in, but before the ball is legally touched inbounds, Team A or Team B commits a foul. **RULING:** Once the throw-in ends – it is too late to change anything. In (a), the throw-in ends when Team A violates and results in a throw-in for Team B as well as the arrow for the next alternating possession. In (b), the alternating-possession throw-in did not end when the foul occurred. Therefore, the alternating-possession mistake is corrected and the arrow now favors Team B; penalize the foul appropriately (4-42-5; 6-4-4; 6-4-5).

Topic 6

Free Throw

Key Terms

A free throw is the opportunity given a player to score one point by an unhindered try for goal from within the free-throw semicircle and behind the free-throw line (4-20-1). The free throw starts and the ball becomes live when the ball is at the disposal of the free thrower (4-20-2; 6-1-2c). The free throw ends when the try is successful, when it is certain the try will not be successful, when the try touches the floor or any player, or when the ball becomes dead (4-20-3).

A multiple throw is a succession of free throws attempted by the same team (4-30-1).

Topic:
Free Thrower

The free throw(s) awarded because of a personal foul shall be attempted by the offended player. If such player must withdraw because of an injury or disqualification, his/her substitute shall attempt the throw(s) unless no substitute is available, in which case any teammate may attempt the throw(s) as selected by the team captain or head coach (8-2).

The free throws awarded because of a technical foul may be attempted by any player of the offended team, including an eligible substitute or designated starter. The coach or captain shall designate the free thrower(s) (8-3).

 COMMENT: When A1 is designated to attempt a free throw(s), no other player shall be permitted to make the attempt unless A1 is injured or disqualified prior to the attempt. If the wrong player attempts the free throw, it may be corrected as prescribed in the correctable error rule. In certain situations, the attempt by the wrong player may be due to a justifiable misunderstanding. In such case, there should be no penalty. But, if it is a situation in which it is reasonable to expect the player to know that he/she is not the proper one to attempt the free throw, a technical foul for unsporting conduct shall be called. In this situation, the proper player is entitled to his/her free throw(s) which will be followed by the administration of the technical foul (8.2).

Free Thrower: Caseplay

8.2 SITUATION A: A1 is unable to attempt either of the two free throws awarded because A1 was injured during the play. A6 enters, replaces A1 and attempts the first free throw. A7 reports and enters to replace A6. **RULING:** A7 must return to the bench and A6 remains in the game to attempt the second free throw. Since A6 replaced A1, A6 must shoot both free throws, unless A6 is injured or disqualified before attempting the second free throw. If this situation involved technical foul free throws, A7 would be allowed to enter and attempt the second free throw (8-3).

8.2 SITUATION B: A1 is fouled and will be shooting two free throws. After A1's first free-throw attempt, B6 (Team B's only remaining eligible substitute) replaces B2. A1's second free-throw attempt is unsuccessful. During rebounding action for A1's missed second free-throw attempt, and before the clock starts, A1 pushes B3 in the back causing B3 to roll an ankle. Team B is in the bonus. B3 is unable to immediately continue playing. Team B requests and is granted a time out in order to allow B3 to recover from the ankle injury so as to remain in the game. B3 is still not able to play after the time out has ended. **RULING:** B2 may return to the game and replace B3 and shoot B3's free throw attempts despite having been replaced since he/she is the only available substitute (3-3-4).

8.3 SITUATION: A technical foul is issued prior to the start of the game and the game begins with free throws. Non-starter, A6, is brought in to the game to attempt the free throws and replaces starter A5. **RULING:** Legal substitute. The ball becomes live to start the game when placed at A6's disposal. A6 and A5 are subject to proper substitution rules. A5 may not re-enter until the next opportunity to substitute after the clock has been properly started (3-2-2a; 3-3-4).

Ten Seconds

The try for goal shall be made within 10 seconds after the ball has been placed at the disposal of the free thrower at the free-throw line. This shall apply to each free throw (8-4). His/her try must cause the ball to enter the basket or touch the ring before the free throw ends (9-1-3).

 # Rationale

The committee felt 10 seconds was adequate enough time for a free thrower to be able to attempt a free thrower without improperly delaying the game.

Where Attempted

The try shall be attempted from within the free-throw semicircle and behind the free-throw line (9-1-1).

Topic:
Lane Spaces

Dimensions

The lane-space marks (2 inches by 8 inches) and neutral-zone marks (12 inches by 8 inches) identify areas which extend 36 inches from the outer edge of the lane lines toward the sidelines. There are three lane spaces on each lane boundary line (1-5-2).

Occupied by Players

During a free throw when lane spaces may be occupied, a maximum of four defensive and two offensive players may occupy said marked lane spaces (8-1-4a).

A player occupying a marked lane space may not have either foot beyond the vertical plane of the outside edge of any lane boundary, or beyond the vertical plane of any edge of the space (2 inches by 36 inches) designated by a lane-space mark or beyond the vertical plane of any edge of the space (12 inches by 36 inches) designated by a neutral zone. A player shall position one foot near the outer edge of the free-throw lane line. The other foot may be positioned anywhere within the designated 36-inch lane space (9-1-3g).

The lane areas from the end line up to, and including, the neutral-zone marks shall remain vacant (8-1-4b).

The first marked lane spaces on each side of the lane, above and adjacent to the neutral-zone marks, shall be occupied by opponents of the free thrower. No teammate of the free thrower shall occupy either of these marked lane spaces (8-1-4c).

The second marked lane spaces on each side may be occupied by teammates of the free thrower (8-1-4d). The third marked lane spaces on each side, nearest the free thrower, may be occupied by opponents of the free thrower (8-1-4e). Players shall be permitted to move along and across the lane to occupy a vacant space within the limitations listed in this rule (8-1-4f). Not more than one player may occupy any part of a marked lane space (8-1-4g).

If the ball is to become dead when the last free throw for a specific penalty is not successful, players shall not occupy any spaces along the free-throw lane (8-1-3).

Any player, other than the free thrower, who does not occupy a marked lane space must be behind the free-throw line extended and behind the three-point line (8-1-5). These players may not have either foot beyond the vertical plane of the free-throw line extended and the three-point line which is farther from the basket (9-1-3f).

Occupied by Players: Caseplays

8.1.3 SITUATION: Players attempt to take positions along the lane when: (a) the free throw is from the first foul of a false double foul and the last part is a double personal foul; (b) the free throw is between quarters; or (c) there is a multiple throw with the first for a personal and last for a technical foul. **RULING:** In (a), the first marked spaces must be occupied by opponents of the thrower during free throw(s) for the personal foul and other marked spaces may properly be occupied. In (b) and (c), the official should order the players away (8-6, 7; 4-19-8a; 7-5-3b; 4-36-1, 2b).

8.1.4 SITUATION: A1 is at the free-throw line for the first attempt of a bonus situation. B4 and B5 are positioned on the lane in the area below the neutral-zone marks and A4 and A5 are positioned in the first marked lane spaces. The official fails to notice the improper alignment and bounces the ball to A1. **RULING:** If the improper alignment is not corrected prior to the free thrower having the ball at his/her disposal, a simultaneous free-throw violation shall be called. Team B occupied an area that must remain vacant and Team A is prohibited from occupying the first marked lane spaces (8-1-4b, c; 9-1-2 Penalty 3).

*8.1.4 SITUATION B: A1 is at the free-throw line for the first attempt of a bonus situation. In (a), two Team B and two Team A players occupy the first and second marked lane spaces, respectively. B3 occupies one of the third marked lane spaces. A3 attempts to occupy the vacant third marked lane space; or (b) two Team B players occupy the first marked lane spaces. The offense chooses not to occupy any marked lane spaces. Two more Team B players choose to occupy the second marked lane spaces. **RULING:** Illegal in (a). In (a), A3 is not permitted to occupy the third marked lane space. Only two offensive players may occupy marked lane spaces during a free throw. If the improper alignment is not corrected prior to the thrower having the ball at his/her disposal, a free-throw violation shall be called on Team A immediately. Legal in (b), four defensive players are permitted in any of the first three vacant marked lane spaces.

Topic:
Free Throw: Live Ball

One of the ways to get a dead ball live is to resume play by a free throw (6-1-1). The ball becomes live on a free throw when it is at the disposal of the free thrower (6-1-2c).

When a free throw is awarded, the ball shall be placed at the disposal of the free thrower (bounced) by the administering official and the free throw count shall begin. Either or both teams may be charged with a violation (8-1-1).

If a free throw for a personal foul, other than intentional or flagrant, is unsuccessful, or if there is a multiple throw for a personal foul(s) and the last free throw is unsuccessful, the ball remains live (8-6-1).

Free Throw: Live Ball: Caseplays

6.1.2 SITUATION A: Is the ball live during a free throw? **RULING:** Yes.

6.7.5 SITUATION: A1 is at the free-throw line for the second of two attempts. After the ball is at A1's disposal, B1 commits a lane violation. The administering official inadvertently sounds his/her whistle after the ball has been released. **RULING:** The whistle does not cause the ball to become dead until the free throw ends. Because B1 violated, in all cases, a substitute throw is awarded if the free-throw attempt by A1 is unsuccessful (4-20-3).

8.1.1 SITUATION A: A1 is awarded two free throws. After the players have had sufficient opportunity and time to take their positions for the first throw, the administering official bounces the ball to the free thrower. Did the official follow proper procedure? **RULING:** Yes. On free throws, the word "disposal," is interpreted to mean that the official shall bounce the ball to the free thrower, but if the free thrower refuses to accept it, the official may place the ball on the floor at the free-throw line and begin the count. This procedure constitutes putting the ball at the free-thrower's disposal. However, in this situation, the ball becomes live when it is caught by the free thrower (4-4-7b).

8.6.1 SITUATION: A1 is about to attempt the first of a one-and-one free-throw situation. The administering official steps in and erroneously informs players that two shots will be taken. A1's first attempt is unsuccessful. The missed shot is rebounded by B2, with several players from both teams attempting to secure the rebound. The officials recognize their error at this point. **RULING:** Both teams made an attempt to rebound despite the official's error and had an equal opportunity to gain possession of the rebound. Play should continue (2-3).

Topic:
Free Throw: Dead Ball

The ball becomes dead, or remains dead, when it is apparent the free throw will not be successful on a free throw which is to be followed by another free throw or throw-in (6-7-2a, b).

Free Throw: Dead Ball: Caseplay

6.7 SITUATION B: After A1 starts the free-throwing motion, A2 commits a foul by pushing B1 along the lane. **RULING:** If the foul occurred after the ball was in flight, the point counts if the throw was successful and no substitute throw is awarded if not successful. If A1 had not released the free-throw attempt before A2 fouled B1, the ball became dead when the team-control foul occurred and A1 is permitted an unhindered free throw. The foul by A2 results in the ball being awarded to Team B at the out-of-bounds spot nearest to where A2 fouled B1, unless the free-throw attempt by A1 is successful in which case B will throw-in from out of bounds anywhere along the end line where the free throw was scored (4-19-7, 9; 7-5-7).

Topic:
Free Throw Penalties

Bonus Throw

A bonus free throw is the second free throw awarded for a common foul (except a player-control or team-control foul) beginning with a team's seventh foul in each half. For the seventh, eighth and ninth foul, the bonus is awarded only if the first free throw is successful. Beginning with a team's 10th foul in each half the bonus is awarded whether or not the first free throw is successful (4-8-1a, b).

Bonus Throw: Caseplay

4.8.2 SITUATION: (a) A1 is charged with a player-control foul; or (b) a Team A member dunks during the pregame warm-ups. **RULING:** In both (a) and (b), the foul counts toward disqualification and it counts as one of the seven team fouls to reach the bonus. In (b), a technical foul is also charged indirectly to the Team A's head coach (10-3-3).

Order of Administration

Penalties for fouls are administered in the order in which the fouls occurred (8-7).

Order of Administration: Caseplays

8.7 SITUATION A: A1 is attempting the second free throw of a two-shot foul. While the second free throw is in flight, A2 and B1 punch each other simultaneously. **RULING:** Both A2 and B1 are disqualified for fighting. Since this is a double personal foul, no free throws are awarded. The ball is put in play at the point of interruption. If A1's free throw is successful, Team B is awarded a throw-in from anywhere along the end line. If A1's free throw is unsuccessful, the alternating-possession procedure is used (4-19-8; 6-4-3g; 7-5-3b; 4-36; 10-3-8; 10 Penalty 1c, 8a(1)).

8.7 SITUATION B: B1 fouls A1 just as the first quarter ends and then A1 retaliates and intentionally contacts B1. A1's foul is a technical foul as it occurred during a dead ball. Team A is in the bonus. The officials by mistake administer the penalty for the technical foul before the free throw(s) by A1. **RULING:** The penalties should have been administered in the order in which the fouls occurred. However, since all merited free throws were attempted it does not constitute a correctable error situation. The second quarter will begin with an alternating-possession throw-in (4-19-5c).

8.7 SITUATION C: During the dead-ball period immediately following a goal by A1, B1 is charged with an unsporting technical foul for using profanity toward A1. A few seconds later, A2 is charged with an unsporting technical foul for taunting B1. Are free throws awarded or are the fouls considered to have occurred simultaneously with offsetting penalties? **RULING:** The fouls did not occur simultaneously and free throws are awarded in the order in which the fouls occurred. Team A will attempt their two free throws followed by Team B's two attempts. Following the second attempt by Team B, they will have a throw-in from the division line opposite the table (4-19-9, 10).

8.7 SITUATION D: A1 and B1 commit personal fouls against each other at the same time. The coach of Team A takes exception to the call and is charged with a technical foul. **RULING:** There are no free throws for the double personal foul committed by A1 and B1. Team B is awarded two free throws and the ball out of bounds at the division line for the technical foul charged directly to the coach of Team A (4-19-8, 9; 10-4-1e; 10 Penalty 1c).

Topic:
Free Throw:
Resumption of Play

Following Made Free Throw

After a free throw which is not followed by another free throw, the ball shall be put in play by a throw-in the same as after a field goal (7-5-7), if the try is for a personal foul other than intentional or flagrant, and is successful (8-5-1).

If the free throw is for a technical foul, the ball shall be put in play by any player of the free-thrower's team from out of bounds at the division line on the side opposite the scorer's and timer's table (8-5-2).

If the free throw is for an intentional personal foul or flagrant personal foul, the ball shall be put in play by any player of the free-thrower's team from the out-of-bounds spot nearest the foul (8-5-3).

Following Missed Free Throw

If a free throw for a personal foul, other than intentional or flagrant, is unsuccessful, or if there is a multiple throw for a personal foul(s) and the last free throw is unsuccessful, the ball remains live (8-6-1) and the clock shall be started when the ball touches or is touched by a player on the court (5-9-3).

Following Multiple Throws

If there is a multiple throw and both a personal and technical foul are involved, the tries shall be attempted in the order in which the related fouls were called, and if the last try is for a technical foul, or intentional or flagrant personal foul, the ball shall be put in play by a throw-in (8-6-2).

Topic 7

Throw-Ins

PlayPic™

Key Terms

A throw-in is a method of putting the ball in play from out of bounds (4-42-2).

Alternating possession is the method of putting the ball in play by a throw-in (4-2-1).

The thrower is the player who attempts to make a throw-in (4-42-1).

It is legal to extend the arms vertically above the shoulders and need not be lowered to avoid contact when guarding the player making a throw-in (4-24-1).

Neither team control nor player control exists during a throw-in (4-12-6).

> ## Fundamental #4
>
> The jump ball, the throw-in and the free throw are the only methods of getting a dead ball live.

On a throw-in, the ball becomes live when the ball is at the disposal of the thrower (6-1-2b).

After a dead ball, any player of the team in control shall make the throw-in from the designated out-of-bounds spot nearest to the ball when it becomes dead (7-4-4; 7-5-4).

Throw-in Begins, Ends

The throw-in and the throw-in count begin when the ball is at the disposal of a player of the team entitled to it (4-42-3).

The throw-in count ends when the ball is released by the thrower so the passed ball goes directly into the court (4-42-4).

The throw-in ends when the passed ball touches or is legally touched by another player inbounds (4-42-5-a), or out of bounds (4-42-5-b) or the throw-in team commits a throw-in violation (4-42-5-c).

◻ Rationale

The word "legally" was added to the definition of when a throw-in ends. The rule change eliminates the possibility of rewarding a team for committing a defensive violation, especially during an alternating-possession throw-in.

Throw-in Begins, Ends: Caseplay

4.42.3 SITUATION: Following a goal by A1 the ball is: (a) deflected under the bleachers; (b) lying on the court just outside the end line; or (c) deflected inbounds but the official has retrieved it and placed it on the floor outside the end line. When does the throw-in begin? **RULING:** In (a), the throw-in will not begin until the ball is at the disposal of

Team B. In (b) and (c), the ball becomes live and the throw-in and throw-in count begin when the ball is available or has been placed on the floor at the disposal of Team B (4-4-7).

4.42.5 SITUATION: Team A is awarded an alternating-possession throw-in. A1's throw-in pass is illegally kicked by B2. **RULING:** As a result of B2's kicking violation, Team A is awarded a new throw-in at the designated spot nearest to where the kicking violation (illegal touching) occurred. Since the throw-in was not contacted legally, the throw-in had not ended, and the arrow remains with Team A the next time an alternating-possession throw-in occurs (6-4-4).

6.1.2 SITUATION A: Is the ball live during a throw-in? **RULING:** Yes.

6.1.2 SITUATION B: Team A has just scored a goal. The ball is bouncing close to the end line when: (a) A1 calls for a time-out; or (b) A1 illegally contacts B1. **RULING:** In order to rule correctly, it depends on whether the bouncing ball is judged to be at the thrower's disposal. If the covering official judges it is at the thrower's disposal, he/she would start the count and the ball becomes live. In this case, in (a) no time-out is granted and the foul in (b) is penalized. If the ball is not at the thrower's disposal, the time-out is granted in (a) and the contact in (b) is ignored unless it is intentional or flagrant.

 COMMENT: In this situation, the covering official must give the new throw-in team a moment or two to recognize it is their ball for a throw-in and get a player into the area to pick up the ball. If the ball is near the end line, it is the throw-in team's responsibility to secure it and throw-in from anywhere out of bounds along the end line. The covering official shall start his/her throw-in count when it is determined the ball is available (4-4-7d).

Topic:
Alternating Possession

To start the second, third and fourth quarters, the ball shall be put in play by a throw-in under the alternating-possession procedure (6-2-3).

In all jump-ball situations, other than the start of the game and each extra period, the teams will alternate taking the ball out of bounds for a throw-in. The team obtaining control from the jump ball establishes the alternating-possession procedure, and the arrow is set toward the opponent's basket. Control may also be established by the results of a violation or foul (4-3; 6-4-1).

To start the second, third and fourth quarters, the throw-in shall be from out of bounds at the division line opposite the scorer's and timer's table (6-4-2).

Alternating-possession throw-ins shall be from the out-of-bounds spot nearest to where the ball was located. An alternating-possession throw-in shall result:

• When a held ball occurs.

• The ball goes out of bounds.

• A simultaneous free-throw violation occurs.

• A live ball lodges between the backboard and ring or comes to rest on the flange, unless a free throw or throw-in follows.

• The ball becomes dead when neither team is in control and no goal, infraction nor end of a quarter/extra period is involved.

• Opponents commit simultaneous goaltending or basket-interference violations.

• Double personal, double technical or simultaneous fouls occur and the point of interruption is such that neither team is in control and no goal, infraction, nor end of quarter/extra period is involved (6-4-3a-g; 7-3).

If the alternating-possession procedure has not been established, the jump ball shall be between the two players involved in the center restraining circle (6-4-3g Note).

The direction of the possession arrow is reversed immediately after an alternating-possession throw-in ends. An alternating-possession throw-in ends when the throw-in ends or when the throw-in team violates (6-4-4).

The opportunity to make an alternating-possession throw-in is lost if the throw-in team violates. If either team fouls during an alternating-possession throw-in, it does not cause the throw-in team to lose the possession arrow (6-4-5).

If the ball goes out of bounds and was last touched simultaneously by two opponents, both of whom are inbounds or out of bounds, or if the official is in doubt as to who last touched the ball or if the officials disagree, play shall be resumed by the team entitled to the alternating-possession throw-in at the spot out of bounds nearest to where the simultaneous violation occurred (7-3-1).

Alternating-Possession: Caseplay

6.4.1 SITUATION C: Following the jump between A1 and B1 to start the first quarter, the jump ball: (a) is touched by A2 and it then goes out of bounds; (b) is touched simultaneously by A2 and B2 and it then goes out of bounds; (c) is simultaneously controlled by A2 and B2; or (d) is caught by A1. **RULING:** In (a), Team B will have a throw-in. The alternating-possession procedure is established and the arrow is set toward A's basket when a player of Team B has the ball for the throw-in. Team A will have the first opportunity to throw-in when the procedure is used. In (b) and (c), A2 and B2 will jump in the center restraining circle regardless of where the ball went out or where the held ball occurred. In (d), Team B will have a throw-in because of the violation and the arrow for the alternating-possession will be pointed towards Team A's basket (4-12-1; 4-28-1).

6.4.3 SITUATION C: A1 is fouled in the act of shooting by B1. A1's try lodges between the ring and the backboard. **RULING:** A1 is awarded two free throws and play continues as per any similar free-throw situation. Even though the ball lodged, alternating possession is not used as the ball is put in play with the free throws resulting from B1's foul. Alternating possession would have been used to resume play in this situation if no foul had been committed.

6.4.5 SITUATION A: Team A is awarded the ball for a throw-in under the alternating procedure. A1 commits a violation. **RULING:** B's ball for a throw-in because of the violation. In addition, the possession arrow is reversed and is pointed towards B's basket. Team B will have the next throw-in opportunity under the alternating procedure. Team A has lost its opportunity by virtue of the violation. A violation by Team A during an alternating-possession throw-in is the only way a team loses its turn under the procedure.

 COMMENT: If a foul by either team occurs before an alternating-possession throw-in ends, the foul is penalized as required and play continues as it normally would, but the possession arrow is not reversed. The same team will still have the arrow for the next alternating-possession throw-in. The arrow is reversed when an alternating-possession throw-in ends (6-4-4).

6.4.5 SITUATION B: During an alternating-possession throw-in, thrower A1 holds the ball through the end-line plane and B1 grabs it, resulting in a held ball. **RULING:** Since the throw-in had not ended and no violation occurred, it is still A's ball for an alternating-possession throw-in (4-42-5).

9.4 SITUATION: At A's basket, the ball enters the net from below and passes through the basket: (a) The officials do not know whether a player of Team A or Team B was responsible; (b) the ball entered the basket after A1's pass was deflected by B1; or (c) A1 and B1 touched the ball simultaneously before it entered the basket. **RULING:** The ball becomes dead when it enters from below and passes through. In (a) and (c), a throw-in will follow by the team entitled to it under the alternating-possession procedure. In (b), it is A's ball for a throw-in, as B1 caused the violation.

Throw-in Replaces Jump Ball

The game and each extra period shall be started by a jump ball in the center restraining circle. In all other jump-ball situations the teams will alternate taking the ball out of bounds for a throw-in. Once the game begins, after any subsequent dead ball, the only way to get the ball live is to resume play by a jump ball in the center restraining circle, by a throw-in or by a free throw (4-28-2; 6-1-1).

Throw-in Replaces Jump Ball: Caseplays

6.4.1 SITUATION A: Twelve minutes before the game is scheduled to start, team member A1 dunks the ball and is charged with a technical foul. B1 is discovered to be wearing an illegal shirt, as the players prepare for the start of the game. **RULING:** The game will be started by awarding Team B two free throws for A1's technical foul. Team A will then be given two free throws and the ball for a division-line throw-in for B1's infraction. When the thrower of Team A has the ball for the throw-in, they have control for purposes of establishing the procedure and the arrow is immediately set toward B's basket. Team B will have the first opportunity for an alternating-possession throw-in (4-3).

6.4.1 SITUATION F: A team member of Team A is detected dunking about five minutes before the game and a team member of B does the same thing about a minute later. **RULING:** The game will start with administration of the technical-foul free throws in the order in which the fouls were called. Team B shoots first followed by Team A. Team A will then be given the ball for a throw-in at the division line opposite the table. When the thrower of Team A is bounced the ball or it is placed at his/her disposal, the possession arrow will be set pointing toward Team B's basket (4-3; 7-5-6a).

Officials' Duties

The referee shall administer the alternating-possession throw-in to start the second, third and fourth quarters (2-5-2).

When a team is entitled to a throw-in, an official shall signal the timer to stop the clock and clearly signal the act which caused the ball to become dead, the team entitled to the throw-in and the throw-in spot unless it follows a successful goal or an awarded goal (2-9-2a through c).

When a throw-in occurs, the official shall silently and visibly count seconds (2-7-9).

Throw-in Plane Violation Warnings

A warning to a team for delay is an administrative procedure by an official which is recorded in the scorebook by the scorer and reported to the coach for throw-in plane violations (4-47-1; 9-2-10).

Throw-in Plane Violation Warnings: Caseplays

9.2.10 SITUATION: A1 is out of bounds for a throw-in. B1 reaches through the boundary plane and knocks the ball out of A1's hands. Team B has not been warned previously for a throw-in plane infraction. **RULING:** B1 is charged with a technical foul and it also results in the official having a team warning recorded and reported to the head coach.

 COMMENT: In situations with the clock running and five or less seconds left in the game, a throw-in plane violation or interfering with the ball following a goal should be ignored if its only purpose is to stop the clock. However, if the tactic in any way interferes with the thrower's efforts to make a throw-in, a technical foul for delay shall be called even though no previous warning had been issued. In this situation, if the official stopped the clock and issued a team warning, it would allow the team to benefit from the tactic (4-47-1; 10-1-10).

10.1.10 SITUATION: Team B is warned in the first half when B1 reaches through the inbounds side of the throw-in boundary plane. Early in the fourth quarter either: (a) B1; or (b) B2 does the same thing. **RULING:** The warning is only given once per game to each team. Thereafter, another violation by a member of that team results in a technical foul. The technical foul in both (a) and (b) is charged to Team B (9-2-10).

Topic:
Point of Interruption

Point of interruption is a method of resuming play due to an official's accidental whistle, an interrupted game, a correctable error or a double personal, double technical or simultaneous foul (2-10-6; 4-19-8; 4-19-10; 4-36-1; 5-4-3).

When point of interruption is required, play shall be resumed by a throw-in to the team that was in control at a spot nearest to where the ball was located when the interruption occurred; a free throw or a throw-in when the interruption occurred during this activity or if a team is entitled to such; or an alternating-possession throw-in when neither team is in control and no goal, infraction, nor end of quarter/extra period is involved when the game is interrupted (4-36-2a through c).

From 1950 through 1986, the official was forced to designate the thrower and that player or that player's substitute had to make the throw-in. The deletion of designating simply means the official points in the direction of play, calls out the shirt color and points to the designated spot.

Did You Know?

Point of Interruption: Caseplay

7.5.3 SITUATION: An official sounds his/her whistle accidentally: (a) while A1 is dribbling and in player control; (b) while Team A is in control and passing among teammates; (c) while A1's unsuccessful try attempt is in flight; or (d) while A's successful try attempt is in flight. **RULING:** The ball is put in play at the point of interruption. In (a) and (b), Team A is awarded a throw-in at the nearest out-of-bounds spot to where the ball was when the whistle was accidentally sounded. In (c) and (d), the ball does not become dead until the try ends. In (c), since there is no team control when the ball becomes dead, the ball is put in play by the team entitled to the throw-in using the alternating-possession procedure. In (d), since a goal has been scored by Team A, the ball is given to Team B for a throw-in anywhere along the end line. (7-4-4; 4-12-3,6; 4-36)

Topic:
Throw-in Designated Spot

The designated throw-in spot is 3 feet wide with no depth limitation and is established by the official prior to putting the ball at the thrower's disposal (4-42-6).

The thrower must keep one foot on or over the spot until the ball is released. Pivot-foot restrictions and the traveling rule are not in effect for a throw-in (4-42-6 Note).

If, on an unofficial court, there is less than 3 feet of unobstructed space outside any sideline or end line, a narrow broken line shall be marked on the court parallel with and 3 feet inside that boundary. This restraining line becomes the boundary line during a throw-in on that side or end. It continues to be the boundary until the ball crosses the line (1-2-2).

If the designated throw-in spot is behind a backboard, the throw-in shall be made from the nearer free-throw lane line extended (7-5-5).

Throw-in Designated Spot: Caseplays

4.42.6 SITUATION: Following a personal foul by B3, the official indicates to Team A that they shall inbound the ball from a spot 10 feet from the sideline. In (a), A1 jumps in the air, over the designated spot, and passes the ball inbounds; (b) A1 has one foot within the designated-spot area but lifts it from the floor as the inbounds pass is made; or (c) A1 moves directly backwards from the designated spot by 6 feet and passes the ball inbounds. **RULING:** Legal in (a), (b) and (c). As long as the thrower maintains any portion of his/her body on or above the 3-foot designated-spot area while making the throw-in, the throw-in shall be legal.

7.4 SITUATION: What and where is the violation when: (a) A1 grabs a rebound at Team A's basket and passes the ball across the division line after which it is touched by A2 in the backcourt; (b) A1, in a corner near B's end line, throws a long pass which crosses the sideline in flight at the division line and touches in the bleachers near A's end-line extended; (c) A1 makes a throw-in at the division line and is first to touch the throw-in near B's basket; or (d) a throw-in by A1 from near the division line goes through A's basket before touching another player on the court? **RULING:** In (a), the violation is not for causing the ball to go into the backcourt, but for A2 touching it first after it went there. The throw-in for Team B is at a spot out of bounds nearest to the spot where A2 touched the ball. In (b), the violation is for causing the ball to be out of bounds, but since the ball is not out of bounds until it touches something, the violation occurs when the ball touches the bleachers and the throw-in by B is at the out-of-bounds spot nearest such touching. In (c), the violation is by A1 for not throwing the ball so that it touches or is touched by another player inbounds or out of bounds before going out of bounds untouched. In (d), the violation is by A1 for throwing the ball so that it enters the basket before touching another player on the court. The throw-in by B in (c) and (d) is from the spot of A1's throw-in (9-2-2, 6; 9-9-1).

7.5.1 SITUATION C: Following a violation, the throw-in spot has been properly designated and the covering official has waited a reasonable amount of time for Team A to provide a thrower. What does the official do now? **RULING:** The

> ## In Simple Terms
>
> During a designated-spot throw-in, only the thrower may be out of bounds.

official shall place the ball on the floor at the spot and begin the five-second throw-in count. Team A thrower must release the ball on a throw-in or request time-out before the five-second count is reached.

7.5.2 SITUATION B: Where is the throw-in when: (a) A1 travels and following the whistle the ball is thrown through the basket; (b) A1 fouls prior to A2's try which goes through the basket; (c) there is goaltending or basket interference by the offense; or (d) A1 is preparing to attempt the second free throw when A2 violates? **RULING:** In (a), (c) and (d), the throw-in will be from the out-of-bounds spot nearest to where the violation occurred. In (b), the throw-in is at the out-of-bounds spot nearest to where the foul occurred unless a free throw(s) results (4-42-6).

7.5.3 SITUATION C: An official sounds his/her whistle accidentally: (a) while A1 is dribbling and in player control; (b) while Team A is in control and passing among teammates; (c) while A1's unsuccessful try attempt is in flight; or (d) while A's successful try attempt is in flight. **RULING:** The ball is put in play at the point of interruption. In (a) and (b), Team A is awarded a throw-in at the nearest out-of-bounds spot to where the ball was when the whistle was accidentally sounded. In (c) and (d), the ball does not become dead until the try ends. In (c), since there is no team control when the ball becomes dead, the ball is put in play by the team entitled to the throw-in using the alternating-possession procedure. In (d), since a goal has been scored by Team A, the ball is given to Team B for a throw-in anywhere along the end line (7-4-4; 4-12-3,6; 4-36).

*9.2.1 SITUATION A: A1 is out of bounds for a designated-spot throw-in. The administering official has designated the spot and put the ball at A1's disposal. In order to avoid some of the defensive pressure near the throw-in spot, A1 takes several steps (a) directly backward, but keeps one foot on or over the designated area prior to releasing the ball on a throw-in pass; or (b) to the left or right. **RULING:** In (a), legal throw-in. It is permissible for the thrower to move backward or forward within the 3-foot-wide designated area without violating. In (b), A1 may move laterally if at least one foot is kept on or over the designated area until the ball is released, if not, a violation has occurred. The thrower may also jump vertically and pass from the designated throw-in spot.

COMMENT: Pivot-foot restrictions and the traveling rule are not in effect for a throw-in. The thrower must keep one foot on or over the spot until the ball is released.

*9.2.1 SITUATION B: A1, out of bounds for a designated spot throw-in: (a) muffs the pass from the official and it rolls forward; or (b) after receiving the ball from the official, fumbles the ball and leaves the designated spot to retrieve the fumble. **RULING:** In (a), the official should sound the whistle to prevent any violations and then start the throw-in procedure again. No throw-in violation should be called in this situation. In (b), a throw-in violation shall be called on A1 for leaving the designated spot.

Topic:
Throw-in Resumption-of-Play Procedure

When a team does not make a thrower available after a time-out or the intermission between any quarter, the resumption-of-play procedure is used to prevent delay. The administering official will sound the whistle to indicate play will resume. In each situation, the ball shall be put in play if Team A is ready or it shall be placed on the floor; the throw-in count shall begin and if a violation occurs, the procedure will be repeated for Team B; following a violation by one team only, if that team continues to delay when authorized to make a throw-in, it is a technical foul; following a violation by both teams, any further delay by either team is a technical foul (6-2-2; 7-4-4; 7-5-1a through d).

◪ Rationale

The resumption of play procedure was put in the rules book to reduce the instances of delay throughout the game. It went into the rules book as an original point of emphasis in 1987 and was so widely accepted and popular, it was written into the rules book language the next year.

Throw-in Resumption-of-Play Procedure: Caseplays

6.5 SITUATION: What is the procedure for putting the ball in play after: (a) a violation; (b) a charged time-out; (c) a substitution; (d) an official's time-out; (e) a successful field goal or free throw; (f) a score followed immediately by a time-out; or (g) after a common foul before the bonus rule applies. **RULING:** In (a), (b), (c), (d) and (g), the official shall hand or bounce (as applicable by NFHS Officials Manual) the ball to the player at the spot designated for the throw-in. In (e), the ball may be thrown in anywhere along the end line. The official shall not handle the ball unless in doing so it will prevent a delay. In (f), the official shall hand or bounce (as applicable by NFHS Officials Manual) the ball to a player of the team entitled to the throw-in, after which the throw-in may be made anywhere along the end line (7-5-7; 8-5).

7.5.1 SITUATION A: The administering official has reached a five-second throw-in count on Team A after placing the ball on the floor when A was not ready to resume play following a time-out. What happens next? **RULING:** The violation is administered and the ball is made available to Team B for a throw-in, at the same spot. If a Team B player is not in position, the same procedure is followed. If both teams have violated, a technical foul will be assessed for any further delay by either team. Team A must now have a thrower available, plus all other players on the court and Team B must be on the court ready to play also. If either or both teams are not in compliance immediately, a technical foul shall be charged.

COMMENT: Each different time a team has delayed returning to the court after a time-out or between quarters (unless either team is not on the court to start the second half), the resumption-of-play procedure should be used. However, if a team refuses to play after technical fouls have been assessed, the game may be forfeited (4-38; 5-4-1).

7.5.1 SITUATION B: Team A does not break the huddle after the second horn for a 60-second time-out. The official puts the ball down at the designated spot and begins the five-second count. The administering official is between four and five on the count when Team B reaches over the boundary and grabs the ball. **RULING**: Delay-of-game warning on Team B for reaching across the plane. No Team A member ever possessed the ball for the throw-in; therefore, a technical foul would not be assessed (9-2 Penalty 3).

Resuming Play After a Goal

After a goal or awarded goal, the team not credited with the score shall make the throw-in from the end of the court where the goal was made and from any point outside the end line. A team retains this privilege if the scoring team commits a violation or common foul (before the throw-in ends and before the bonus is in effect) and the ensuing throw-in spot would have been on the end line (7-5-7b). Any player of the team may make a direct throw-in or he/she may pass the ball along the end line to a teammate(s) outside the boundary line (7-4-3; 7-5-7a).

Resuming Play After a Goal: Caseplays

6.5 SITUATION: What is the procedure for putting the ball in play after a successful field goal or free throw? **RULING:** The ball may be thrown in anywhere along the end line. The official shall not handle the ball unless in doing so it will prevent a delay (7-5-7; 8-5).

7.5.7 SITUATION D: Team A scores a field goal. B1 picks up the ball and steps out of bounds at the end line to prepare for a throw-in. Before the throw-in is completed, A2 is called for an intentional (or flagrant) foul on B3 near the end line. **RULING:** B3 would shoot the two free throws for the intentional (or flagrant) foul with the lane cleared. Team B will then have a designated spot throw-in on the end line (7-5-4b).

Resuming Play After a Foul

A penalty is an action assessed by an official to a player or team for a rules infractions (4-32). The penalty for a foul is the charging of the offender with the foul and awarding a free throw(s) and/or the ball for a throw-in as specified by the type of infraction committed.

After a player-control foul, a team-control foul or a common foul prior to the bonus rule being in effect, any player of the offended team shall make the throw-in from the designated out-of-bounds spot nearest the foul (4-19-2; 4-19-6; 4-19-7; 7-5-5).

After a technical foul, any player of the team to whom the free throws have been awarded shall make the throw-in from out of bounds at the division line on the side of the court opposite the scorer's and timer's table (4-19-5; 7-5-8).

After a double personal foul, a double technical foul or a simultaneous foul, play shall be resumed at the point of interruption (4-19-8a; 4-19-8b; 4-19-10; 4-36; 7-5-3b).

After an intentional personal foul or flagrant personal foul, any player of the team to whom the free throws have been awarded shall make the throw-in from the out-of-bounds spot nearest the foul (4-19-3; 4-19-4; 7-5-10).

Resuming Play After a Foul: Caseplays

6.5 SITUATION: What is the procedure for putting the ball in play after a common foul before the bonus rule applies? **RULING:** The official shall hand or bounce (as applicable by NFHS Officials Manual) the ball to the player at the spot designated for the throw-in (7-5-7; 8-5).

6.7 SITUATION B: After A1 starts the free-throwing motion, A2 commits a foul by pushing B1 along the lane. **RULING:** If the foul occurred after the ball was in flight, the point counts if the throw was successful and no substitute throw is awarded if not successful. If A1 had not released the free-throw attempt before A2 fouled B1, the ball became dead when the team-control foul occurred and A1 is permitted an unhindered free throw. The foul by A2 results in the ball being awarded to Team B at the out-of-bounds spot nearest to where A2 fouled B1, unless the free-throw attempt by A1 is successful in which case B will throw-in from out of bounds anywhere along the end line where the free throw was scored (4-19-7, 9; 7-5-7).

6.7 SITUATION D: A1 has started a try for a goal (is in the act of shooting), but the ball is not yet in flight when the official blows the whistle for B2 fouling A2. A1's try is successful. **RULING:** Score the goal by A1. If Team A is in the bonus, A2 will shoot free throws. If not, Team A will have a designated spot throw-in nearest to where the foul occurred.

7.5.4 SITUATION: Where is the ball awarded to the offended team when prior to the bonus: (a) while trying for goal A1 charges B1 and then releases the ball and it goes through Team A's basket; or (b) airborne shooter A1 charges into B1 after which A2 touches the ball while it is in the cylinder? **RULING:** In both (a) and (b), the goal does not count and the throw-in by B will be from the spot nearest the foul (2-9-2).

7.5.7 SITUATION C: Team B has scored a field goal and A1 has the ball along the end line for a throw-in. Team A is not in the bonus. Prior to the ball being thrown inbounds by A1: (a) B1 fouls A2 inbounds near A1; (b) B1 fouls A2 at the division line; (c) B1 fouls A2 beyond the division line; or (d) A2 requests a time-out. **RULING:** In (a) and (d), Team A may throw-in from anywhere out of bounds along the end line following the foul reporting and the time-out. In (b) and (c), the ball will be given to Team A for a throw-in from the spot out of bounds nearest to where the foul occurred.

7.5.7 SITUATION D: Team A scores a field goal. B1 picks up the ball and steps out of bounds at the end line to prepare for a throw-in. Before the throw-in is completed, A2 is called for an intentional (or flagrant) foul on B3 near the end line. **RULING:** B3 would shoot the two free throws for the intentional (or flagrant) foul with the lane cleared. Team B will then have a designated spot throw-in on the end line (7-5-4b).

7.5.7 SITUATION E: While A1's three-point field-goal attempt is in flight, A3 fouls B1 (B is not in the bonus) near the bottom block area. The three-point field-goal attempt is successful. **RULING:** Score the three-point goal for A1. Team B will be permitted to run the end line on the ensuing throw-in (6-7-7 Exception 2).

Resuming Play After a Free Throw

After a free throw which is not followed by another free throw, the ball shall be put in play by a throw-in as after a field goal if the try is for a personal foul other than intentional or flagrant, and is successful (7-5-7; 8-5-1); by any player of the free-thrower's team from out of bounds at the division line on the side opposite the scorer's and timer's table if the free throw is for a technical foul (7-5-6a; 8-5-2); or by any player of the free-thrower's team from the out-of-bounds spot nearest the foul if the free throw is for an intentional personal foul or flagrant personal foul (7-5-4b; 8-5-3).

If there is a multiple throw and both a personal and technical foul are involved, the tries shall be attempted in the order in which the related fouls were called, and if the last try is for a technical foul, or intentional or flagrant personal foul, the ball shall be put in play by a throw-in (8-6-2).

Resuming Play After a Free Throw: Caseplays

6.5 SITUATION: What is the procedure for putting the ball in play after a successful field goal or free throw? **RULING:** The ball may be thrown in anywhere along the end line. The official shall not handle the ball unless in doing so it will prevent a delay (7-5-7; 8-5).

6.7.4 SITUATION: Airborne A1 is fouled by B1 during a field-goal try or tap. After the ball is in flight, A1 illegally contacts B2 in returning to the floor. The ball goes through the basket. **RULING:** The foul by B1 did not cause the ball to become dead since A1 had started the trying or tapping motion. However, airborne shooter A1's foul is a player-control foul which does cause the ball to become dead immediately. No goal can be scored even if the ball had already gone through the basket before the foul. Since the goal is unsuccessful, A1 is awarded two free throws for the foul by B1. No players are allowed in the lane spaces as Team B will be awarded the ball following the last free throw. If the last throw is successful, the throw-in is from anywhere along the end line. If the last throw is unsuccessful, the throw-in is from a designated spot nearest the foul. The situation is a false double foul (4-11; 4-19-6, 9).

7.5.7 SITUATION F: A1 is fouled during an unsuccessful try and is awarded two free throws. While A1's successful first free throw is in flight, A2 fouls B1 along the lane. Team B is not in the bonus. The lane is cleared for A1's second attempt. A1 then violates by having a foot through the free-throw-line plane prematurely. **RULING:** The free-throw violation by A1 cancels the second attempt. Since Team B is not in the bonus, it results in a designated spot throw-in from the nearest spot out of bounds from where A2's foul occurred. Team B may not run the end line as the last free throw was unsuccessful (9-1-3e).

7.5.2 SITUATION C: A1 is awarded two free throws and makes the first one. A2 violates on A1's second attempt and B is awarded the ball for a throw-in. Can the thrower of B run the end line? **RULING:** No. The throw-in shall be from a designated spot outside the end line.

Resuming Play After a Free-Throw Violation

If the first or only free-throw lane violation is committed by the free-thrower or a teammate, the ball becomes dead when the violation occurs and no point can be scored by that throw. If the violation occurs during a free throw for a personal foul, other than intentional or flagrant, the ball is awarded to the opponents for a throw-in from the designated out-of-bounds spot nearest the violation (9-1-4-1a). If the violation occurs during a free throw for a technical foul, the ball is awarded to the thrower's team for a throw-in at the division line on the side of the court opposite the scorer's and timer's table (9-1-4-1b). If the violation occurs during a free throw for a flagrant personal foul or an intentional personal foul, the ball is awarded to the thrower's team for a throw-in from the designated out-of-bounds spot nearest the foul (9-1-4-1c).

Resuming Play After a Violation

A penalty is an action assessed by an official to a player or team for a rules infraction (4-32). The penalty for a violation is the awarding of the ball to the opponents for a throw-in, or the awarding of one or more points, or the awarding of a substitute free throw.

When any of the following violations occurs, the ball is dead and is awarded to the opponents for a throw-in from the designated out-of-bounds spot nearest the violation:

• Out of bounds (9-3-1; 9-3-2).

• Traveling, kicking the ball, striking the ball with the fist or causing the ball to enter and pass through the basket from below (4-29; 4-44; 9-4).

• Dribbling the ball a second time after his/her first dribble has ended, unless it is after he/she has lost control because of a try for field goal (9-5-1); a touch by an opponent (9-5-2); or a pass or fumble which has then touched, or been touched by, another player (9-5-3).

- Three seconds in the lane (9-7-1).

- 10 seconds in the backcourt (9-8).

- Backcourt violations (9-9-1 through 3).

- Basket interference at the team's own basket (4-6; 9-11).

- Goaltending (4-22; 9-12).

- Excessively swinging of arm(s) or elbow(s) (9-13).

The first violation of the throw-in boundary-line plane by an opponent(s) of the thrower shall result in a team warning for delay being given (one delay warning per team per game). The warning does not result in the loss of the opportunity to move along the end line when applicable (9-2-10 Penalties 2).

If an opponent of the thrower reaches through the throw-in boundary-line plane and touches or dislodges the ball while in possession of the thrower or being passed to a teammate outside the boundary line, a technical foul shall be charged to the offender. No warning for delay required 9-2-10 Penalty 3; 10-3-11 Penalty).

If an opponent of the thrower reaches through the boundary-line plane and fouls the thrower, an intentional personal foul shall be charged to the offender. No warning for delay required (9-2-10 Penalty 4).

 # Rationale

No throw-ins are to occur behind the backboard. Such a change was made in 1964 to permit the thrower an unimpeded area in case he/she should wish to throw the ball to a teammate who is at some distance down the court.

Resuming Play After a Violation: Caseplays

4.29 SITUATION: During A1's attempt to pass to A2, B1 (a) intentionally uses his/her thigh to deflect the pass; (b) intentionally kicks the ball with his/her foot; or (c) has the ball accidentally hit his/her lower leg. **RULING:** In (a) and (b), there is a kicking violation and Team A will receive the ball out of bounds nearest the violation. In (c), the ball remains live and there is no violation (9-4).

6.5 SITUATION: What is the procedure for putting the ball in play after a violation? **RULING:** The official shall hand or bounce (as applicable by NFHS Officials Manual) the ball to the player at the spot designated for the throw-in (7-5-7; 8-5).

7.2.2 SITUATION: A throw-in by A1 (a) strikes B1 who is inbounds and rebounds in flight directly from B1 and then strikes A1 who is still out of bounds; (b) is batted by B1, who is inbounds and the ball is next touched by A1 who is still out of bounds. **RULING:** A1 caused the ball to go out of bounds and it is awarded to Team B at that spot for a throw-in for both (a) and (b).

7.5.7 SITUATION A: B1 goaltends on airborne shooter A1's try. A1 fouls B1 in returning to the floor. **RULING:** Since no free throws result from the player-control foul, B's throw-in is from anywhere along the end line because of the awarded goal for B1's goaltending violation (9-12 Penalty 1).

7.5.7 SITUATION B: Team A scores a field goal. B1 picks up the ball after the made basket, then proceeds out of bounds to start the throw-in process. B1 runs along the end line out of bounds while attempting to find an open teammate for the throw-in. Immediately after B1 releases the throw-in pass, (a) the ball is kicked by A2 near the end line; (b) the ball is kicked by A2 near the division line; or (c) the ball is deflected out of bounds across the end line off of A2. **RULING:** In (a) and (b), A2 has violated by kicking the ball. In (a), Team B will be awarded a throw-in and retain the right to run the end line on the ensuing throw-in. In (b), Team B will put the ball in play at a designated spot nearest the violation, which is the division line. In (c), A2 legally contacted the ball and subsequently hit it out of bounds, ending the throw-in. Team B is awarded a designated spot throw-in on the end line.

Topic:
Throw-in Administration

The official shall hand or bounce the ball to the thrower for a throw-in unless the throw-in is from outside an end line following a successful goal (7-6-1).

The throw-in starts when the ball is at the disposal of a player of the team entitled to the throw-in. The thrower shall release the ball on a pass directly into the court within five seconds after the throw-in starts. The throw-in pass shall touch another player (inbounds or out of bounds) on the court before going out of bounds untouched. The throw-in pass shall not touch a teammate while it is on the out-of-bounds side of the throw-in boundary plane (7-5-7; 7-6-2).

The thrower shall not leave the designated throw-in spot until the ball has been released on a throw-in pass (4-42-6; 7-6-3).

The opponent(s) of the thrower shall not have any part of his/her person through the inbounds side of the throw-in boundary plane until the ball has been released on a throw-in pass (7-6-4; 9-2-11 Penalty).

Throw-in Administration: Caseplays

7.5.2 SITUATION A: Team A is awarded a throw-in near the division line. The administering official by mistake, puts the ball at B1's disposal. B1 completes the throw-in and Team B subsequently scores a goal. **RULING:** No correction can be made for the mistake by the official after the throw-in ends.

7.6.4 SITUATION A: While attempting a throw-in, A1 holds the ball through the plane of the end line. B1: (a) slaps the ball from A1's hand(s); or (b) simply grabs the ball and then throws it through B's basket. **RULING:** In (a), no violation has occurred and play continues. In (b), score two points for Team B.

7.6.4 SITUATION B: During an attempted throw-in, A1: (a) holds the ball through the plane of the end line and then passes it; (b) steps through the plane (makes contact with the floor inbounds) before passing the ball to A2; or (c) holds the ball through the plane and hands it to A2. **RULING:** A legal throw-in in (a), but a throw-in violation in (b) and (c) (9-2-2; 9-2-5).

7.6.4 SITUATION C: A1 is attempting to make a throw-in and Team B is applying a great deal of pressure. B1 reaches through the boundary-line plane and waves his/her hand in an effort to prevent the pass. The action takes place on a court which has more than 3 feet of unobstructed space outside the boundary line. **RULING:** Team B is warned for violation of the boundary plane. The warning is reported to the scorer and to the coach and applies for the rest of the game. Any subsequent delay-of-game situation by Team B shall result in a technical foul charged to Team B (9-2-10; 10-1-5c).

7.6.4 SITUATION D: The sideline is very near the spectators leaving little space out of bounds for A1 to make a throw-in. As a result, the administering official has directed B1 to move back a step to give the thrower some room: (a) as soon as the ball is handed or bounced to A1, B1 moves right back to the boundary line in front of A1; or (b) A1 attempts to complete the throw-in just inside the boundary line and B1 moves to his/her original position in order to defend. **RULING:** In (a), it is a violation by B1 and will also result in a warning for Team B which is reported to the scorer and to the head coach. Any subsequent delay-of-game situation or noncompliance with the verbal order will result in a technical foul charged to Team B. In (b), B1 is expected to stay back one step unless the throw-in is attempted between this area and the boundary line. No violation in this case as B1 is allowed to defend the area if the throw-in is attempted there (10-1-5c).

7.6.4 SITUATION E: Following a goal, A1 is running the end line when B1 reaches through the plane in an attempt to prevent the throw-in. **RULING:** Team B is warned for the violation which is reported to the scorer and to the head coach. A1 may run the end line during the subsequent throw-in.

7.6.4 SITUATION F: Thrower A1 inadvertently holds the ball through the end-line plane during a throw-in. B1 is able to get his/her hands on the ball and A1 cannot pull it back. **RULING:** There is no player or team control during a throw-in, therefore a held ball is called, resulting in an alternating-possession throw-in. If the original throw-in is an alternating-possession throw-in, Team A still has the arrow following the held ball.

7.6.5 SITUATION: Prior to a throw-in on the end line near A's basket, A1, A2 and A3 line up shoulder-to-shoulder parallel to the line and: (a) within 3 feet of it; or (b) more than 3 feet from it. In both cases, Team B requests space between the Team A players. **RULING:** In (a), the request is granted and a Team B player may position between each of the Team A players. In (b), the request is denied.

10.3.10 SITUATION A: After a field goal, A1 has the ball out of bounds for a throw-in. Thrower A1 holds the ball: (a) B2 crosses the boundary line and fouls A1; or (b) B2 reaches through the out-of-bounds plane and touches the ball while in the hands of A1. **RULING:** It is an intentional personal foul in (a), and a technical foul in (b). In (a), such a contact foul with the thrower during a throw-in shall be considered intentional, or if it is violent, it should be ruled flagrant (4-19-3,4; 9-2-11 Pen. 3.4).

 COMMENT: Either act is a foul and it should be called whenever it occurs during a game without regard to time or score or whether the team had or had not been warned for a delay-of-game situation. If the player making the throw-in (A1) reaches through the out-of-bounds plane into the court and B1 then slaps the ball from the hand of A1, no violation has occurred. B1 has merely slapped a live ball from the hands of A1 (4-19-3, 4; 9-2-11 Penalty).

10.3.10 SITUATION B: After a field goal, the score is A-55, B-54. A1 has the ball out of bounds for a throw-in with two seconds remaining in the game. A1 throws the ball toward A2 who also is out of bounds along the end line. B2 reaches across the end line and grabs or slaps the ball while it is in flight. Time expires close to the moment the official indicates the infraction. **RULING:** A technical foul is charged against B2. The remaining time or whether Team B had been previously warned for a delay-of-game situation is not a factor. No free throws are awarded as the winner of the game has been determined (9-2-11 Penalty 3, 4).

10.3.10 SITUATION C: Team A scores near the end of the fourth quarter and is trailing by one point. B1 has the ball and is moving along the end line to make the throw-in. A2 steps out of bounds and fouls B1. Is the foul personal or technical? **RULING:** This is an intentional personal foul. The time remaining to be played or whether Team A had been previously warned for a delay-of-game situation is not a factor. If the team had not been warned, the foul constitutes the warning (4-19-1; 9-2-11 Penalty 4).

10.3.11 SITUATION D: A1 is out of bounds for a throw-in. B1 reaches through the boundary plane and knocks the ball out of A1's hands. Earlier in the game, Team B had received a team warning for delay. **RULING:** Even though Team B had already been issued a warning for team delay, when B1 breaks the plane and subsequently contacts the ball in the thrower's hand, it is considered all the same act and the end result is penalized. A player technical foul is assessed to B1; two free throws and a division line throw-in for Team A will follow. The previous warning for team delay still applies with any subsequent team delay resulting in a team technical foul (4-47; 9-2-10 Penalty 3; 10-1-5c).

Ball Status

On a throw-in, the ball becomes live when the ball is at the disposal of the thrower (6-1-2b).

Clock Starts After Throw-in

If play is resumed by a throw-in, the clock shall be started when the ball touches, or is touched by, a player on the court after it is released by the thrower (5-9-4).

Clock Starts After Throw-in: Caseplays

5.9.4 SITUATION: Thrower A1 holds the ball through the throw-in boundary plane and B1 slaps the ball out of his/her hands. **RULING:** The clock starts when it is released by A1 as it simultaneously has been touched on the court by B1. If this had been an alternating-possession throw-in, the arrow would be reversed.

Scoring After a Throw-in

No goal is scored if an untouched throw-in goes through the basket (5-1-1).

When play is resumed with a throw-in or free throw and three-tenths (.3) of a second or less remains on the clock, a player may not gain control of the ball and try for a field goal. In this situation only a tap could score (5-2-5). This rule does not apply if the clock does not display tenths of a second (5-2-5 Note).

Scoring After a Throw-in: Caseplays

5.2.1 SITUATION D: Following the free throws for a technical foul, A1 makes a throw-in from out of bounds at the division line opposite the table. The throw-in pass is deflected at A's free-throw line by: (a) A2; or (b) B1 and it then goes directly through A's basket. **RULING:** Score two points for Team A in both (a) and (b). The throw-in ended when the ball was touched by an inbounds player and the live ball subsequently passed through the basket. The fact it was not a tap or a try for goal does not affect the scoring of two points (4-41-4).

Topic:
Throw-in Violations

The thrower shall not leave the designated throw-in spot until the ball has been released on a throw-in pass (9-2-1).

The ball shall be passed by the thrower directly into the court from out-of-bound so it touches or is touched by another player (inbounds or out of bounds) on the court before going out of bounds untouched (9-2-2).

The thrown ball shall not be touched by a teammate of the thrower while the ball is on the out-of-bounds side of the throw-in boundary-line plane except during a non-designated spot throw-in (7-5-7; 9-2-3).

Once the throw-in starts, the ball shall be released on a pass directly into the court before five seconds have elapsed (9-2-4).

The thrower shall not carry the ball onto the court (9-2-5).

The thrown ball shall not touch the thrower in the court before it touches or is touched by another player (9-2-6); shall not enter the

In Simple Terms

The thrower may step on but not over the boundary line.

basket before it touches or is touched by another player (9-2-7); nor shall not become lodged between the backboard and ring or come to rest on the flange before it touches or is touched by another player (9-2-8).

The thrower shall not be replaced by a teammate after the ball is at the thrower's disposal (9-2-9).

No player shall be out of bounds when he/she touches or is touched by the ball after it has been released on a throw-in pass (9-2-10).

The opponent(s) of the thrower shall not have any part of his/her person through the inbounds side of the throw-in boundary-line plane until the ball has been released on a throw-in pass (9-2-11). The thrower may penetrate the plane provided he/she does not touch the inbounds area before the ball is released on the throw-in pass. The opponent in this situation may legally touch or grasp the ball (9-2-11 Note).

In Simple Terms

The thrower may not hand nor carry the ball onto the court.

The thrower shall have a minimum of 3 feet horizontally. If the court is not marked accordingly, an imaginary restraining line shall be imposed by the administering official (1-2-2; 7-6-3 Note).

Teammates shall not occupy adjacent positions which are parallel to and within 3 feet of the boundary line if an opponent desires one of the positions. The 3-foot restraining line is sometimes the temporary boundary line as in (1-2-2; 7-6-5).

Throw-in Violations: Penalties

The first violation of the throw-in boundary-line plane by an opponent(s) of the thrower shall result in a team warning for delay being given (one delay warning per team per game). The warning does not result in the loss of the opportunity to move along the end line when and if applicable (9-2-10-1).

The second or additional violations will result in a technical foul assessed to the offending team (9-2-10-2; 10-1-10 Penalty).

If an opponent(s) of the thrower reaches through the throw-in boundary-line plane and touches or dislodges the ball while in possession of the thrower or being passed to a teammate outside the boundary line, a technical foul shall be charged to the offender. No warning for delay required (7-5-7; 9-2-10-3; 10-3-11 Penalty).

If an opponent(s) of the thrower reaches through the throw-in boundary-line plane and fouls the thrower, an intentional personal foul shall be charged to the offender. No warning for delay required (9-2-10-4).

No teammate of the thrower shall be out of bounds after a designated-spot throw-in begins (9-2-11). The ball becomes dead when the violation or technical foul occurs. Following a violation, the ball is awarded to the opponents for a throw-in at the original throw-in spot (9-2-12 Penalty 2).

Rationale

The throw-in count ends when the ball is released onto the court. The committee felt the risk of interception and defensive pressure was enough of a factor to stop the count upon release.

Throw-in Violations: Caseplays

*9.2.2 SITUATION A: Thrower A1 (a) causes the ball to carom from the wall behind him/her, or from the floor out of bounds and then into the court; (b) caroms the ball from the back of the backboard to a player in the court; or (c) throws the ball against the side or the front face of the backboard, after which it rebounds into the hands of A2. **RULING:** Violation in (a) and (b), since the throw touched an object out of bounds. The throw-in in (c) is legal. The side and front face of the backboard are inbounds and, in this specific situation, are treated the same as the floor inbounds.

9.2.2 SITUATION B: The throw-in by A1 is: (a) first touched in the court by A1; or (b) touched or caught by A2 whose hand(s) is on the out-of-bounds side of the throw-in boundary plane. **RULING:** Violation in both (a) and (b), B's ball at the spot of the throw-in (9-2-3; 9-2-6).

9.2.2 SITUATION C: A1 scores a basket. After the ball goes through the net, B1 grabs it and makes a move toward the end line as though preparing to make a throw-in. However, B1 never legally steps out of bounds, both feet remain inbounds. B1 immediately passes the ball up the court to a fast-breaking teammate, who scores a basket. **RULING:** Cancel Team B's goal, throw-in violation on B1. The ball was at B1's disposal after the made basket to make a throw-in. B1 must be out of bounds to make a legal throw-in (7-4-3; 7-5-7).

9.2.2 SITUATION D: A1 dribbles the ball on floor on the out-of-bounds area before making a throw-in. **RULING:** Legal, a player may bounce the ball on the out-of-bounds area prior to making a throw-in.

*9.2.5 SITUATION: Thrower A1 inadvertently steps onto the court inbounds. A1 immediately steps back into normal out-of-bounds throw-in position. The contact with the court was during a situation: (a) with; or (b) without defensive pressure on the throw-in team. **RULING:** A violation in both (a) and (b).

COMMENT: Whether or not there was defensive pressure or whether or not stepping on the court was inadvertent, it is a violation and no judgment is required in making the call.

9.2.8 SITUATION: Team A is awarded an alternating-possession throw-in. A1 lobs the throw-in pass toward A2 who is breaking to the basket. The throw-in pass is too high and lodges between the ring and backboard. **RULING:** Violation by A1 for lodging the untouched throw-in pass. Team B's ball at the throw-in spot. Since A1 violated during an alternating-possession throw-in, Team A has lost the arrow. Team B will have the arrow for the next alternating-possession throw-in (6-4-5).

9.2.9 SITUATION: Following a violation, the official has properly signaled and awarded a throw-in to Team A at a designated spot. No Team A player comes to the spot even though the official has allowed ample time for them to respond. The official then places the ball on the floor and begins the five-second count (a) Both A1 and A2 step out of bounds and A1 picks up the ball; or (b) both A1 and A2 step out of bounds and A1 picks up the ball and hands it to A2. **RULING:** In (a), A2 must immediately return inbounds. In (b), it is a throw-in violation when A1 hands the ball to A2 (9-2-12).

10.1.8 SITUATION: Immediately following a goal or free throw by Team A, A1 inbounds the ball to A2 and A2 subsequently throws the ball through A's basket. **RULING:** The following procedure has been adopted to handle this specific situation if it is recognized before the opponents gain control or before the next throw-in begins: (a) charge Team A with a technical foul; (b) cancel the field goal; (c) cancel any common foul(s) committed and any nonflagrant foul against A2 in the act of shooting; and (d) put "consumed" time back on the clock.

COMMENT: If there is no doubt the throw-in was a result of confusion, the entire procedure would be followed except no technical foul would be charged. This procedure shall not be used in any other throw-in situation in which a mistake allows the wrong team to inbound the ball.

Topic 8

Clock and Scorers/Timers

POSS

Key Terms

The game and each extra period shall be started by a jump ball in the center restraining circle.

Each quarter or extra period begins when the ball first becomes live (5-5-6).

Topic:
Clock Starts

If play is started or resumed by a jump, the clock shall be started when the tossed ball is legally touched (5-9-2).

After time has been out, the clock shall be started when the official signals time-in. If the official neglects to signal, the timer is authorized to start the clock as per rule, unless an official specifically signals continued time-out (5-9-1).

If a free throw is not successful and the ball is to remain live, the clock shall be started when the ball touches or is touched by a player on the court (5-9-3).

If play is resumed by a throw-in, the clock shall be started when the

Fundamental #18
Whether the clock is running or is stopped has no influence on the counting of a goal.

ball touches, or is touched by a player on the court after it is released by the thrower (5-9-4).

The timer shall note when each half is to start and shall notify the referee more than three minutes before this time so the referee may notify the teams, or cause them to be notified, at least three minutes before the half is to start (2-12-1) and signal the scorer three minutes before starting time (2-12-2).

Clock Starts: Caseplay

5.9.3 SITUATION: With two seconds on the clock in the fourth quarter, A1 is awarded one free throw with Team B leading 68-66. A1 throws the ball against the backboard and it ricochets off the ring with such force that A1 secures the rebound. A1's try for goal is successful as time expires. **RULING:** Legal goal by A1. The clock started when A1 touched the ball (5-9-3; 9-1-3a).

Topic:
Clock Stops

The clock, if running, shall be stopped when an official signals a foul, a held ball or a violation (5-8-1).

The clock shall also be stopped when an official stops play because of an injury or a player with blood; to confer with the scorer or timer; because of unusual delay in getting a dead ball live or for any other situations or any emergency (5-8-2).

 COMMENT: When a player is injured, the official may suspend play after the ball is dead or is in control of the injured player's team or when the opponents complete a play. A play is completed when a team loses control (including throwing for goal) or withholds the ball from play by ceasing to attempt to score or advance the ball to a scoring position. When necessary to protect an injured player, the official may immediately suspend play.

The clock shall also be stopped when an official grants a player's/head coach's oral or visual request for a time-out, such request being granted only when the ball is in control or at the disposal of a player of his/her team or the ball is dead, unless replacement of a disqualified, or injured player(s), or a player directed to leave the game is pending, and a substitute(s) is available and required (5-8-3).

Clock Stops: Caseplays

5.8.3 SITUATION A: A1 fouls B1. The official who made the call moves toward the reporting area. A2 immediately signals the free official for a time-out. Momentarily thereafter, the scorer notifies the calling official that A1 has fouled out. **RULING:** A1 must be replaced before the time-out is granted (2-8-4; 10-5-3).

 COMMENT: The first responsibility the calling official has is to report the foul to the scorer. Officials should not be hasty in granting an immediate time-out after the game has reached a point that players may begin to foul out. Rather, they should take a second or two after reporting the foul to see if the scorer may indicate a disqualification.

5.8.3 SITUATION B: Following a time-out, both teams are at the sideline with respective coaches after all signals have been given prior to a throw-in by Team A. Team A or Team B requests a time-out: (a) before; or (b) after, the official places the ball on the floor at the throw-in spot. **RULING:** In (a), either team may be granted a time-out. In (b), Team A may, but Team B may not be granted a time-out after the ball is at A's disposal.

5.8.3 SITUATION C: A1 fouls B2. The scorer notifies the nearest official that this is A1's fifth foul. The official notifies the coach of Team A of the disqualification. The official then instructs the timer to begin the 20-second replacement period. The official then notifies A1. After 10 seconds have elapsed: (a) the captain of Team A; or (b) the captain of Team B requests a time-out. **RULING:** In (a) and (b), the time-out request is denied as disqualified A1 must be replaced prior to any time-out being granted to either team (2-8-4; 10-5-2).

5.8.3 SITUATION D: A1 or A2 requests a time-out: (a) while airborne A1 is holding the ball; (b) while A1's throw-in is in flight toward A2; or (c) when the ball is on the floor at A1's disposal for a throw-in. **RULING:** The request is granted in (a) and (c), but denied in (b), as there is no player control while the ball is loose between players.

5.8.3 SITUATION E: A1 is dribbling the ball in his/her backcourt when: (a) the Team B head coach requests and is erroneously granted a time-out by an official; or (b) the Team A head coach is yelling "side out" offensive instructions to his/her team and the official stops play believing the coach requested a time-out. **RULING:** In (a), Team B is entitled to use the time-out since it was requested and granted; once granted it cannot be revoked and is charged to Team B. All privileges and rights permitted during a charged time-out are available to both teams. Play will resume with a Team A throw-in nearest to where play was stopped. In (b), an accidental whistle has occurred. Team A was not requesting a time-out, and therefore, should not be granted or charged with one. Play is resumed at the point of interruption (4-36-1; 4-36-2a).

5.8.3 SITUATION F: A1's dribble is "interrupted" when the ball deflects off his/her shoe. A1 or a teammate asks or signals for a time-out as the ball bounces toward: (a) the sideline; or (b) the division line. **RULING:** The request cannot be granted in (a) or (b), since A1's dribble has been "interrupted" and the ball is loose (4-15-6c).

Topic:
Scorer's Duties

The scorer shall keep a record of the names and numbers of players who are to start the game and of all substitutes who enter the game (2-11-1) and notify the nearer official when there is an infraction of the rules pertaining to submission of the roster, substitutions or numbers of players (2-11-2).

It is recommended the team member's numbers be entered into the scorebook in numerical order (2-11-1 Note).

The scorer shall signal the officials by using the game horn or a sounding device unlike that used by the referee and umpire(s). This may be used immediately if, or as soon as, the ball is dead or is in control of the offending team (2-11-3).

The scorer shall record the field goals made, the free throws made and missed, and keep a running summary of the points scored (2-11-4).

The scorer shall record the jump balls for the alternating-possession procedure and be responsible for the possession arrow (2-11-7).

The scorer shall record the personal and technical fouls called on each player and notify an official immediately when the fifth foul (personal and technical) is charged to any player, the second technical foul is charged to any team member, bench personnel, or directly to the head coach, or the third technical foul is charged to the head coach (2-11-5).

The scorer shall signal in each half when a player commits a common foul beginning with his/her team's seventh and 10th foul (2-11-10).

The scorer shall record the time-out information charged to each team (who and when) and notify a team and its coach, through an official, whenever that team is granted its final allotted charged time-out (2-11-6), and signal the nearer official each time a team is granted a time-out in excess of the allotted number (2-11-9).

Scorer's Duties: Caseplay

2.11.3 SITUATION: When may the scorer signal? **RULING:** If the scorer desires to call attention to a player who is illegally in the game, he/she may signal the official when the ball is in control of that player's team. If it is for a substitution, the scorer may signal when the ball next becomes dead and the clock is stopped. If it is for conferring with an official, he/she may signal when the ball is dead. If the scorer signals while the ball is live, the official should ignore the signal if a scoring play is in progress. Otherwise, the official may stop play to determine the reason for the scorer's signal.

 **Did You Know?** The original rules of basketball designated the game to be played in two 15-minute halves, with five minutes rest in between.

Topic:
Timer's Duties

The timer shall indicate by signal the expiration of playing time in each quarter or extra period. If a red/LED light is used, the light is the official expiration of playing time (2-12-7).

If the red/LED light fails to illuminate and the timer's signal fails to sound, or is not heard, the timer shall go onto the court or use other means to immediately notify the referee. If in the meantime, a goal has been made or a foul has occurred, the referee shall consult the timer. If table officials agree that time expired before the ball was in flight, the goal shall not count (2-13-1). If table officials agree that the quarter or extra period ended before the foul occurred, the foul shall be disregarded, unless it was intentional or flagrant (2-13-2). If table officials disagree, the goal shall count and/or the foul shall be penalized, unless the referee has knowledge which alters such ruling (2-13-3).

The timer shall stop the clock at the expiration of time for each quarter or extra period, and when an official signals time-out (2-12-6).

The timer shall sound a warning signal 15 seconds before the expiration of a 60-second charged time-out and at 15 seconds of a 30-second time-out, immediately after which the players shall prepare to be ready to resume play, and signal again at the end of the time-out (2-12-4); and sound a warning signal 15 seconds before the expiration of the 20 seconds (maximum) permitted for replacing a disqualified or injured player, or for a player directed to leave the game (2-12-5). The official shall signal the timer to begin the 20-second interval for replacing an injured player after the injured player has been removed from the court and the coach has been notified that a replacement player is required, except when a time-out is used to keep the player in the game (2-12-5 Note).

The timer shall also stop the clock at the expiration of time for each quarter or extra period and when an official signals time-out; and, for an intermission or a charged time-out, start the stopwatch and signal the referee (2-12-6).

In Simple Terms

If an official is uncertain as to whether or not time expired before a basket, he/she shall always consult the scorer and timer, but ultimately has the final say in the decision.

Timer's Duties: Caseplay

2.13 SITUATION: The signal to end the fourth quarter cannot be heard by the officials. The table officials disagree as to whether the ball was in flight during a try for field goal when time expired or if a foul occurred before the ball became dead. **RULING:** The final decision shall be made by the referee, and unless he/she has knowledge to alter the ruling, the goal shall count if it was successful and the foul shall be charged and penalized (2-5-5).

Topic 9

Guarding

PlayPic™

Key Terms

Guarding is the act of legally placing the body in the path of an offensive opponent. There is no minimum distance required between the guard and opponent, but the maximum is 6 feet when closely guarded. Every player is entitled to a spot on the playing court provided such player gets there first without illegally contacting an opponent. A player who extends an arm, shoulder, hip or leg into the path of an opponent is not considered to have a legal position if contact occurs (4-23-1).

Topic:

Legal Guarding Position

To obtain an initial legal guarding position, the guard must have both feet touching the playing court and the front of the guard's torso must be facing the opponent (4-23-2a, b).

After the initial legal guarding position is obtained, the guard may have one or both feet on the playing court or be airborne, provided he/she has inbound status. The guard is not required to continue facing the opponent; may move laterally or obliquely to maintain position, provided it is not toward the opponent when contact occurs; may raise hands or jump within his/her own vertical plane; and may turn or duck to absorb the shock of imminent contact (4-23-3a through e).

A player who is moving with the ball is required to stop or change direction to avoid contact if a defensive player has obtained a legal guarding position in his/her path (4-7-2a).

If a guard has obtained a legal guarding position, the player with the ball must get his/her head and shoulders past the torso of the defensive player. If contact occurs on the torso of the defensive player, the dribbler is responsible for the contact (4-7-2b).

The player with the ball may not push the torso of the guard to gain an advantage to pass, shoot or dribble (4-7-2d).

Legal guarding position must be obtained initially and movement thereafter must be legal (4-45-1).

Legal Guarding Position: Caseplays

4.23.2 SITUATION: B1 jumps in front of dribbler A1 and obtains a legal guarding position with both feet touching the court and facing A1. Dribbler A1 contacts B1's torso. **RULING:** Player-control foul on A1 (4-7-2).

4.23.3 SITUATION A: B1 has obtained a legal guarding position on A1 and moves to maintain it. A1 moves laterally and contacts defender B1 but does not get his/her head and shoulders past the torso of B1. Contact occurs on the side of B1's torso. **RULING:** Player-control foul by A1 (4-7-2).

4.23.3 SITUATION B: A1 is dribbling near the sideline when B1 obtains legal guarding position. B1 stays in the path of A1 but in doing so has (a) one foot touching the sideline or (b) one foot in the air over the out-of-bounds area when A1 contacts B1 in the torso. **RULING:** In (a), B1 is called for a blocking foul because a player may not be out of bounds and obtain or maintain legal guarding position. In (b), A1 is called for a player-control foul because B2 had obtained and maintained legal guarding position (4-23-2; 4-23-3a).

Guarding a Moving Opponent Without the Ball

When guarding a moving opponent without the ball, time and distance are factors required to obtain an initial legal position. The guard must give the opponent the time and/or distance to avoid contact. The distance need not be more than two strides. If the opponent is airborne, the guard must have obtained legal position before the opponent left the floor (4-23-5a through d).

Guarding an Opponent With the Ball or a Stationary Opponent

When guarding an opponent with the ball or a stationary opponent without the ball, no time or distance is required to obtain an initial legal position. If the opponent with the ball is airborne, the guard must have obtained legal position before the opponent left the floor (4-23-4).

Topic:
Closely Guarded

A closely-guarded situation occurs when a player in control of the ball in his/her team's frontcourt, is continuously guarded by any opponent who is within six feet of the player who is holding or dribbling the ball. The distance shall be measured from the forward foot/feet of the defender to the forward foot/feet of the ball handler. A closely guarded count shall be terminated when the offensive player in control of the ball gets his/her head and shoulders past the defensive player (4-10).

A player shall not, while closely guarded in his/her frontcourt, hold the ball for five seconds or dribble the ball for five seconds; or, in his/her frontcourt, control the ball for five seconds in an area enclosed by screening teammates (9-10-1a, b).

An interrupted dribble occurs when the ball is loose after

In Simple Terms

During an interrupted dribble, no time-out can be granted, a five-second count is not in effect and a player-control foul cannot occur.

deflecting off the dribbler or after it momentarily gets away from the dribbler. There is no player control during an interrupted dribble (4-15-5). During an interrupted dribble, a closely-guarded count shall not be started or shall be terminated (4-15-6a; 9-10-2; 9-10-3).

Closely-Guarded: Penalty

The ball is dead when the violation occurs and is awarded to the opponents for a throw-in from the designated out-of-bounds spot nearest the violation (9-10 Penalty).

Closely Guarded: Caseplays

9.10.1 SITUATION A: A1 while closely guarded, dribbles across the division line and while in A's frontcourt: (a) dribbles for five seconds; or (b) dribbles for three seconds and then holds the ball for four seconds before passing the ball to A2. RULING: Violation in (a) and Team B's ball because the five-second count was reached during the dribble. Legal action in (b).

9.10.1 SITUATION B: While dribbling in A's frontcourt, A1 is closely guarded by B1. After two seconds, B2 also assumes a closely-guarded position on A1 and B1 leaves to guard A2. **RULING:** The closely-guarded count continues. There is no requirement for the defensive player to remain the same during the count as long as A1 is closely-guarded throughout.

9.10.1 SITUATION C: Team A has the ball in its own frontcourt. B1 stands within 6 feet and facing A1 while A1 is holding the ball near the division line. **RULING:** In five seconds this would be a violation. In the situation outlined, as soon as B1 has assumed a guarding position, both feet on the court, facing the opponent, no other specific requirement is in effect. The amount of movement or the actual body position of the player is irrelevant.

9.10.1 SITUATION D: Team A, while in possession of the ball in its frontcourt: (a) positions four players parallel with the sideline and they pass the ball from one to another with their arms reaching beyond the sideline plane; or (b) has four teammates surround dribbler A1. In both (a) and (b), the opponents are unable to get close to the ball. **RULING:** This is considered to be a closely-guarded situation and a violation in five seconds in both (a) and (b), if any B player is within 6 feet of the ball or within 6 feet of the screening teammates and is attempting to gain control of the ball. Preventing opponents from getting to the ball by using screening teammates becomes a violation in five seconds if the opponents are attempting to gain control.

9.10.3 SITUATION: Dribbler A1 is closely-guarded by B1 in A's frontcourt and the covering official's count is at three when A1's dribble is interrupted when the ball bounces off his/her foot. An additional two seconds goes by as A1 turns to get the loose ball and B1 remains within 6 feet. **RULING:** The closely-guarded count shall be terminated when the dribble is interrupted, but it will start over if A1 continues the dribble or holds the ball and is again closely-guarded.

 **Did You Know?** The original penalty for a five-second closely-guarded count resulted in a jump ball.

Topic 10

Violations

Key Terms

A violation is one of three types of rule infractions: floor violations including basket interference by a teammate of the player attempting a field goal or free throw, or goaltending a field goal and other violations which are not connected with a free throw or try or tap for goal (4-46-1); basket interference or goaltending by a player at the opponent's basket (4-46-2); or free-throw violations other than those involving basket interference or goaltending (4-46-3).

Fundamental #8

There are three types of violations and each has its own penalty.

If a violation occurs so near the expiration of time that the clock is not stopped before time expires, the quarter or extra period ends with the violation (5-6-2 Exception 2).

Dead Ball

The ball becomes dead, or remains dead, when a floor violation occurs (6-7-9), or a free throw violation by the throwing team occurs (6-7-8). It does not become dead until the try or tap ends, or until the airborne shooter returns to the floor when a violation for leaving the court or excessively swinging arms or elbows occurs by an opponent (6-7-9 exception d).

Penalty

After any violation, the official shall place the ball at the disposal of an opponent of the player who committed the violation for a throw-in from the designated out-of-bounds spot nearest the violation (7-5-2a).

 COMMENT: If the violation involves basket interference or goaltending at the opponent's basket, the penalty is the awarding of points and the subsequent procedure is the same as after a successful goal, except that the official must hand or bounce the ball to the thrower.

Clock

Time-out occurs and the clock, if running, shall be stopped when an official signals a violation (5-8-1c).

Court Location

The frontcourt of a team consists of that part of the court between its end line and the nearer edge of the division line, including its basket and the inbounds part of the backboard (4-13-1).

The backcourt of a team consists of the rest of the court, including the entire division line and the opponent's basket and inbounds part of the opponent's backboard (4-13-2).

Ball Location

A ball which is in contact with a player or with the court is in the backcourt if either the ball or the player (either player if the ball is touching more than one) is touching the backcourt (4-4-1).

A ball which is in contact with a player or with the court is in the frontcourt if neither the ball nor the player is touching the backcourt (4-4-2).

A ball which is in flight retains the same location as when it was last in contact with a player or the court (4-4-3).

> ## Fundamental #9
>
> A ball in flight has the same relationship to frontcourt or backcourt, or inbounds or out of bounds, as when it last touched a person or the floor (except during a throw-in).

A ball which touches a player or an official is the same as the ball touching the floor at that individual's location (4-4-4).

During a dribble from backcourt to frontcourt, the ball is in the frontcourt when the ball and both feet of the dribbler touch the court entirely in the frontcourt (4-4-6).

Player Location

The location of a player or nonplayer is determined by where the player is touching the floor as far as being in the frontcourt or backcourt (4-35-1b).

When a player is touching the backcourt, the player is located in backcourt (4-35-2). The location of an airborne player with reference to the backcourt is the same as at the time such player was last in contact with the floor or an extension of the floor, such as a bleacher (4-35-3).

Topic:
Backcourt Violation

A player shall not be the first to touch a ball after it has been in team control in the frontcourt, if he/she or a teammate last touched or was touched by the ball in the frontcourt before it went to the backcourt (9-9-1).

While in team control in its backcourt, a player shall not cause the ball to go from backcourt to frontcourt and return to backcourt, without the ball touching a player in the frontcourt, such that he/she or a teammate is the first to touch it in the backcourt (9-9-2).

A player from the team not in control (defensive player or during a jump ball or throw-in) may legally jump from his/her frontcourt, secure

In Simple Terms

A player dribbling the ball must have all three points in the frontcourt before such status is achieved (left foot, right foot and the ball).

control of the ball with both feet off the floor and return to the floor with one or both feet in the backcourt. The player may make a normal landing and it makes no difference whether the first foot down is in the frontcourt or backcourt (9-9-3).

Backcourt Violation: Penalty

The ball is dead when the violation occurs and is awarded to the opponents for a throw-in from the designated out-of-bounds spot nearest the violation.

Backcourt Violation: Caseplays

4.4.1 SITUATION: As Team A is advancing the ball from its backcourt toward its frontcourt, A1 passes the ball to A2. A2 catches the ball while both feet are on the floor – with one foot on either side of the division line. In this situation, either foot may be the pivot foot. (a) A2 lifts the foot which is in the backcourt and then puts it back on the floor in the backcourt; or (b) A2 lifts the foot which is in the frontcourt, pivots and puts it on the floor in the backcourt. **RULING:** In (a), it is a backcourt violation. When A2, while holding the ball, lifts the foot which was in the backcourt, the ball is now in the frontcourt. When A2's foot then touches in the backcourt, it is a violation. In (b), when A2 lifts the foot which is in the frontcourt and places it down in the backcourt, the location of the ball has not changed. The ball is still in the backcourt and no violation has occurred (4-35-2).

4.4.4 SITUATION: The official is in Team A's frontcourt when he/she is contacted by a pass thrown by A1 from Team A's backcourt. After touching the official, the ball: (a) goes out of bounds; or (b) rebounds to the backcourt where it is recovered by A2. **RULING:** Touching the official is the same as touching the floor where the official is standing. In (a), the ball is awarded to B for a throw-in. In (b), the ball has been in the frontcourt and then has gone to the backcourt while in Team A's control. It is a violation for A1 to cause the ball to go from A's backcourt to frontcourt and return to backcourt untouched if A1 or a teammate is first to touch it after it has returned to backcourt (9-9-2).

9.9.1 SITUATION A: A1 catches the throw-in pass with one foot on the floor in A's frontcourt and the other foot not touching the floor. The non-pivot foot then comes down in A's backcourt. **RULING:** Violation. Team control is established in A's frontcourt when A1 catches the throw-in pass. The violation occurs when A1 subsequently touches the backcourt with the non-pivot foot (4-12-6; 9-9-3).

9.9.1 SITUATION B: During a jump ball, A1 taps the ball. A2 takes off from Team A's frontcourt and catches the ball while in the air. A2 lands with: (a) both feet in frontcourt and then steps to backcourt with one foot; (b) one foot in backcourt and one in the frontcourt; or (c) both feet in the backcourt. **RULING:** Team control is not established until A2 catches the ball. Violation in (a). Legal in (b) and (c) (4-12-6; 9-9-3).

9.9.1 SITUATION C: A1 is dribbling in his/her backcourt and throws a pass to the frontcourt. While standing in A's frontcourt: (a) A2 or (b) B3 touches the ball and deflects it back to A's backcourt. A2 recovers in the backcourt. **RULING:** In (a), it is a violation. The ball was in control of Team A, and a player from A was the last to touch the ball in frontcourt and a player of A was the first to touch it after it returned to the back court. In (b), legal play. A Team A player was not the last to touch the ball in the frontcourt. Team A is entitled to a new 10-second count.

9.9.1 SITUATION D: Team A is awarded a throw-in near the division line. A1's throw-in is deflected by B1; A2 jumps from Team A's frontcourt, catches the ball in the air and lands in the backcourt. **RULING:** Backcourt violation on Team A. The throw-in ends when it is legally touched by B1. A2 gains player and team control in the air after having left the floor from Team A's frontcourt, therefore having frontcourt status. As soon as A2 lands in the backcourt, he/she has committed a backcourt violation. The exception granted during a throw-in ends when the throw-in ends and is only for the player making the initial touch on the ball (9-9-3).

Topic:

Basket Interference

Basket interference occurs when a player: touches the ball or any part of the basket (including the net) while the ball is on or within either basket (4-6-1); touches the ball while any part of the ball is within the imaginary cylinder which has the basket ring as its lower base (4-6-2); touches the ball outside the cylinder while reaching through the basket from below (4-6-3); or pulls down a movable ring so that it contacts the ball before the ring returns to its original position (4-6-4).

If a player has his/her hand legally in contact with the ball, it is not a violation if such contact with the ball continues after it enters a basket cylinder or if in such action, the player touches the basket. Dunking or stuffing is legal and is not basket interference.

A player shall not commit basket interference (9-11).

In Simple Terms

A basket interference violation can occur whenever a ball is touched when the ball is in, on, or directly above the basket, regardless of how it got there.

Basket Interference: Penalty

If the violation is at the opponent's basket, the opponents are awarded one point if during a free throw, three points if during a three-point try and two points in any other case. The crediting of the score and subsequent procedure are the same as if the awarded score had resulted from the ball having gone through the basket, except that the team not credited with the score shall make a throw-in from the end of the court where the goal was made and from any point outside the end line (7-5-7).

If the violation is at a team's own basket, no points can be scored, and the ball is awarded to the opponents for a throw-in from the designated out-of-bounds spot nearest the violation.

If the violation results from touching the ball while it is in the basket after entering from below, no points are scored and the ball is awarded to the opponents for a throw-in from the designated out-of-bounds spot nearest the violation.

If there is a violation by both teams, play shall be resumed by the team entitled to the alternating-possession throw-in at the out-of-bounds spot nearest to where the simultaneous violations occurred.

Basket Interference: Caseplays

4.41.4 SITUATION A: While the ball is in flight on a try for goal by A1: (a) B1 touches the ball and then time expires; or (b) time expires and then B1 touches the ball. The ball continues in flight and enters Team A's basket. **RULING:** The goal is scored in both (a) and (b), as B1's touching did not cause the try to end. However, in both (a) and (b), if B1's touching is either goaltending or basket interference, the ball becomes dead and two points will be awarded (6-7 Exception a; 9-11, 12).

6.7 SITUATION A: The ball is in flight during a try or a tap for goal by A1 when time for the third quarter expires. After time expires, the ball is on the ring or in the basket or is touching the cylinder above the basket when it is touched by: (a) A2; or (b) B1. The ball then goes through the basket or does not go through. **RULING:** In (a) and (b), the ball became dead as the try ended with the violation. In (a), no points can be scored because of the offensive basket interference by A2. However, in (b), since the touching is defensive basket interference by B1, two points are awarded to A1. Whether or not the ball goes through the basket has no effect upon either ruling (4-6; 6-7 Note; 9-11).

6.7.9 SITUATION: A1 is fouled in the act of shooting by B1. While the ball is in the cylinder above the basket, A2 touches the ball. **RULING:** The basket interference by A2 causes the ball to become dead and no goal can be scored. However, A1 is awarded two free throws for being fouled in the act of shooting an unsuccessful try. Players must occupy lane spaces as required and play continues as per rule when the last free throw is made or missed (9-11).

9.11 SITUATION: Both A1 and B1 jump to grab a rebound at the basket of Team A. Each has a hand on the ball which is entirely outside of the cylinder above the basket. While both have contact with the ball, it is carried or forced into the cylinder above the basket. **RULING:** There is no violation by either player for having hand(s) on the ball while it is in the cylinder or basket in this situation (4-6; 9-11 Exception).

9.11.1 SITUATION A: A1 taps the ball toward Team A's basket. While the ball is in the cylinder above the basket or on the basket ring: (a) B1 touches the ball; or (b) A2 touches the ball. **RULING:** In (a), basket interference by B1 causes the ball to become dead and the official shall award Team A two points. In (b), the basket interference by A2 causes the ball to become dead. No basket. The ball is awarded to Team B for a throw-in from the out-of-bounds spot nearest the violation (4-6; 6-7-9).

9.11.1 SITUATION B: While the ball is touching the ring of the basket on a field-goal attempt, B1 grasps the ring when there is no threat of injury. **RULING:** This is a double infraction and both acts are penalized. It is both basket interference and a technical foul. The moment the hand touched the ring, it was basket interference. When the player grasped the ring, a technical foul occurred. Award two points to Team A, followed by two free throws and a division line throw-in (10-3-3 Exception).

9.11.1 SITUATION C: The ball is in flight during a three-point field-goal try by A1 when time for a quarter expires. Following the expiration of time and while the ball is rolling on the ring, B1 tips it into the basket. **RULING:** Violation by B1. The ball was live until the violation, it then became dead. Consequently, the field goal does not count. However, the action by B1 is basket interference. Three points are awarded to A1 because of the basket interference by B1 during a three-point try (4-6; 6-7-9).

9.11.1 SITUATION D: The ball is on the ring of Team A's basket when A1 hits the net. **RULING:** Basket interference by A1. No goal. The ball became dead when A1 touched the net as it is part of the basket (4-6; 6-7-9).

9.11.1 SITUATION E: The bonus rule is in effect. While the ball is in flight during a try for field goal by A1, A2 fouls B1. B2 then commits a basket-interference violation. **RULING:** Both the violation and personal foul are penalized. Team A is awarded two points for the basket interference by B2 and then B1 is awarded a free throw(s) for the foul by A2 (6-7 Exception b).

9.11.1 SITUATION F: The ball is touching the side of the basket ring of Team A. B1 jumps and B1's hand contacts the net. The ball definitely is not touching the top of the basket ring. **RULING:** This is not a violation. The ball remains live (4-6-1).

9.11.2 SITUATION A: A1 tries for a field goal. B1 rebounds, but A2 slaps the ball from the grasp of B1. The ball is above the level of the basket and is partly in the cylinder when B2 slaps the ball away to teammate B3. **RULING:** Basket interference by B2. Two points for Team A. The throw-in by B may be from anywhere out of bounds along the end line (4-6; 6-7-9; 7-4-3; 7-5-7).

9.11.2 SITUATION B: A1 throws the ball into the basket from above, but from outside the cylinder. A1's hand loses contact with the ball before the ball enters the cylinder. However, on the follow-through, A1's hand enters the cylinder and again contacts the ball. **RULING:** Violation. It is not a violation for a player to have a hand within the cylinder above the basket provided it is not touching the ball. The rules do allow a player to carry the ball into the cylinder above the ring or place the ball into the basket itself. It is basket interference; however, when a player touches the ball or the basket when the ball is in or on the basket, or touches the ball while any portion of the ball is touching the cylinder directly above the basket and the player did not carry the ball into the cylinder or basket (4-6).

9.11.2 SITUATION C: Since it is a violation for thrower A1 to throw the ball directly into the basket from out of bounds, what happens if B1 touches the throw-in pass while the ball is in the cylinder above A's basket? **RULING:** B1 is charged with basket interference and a two-point goal is scored. Team B is awarded the ball for a throw-in anywhere along the end lines as after a scored goal except the official shall place the ball at the disposal of a player of Team B for a throw-in from any point outside the end line (4-6).

9.11.2 SITUATION D: After A1's free-throw attempt strikes the ring and rebounds in the cylinder above the basket: (a) A2; or (b) B1 touches the ball. RULING: Basket interference in both (a) and (b). No point in (a). In (b), the free throw is scored because of the basket interference (9-11 Penalty 1, 2).

9.11.2 SITUATION E: A1 is fouled in the act of shooting by B1. While the ball is in the cylinder above the basket, A2 touches the ball. **RULING:** The basket interference by A2 causes the ball to become dead and no goal can be scored. A1 is awarded two free throws and players occupy spaces and play continues as normal when the last free throw is made or missed.

9.11.4 SITUATION: Defender B4 attempts to stop an apparent lob pass. While B4 is airborne, A3 moves beneath B4. To avoid injury, B4 grasps the basket ring. While B4 grasps the ring, A1 shoots from about 12 feet away. Just after A1 releases the shot, B4 lets go of the ring and lands safely. The ring is still moving when (a) the ball hits the moving ring and bounces out; (b) the ball, despite the moving ring, enters and passes completely through the basket; or (c) the ring stops vibrating (returns to its normal position) and the ball bounces off the ring. **RULING:** Since B4 grasped the ring to prevent injury, no technical foul is called. However, the basket interference rule applies. In (a), basket interference is called on B4 because the ball struck a still-vibrating ring. Award A1 two points. In (b), since the ball entered and passed completely through the basket, basket interference is not called. Play continues. In (c), because the ring returned to its original position before the ball struck the ring, basket interference is not called. Play continues (4-6-4; 10-3-3 Exception).

10.6.1 SITUATION B: The bonus is in effect and while the ball is in flight during a try for a field goal by A1, A2 charges into B1. Following this there is a basket-interference violation by: (a) B2 or (b) A3. **RULING:** In (a), both the foul by A2 and the violation by B2 are penalized, but in the reverse order of occurrence. Two points are first awarded to Team A because of the violation by B2. B1 is then awarded a one-and-one. Had the bonus not been in effect in (a), B would have been awarded the ball out of bounds at its end line where the basket was awarded. In (b), there are no rule complications. The violation by A3 caused the ball to become dead. Ordinarily, the ball would go to B out-of-bounds at the spot nearest the violation. However, this penalty is ignored because of the penalty enforcement for the foul by A2 (7-5-7; 9-11 Penalty).

Topic:
Closely-Guarded Violation

There is no minimum distance required between the guard and the opponent, but the maximum is 6 feet when closely guarded (4-23-1). A player shall not while closely guarded hold the ball or dribble the ball for five seconds while in his/her frontcourt (9-10-1a). A player shall not control the ball for five seconds in an area enclosed by screening teammates while in his/her frontcourt (9-10-1b).

A closely-guarded count shall not be started during an interrupted dribble (9-10-2). A closely-guarded count shall be terminated during an interrupted dribble (9-10-3).

▨ Rationale

The closely-guarded rule was developed to eliminate game-delaying tactics used by the dribbler to withhold the ball from play by controlling it for long periods of time.

Closely-Guarded Violation: Penalty

The ball is dead when the violation occurs and is awarded to the opponents for a throw-in from the designated out-of-bounds spot nearest the violation.

Closely-Guarded Violation: Caseplays

*9.10.1 SITUATION A: A1 while closely guarded, dribbles across the division line and while in A's frontcourt: (a) dribbles for five seconds; or (b) dribbles for three seconds and then holds the ball for four seconds before passing the ball to A2. **RULING:** Violation in (a) and Team B's ball because the five-second count was reached during the dribble in the frontcourt. Legal action in (b).

9.10.1 SITUATION B: While dribbling in A's frontcourt, A1 is closely guarded by B1. After two seconds, B2 also assumes a closely-guarded position on A1 and B1 leaves to guard A2. **RULING:** The closely-guarded count continues. There is no requirement for the defensive player to remain the same during the count as long as A1 is closely-guarded throughout.

9.10.1 SITUATION C: Team A has the ball in its own frontcourt. B1 stands within 6 feet and facing A1 while A1 is holding the ball near the division line. **RULING:** In five seconds this would be a violation. In the situation outlined, as soon as B1 has assumed a guarding position, both feet on the court, facing the opponent, no other specific requirement is in effect. The amount of movement or the actual body position of the player is irrelevant.

9.10.1 SITUATION D: Team A, while in possession of the ball in its frontcourt: (a) positions four players parallel with the sideline and they pass the ball from one to another with their arms reaching beyond the sideline plane; or (b) has four teammates surround dribbler A1. In both (a) and (b), the opponents are unable to get close to the ball. **RULING:** This is considered to be a closely-guarded situation and a violation in five seconds in both (a) and (b), if any B player is within 6 feet of the ball or within 6 feet of the screening teammates and is attempting to gain control of the ball. Preventing opponents from getting to the ball by using screening teammates becomes a violation in five seconds if the opponents are attempting to gain control.

9.10.3 SITUATION: Dribbler A1 is closely-guarded by B1 in A's frontcourt and the covering official's count is at three when A1's dribble is interrupted when the ball bounces off his/her foot. An additional two seconds goes by as A1 turns to get the loose ball and B1 remains within 6 feet. **RULING:** The closely-guarded count shall be terminated when the dribble is interrupted, but it will start over if A1 continues the dribble or holds the ball and is again closely guarded.

Topic:
Excessive Swinging of Arms/Elbows Violation

It is not legal to swing arms and elbows excessively. This occurs when arms and elbows are swung about while using the shoulders as pivots, and the speed of the extended arms and elbows is in excess of the rest of the body as it rotates on the hips or on the pivot foot (4-24-8a). The aggressiveness with which the arms and elbows are swung could cause injury to another player if contacted (4-24-8b). Using this description as a basis, an official will promptly and unhesitatingly call such action with arms and elbows a violation.

A player shall not excessively swing his/her arms(s) or elbow(s), even without contacting an opponent (9-13-1).

A player may extend arm(s) or elbow(s) to hold the ball under the chin or against the body (9-13-2).

Action of arm(s) and elbow(s) resulting from total body movements as in pivoting or movement of the ball incidental to feinting with it, releasing it, or moving it to prevent a held ball or loss of control shall not be considered excessive (9-13-3).

Rationale

The excessive swinging of elbows violation was changed from a technical foul to a violation in order to make the penalty less severe with the hopes it would be called more often. The purpose of penalizing these types of movements is to reduce rough play.

Excessive Swinging of Arms/Elbows Violation: Penalty

The ball is dead when the violation occurs and is awarded to the opponents for a throw-in from the designated out-of-bounds spot nearest the violation. The ball does not become dead until the try or tap ends, or until the airborne shooter returns to the floor, when the violation occurs by an opponent (6-7-9 Exception d).

Excessive Swinging of Arms/Elbows Violation: Caseplays

9.13.1 SITUATION: The ball has been released on a field-goal try or tap by A1 towards A's basket: (a) A2, or (b) B1, excessively swings arm(s) or elbow(s) without contacting an opponent. The ball goes through the basket. **RULING:** In (a), the official will sound the whistle immediately for a violation. The ball is dead, the goal is not scored. In (b), the ball is dead when the try ends. The goal is scored and Team A is awarded a throw-in at the spot closest to the violation (6-7-9 Exception d).

Topic:

Free-Throw Violation

The try shall be attempted from within the free-throw semicircle and behind the free-throw line (9-1-1).

Teams shall properly occupy marked lane spaces according to number and space requirements (9-1-2).

During a free throw, lane spaces may be occupied as follows:

• Marked lane spaces may be occupied by a maximum of four defensive and two offensive players (8-1-4a).

• The lane areas from the end line up to, and including, the neutral-zone marks, shall remain vacant (8-1-4-b).

• The first marked lane spaces on each side of the lane, above and adjacent to the neutral-zone marks, shall be occupied by opponents of the free thrower. No teammate of the free thrower shall occupy either of these marked lane spaces (8-1-4-c).

• The second marked lane spaces on each side may be occupied by teammates of the free thrower (8-1-4-d).

• The third marked lane spaces on each side, nearest the free thrower, may be occupied by the opponents of the free thrower (8-1-4-e).

• Players shall be permitted to move along and across the lane to occupy a vacant marked lane space within the limitations listed in this rule (8-1-4-f).

• Not more than one player may occupy any part of a marked lane space (8-1-4-g).

Any player, other than the free thrower, who does not occupy a marked lane space must be behind the free-throw line extended and behind the three-point line (8-1-5).

The ball is at the disposal of the free thrower when it is handed to a free thrower (4-4-7a), caught by a player after it is bounced to him/her (4-4-7b), or placed on the floor at the spot (4-4-7c).

After the ball is placed at the disposal of the free thrower:

Fundamental #14

The first or only free-throw violation by the offense causes the ball to become dead immediately.

• He/she shall throw within 10 seconds to cause the ball to enter the basket or touch the ring before the free throw ends (9-1-3a).

• The free thrower shall not fake a try, nor shall any player in a marked lane space fake to cause an opponent to violate (9-1-3b).

• No opponent shall disconcert the free thrower (9-1-3c).

• No player shall enter or leave a marked lane space by contacting the court outside the 36 inch by 36 inch space (9-1-3d).

• The free thrower shall not have either foot beyond the vertical plane of the edge of the free-throw line which is farther from the basket or the free-throw semicircle line (9-1-3e).

• A player, other than the free thrower, who does not occupy a marked lane space, may not have either foot beyond the vertical plane of the free-throw line extended and the three-point line which is farther from the basket (9-1-3f).

• A player occupying a marked lane space may not have either foot beyond the vertical plane of the outside edge of any lane boundary, or beyond the vertical plane of any edge of the space (2 inches by 36 inches) designated by a lane-space mark or beyond the vertical plane of any edge of the space (12 inches by 36 inches) designated by a neutral zone. A player shall position one foot near the outer edge of the free-throw lane line. The other foot may be positioned anywhere within the designated 36-inch lane space (9-1-3g).

• The restrictions for all players apply until the ball touches the ring or backboard or until the free throw ends (9-1-4).

Free-Throw Violation: Penalties

After a free-throw violation by the throwing team, provided there are no additional free throws to be awarded, any opponent of the throwing team shall make the throw-in (7-5-2c).

If the first or only violation is by the free thrower or a teammate, the ball becomes dead when the violation occurs and no point can be scored by that throw. The following out-of-bounds provisions apply if no further free throws are to be administered: If the violation occurs during a free throw for a personal foul,  other than intentional or flagrant, the ball is awarded to the opponents for a throw-in from the designated out-of-bounds spot nearest the violation; if the violation occurs during a free throw for a technical foul, the ball is awarded to the thrower's team for a throw-in at the division line on the side of the court opposite the scorer's and timer's table; or if the violation occurs during a free throw for a flagrant personal foul or an intentional personal foul, the ball is awarded to the thrower's team for a throw-in from the designated out-of-bounds spot nearest the foul.

If the violation is by the free-thrower's opponent only: If the try is successful, the goal counts and the violation is disregarded; if the try is not successful, the ball becomes dead when the free throw ends, and a substitute throw shall be attempted by the same free thrower under conditions the same as for the free throw for which it is substituted.

If there is a simultaneous violation by each team, the ball becomes dead and no point can be scored. Remaining free throws are administered or play is resumed by the team entitled to the alternating-possession throw-in from the designated out-of-bounds spot nearest to where the simultaneous violation occurred.

If there is a violation first by the free-thrower's opponent followed by the free thrower or a teammate: If both offenders are in a marked lane-space, the second violation is ignored; if the second violation is by the free thrower or a teammate behind the free-throw line extended and the three-point line, both violations are penalized; if a violation by the free thrower follows disconcertion by an opponent, a substitute free throw shall be awarded; or if a fake by an opponent causes the free thrower or a teammate of the free thrower to violate, only the fake is penalized.

 COMMENT: While Rule 8-1 clearly states which marked lane spaces must be occupied and by whom, a team forfeits its right to any space not occupied before the free throw starts (when the ball is placed at the disposal of the free thrower). Once a free throw starts, no player occupying a marked lane space may enter or leave such space or break with either foot the vertical plane of any lane or lane-space boundary until the ball touches the ring or backboard or until the free throw ends. Players who do not occupy a marked lane space may not have either foot break the vertical plane of the free-throw-line extended and the vertical plane of the three-point line until the ball touches the ring, or the backboard, or the free throw ends. No player may enter or leave a marked lane space after the ball is placed at the disposal of the free thrower until the restrictions have ended as outlined.

Free-Throw Violation: Caseplays

6.4.3 SITUATION B: B1, in a marked lane space, enters the lane prematurely. The administering official properly signals the violation and A1 attempts the free throw. However, A1's attempt does not enter the basket or touch the ring. **RULING:** The violations by B1 and A1 constitute a simultaneous free-throw violation. Unless another free throw follows, play resumes with an alternating-possession throw-in from a designated spot outside the end line.

9.1.1 SITUATION: A1, at the free-throw line to attempt a free throw: (a) muffs the pass from the official and it rolls forward; or (b) while performing his/her habitual dribbles prior to the release, accidentally allows the ball to deflect off his/her foot into the lane. **RULING:** In (a), the official should sound the whistle to prevent any violations and then start the free throw procedure again. No free-throw violation should be called in this situation. In (b), a free-throw violation shall be called on A1 (9-1-3a, e).

9.1.2 SITUATION A: Following a time-out by Team B, A1 is given the ball for the first of two free throws even though Team B is still huddling at the bench and the first marked spaces on each side of the lane are not occupied. In this case, the lead official uses the resumption-of-play procedure even though the first spaces are not occupied, whereas in other cases, the spaces would have to be properly occupied before the official would proceed with the free throw administration. A1's first attempt is successful. The lead official then bounces the ball to A1 for the second attempt. Team B is still at the sideline. The official again gives the signal which indicates a violation by Team B if the attempt is missed. A1 misses the second free-throw attempt. **RULING:** The violation will result in A1 being given a substitute attempt. Team B will be assessed a technical foul if they delay further by not occupying the first marked spaces on each side of the lane before the ball becomes live for the substitute throw (4-38; 8-1-2; 10-1-5b).

9.1.2 SITUATION B: A1 is shooting the first of a bonus free-throw situation. A4 and A5 are positioned in the first two marked lane spaces (near the end line) and B4 and B5 are positioned in the second two marked lane spaces. The incorrect alignment is discovered by the officials (a) before the ball is at the disposal of A1; (b) after the ball is at A1's disposal, but before the try is in flight; (c) when the try is in flight; (d) when the successful try goes through the cylinder; (e) when the unsuccessful try is rebounding off the basket ring; or (f) when the rebound of the unsuccessful try is securely in A4's possession. **RULING:** In (a), the administering official shall "reset" the free throw and put the players in their proper marked lane spaces. In (b) and (c) an official shall sound his/her whistle immediately and call a simultaneous violation, utilizing the alternating-possession procedure to put the ball in play. In (d), (e) and (f) the free throw has ended and the improper alignment is ignored (4-20-3; 9-1-2 Penalty 3).

9.1.3 SITUATION A: A1, at the free throw line to attempt a final free throw, fakes the release of the ball. **RULING:** A violation by A1, Team B will be awarded a throw-in at the nearest spot.

COMMENT: The faking of a free throw try is a violation. However, if A1 does not feel comfortable after starting his/her motion and stops to adjust, the players in the lane spaces are expected to hold their positions (9-1-3b).

9.1.3 SITUATION B: While A1's free-throw attempt is in flight toward the basket: (a) B1; or (b) A2, in a marked lane space, fakes by rocking forward causing an opponent to enter the lane prematurely. **RULING:** In (a), the official will use the proper signal indicating a violation by B1 and a substitute free throw is awarded if A1's attempt is unsuccessful. If it is successful, the violation is ignored. In (b), the official will sound his/her whistle immediately when A2 violates. The violation cancels A1's attempt and it is B's ball for a throw-in, unless an additional free throw(s) is involved.

COMMENT: If a player uses verbal tactics like "you're in my space" or a time-out request to fake an opponent into violations, only the fake is penalized (9-1-3b Penalty 1 4d).

9.1.3 SITUATION C: A1 is preparing to attempt a free throw. Prior to A1's release of the ball, B1 fakes causing A2 to enter the lane prematurely. A1 then requests and is granted a time-out. **RULING:** Upon resuming play, A1 is entitled to a free throw and the official shall use the proper signal indicating a violation by B1 prior to the granting of the time-out. If the free throw is successful, the violation is ignored, if unsuccessful a substitute throw is awarded (9-1-3b).

9.1.3 SITUATION D: The ball is at the disposal of free thrower A1. B1, within the visual field of A1: (a) raises his/her arms above the head; or (b) after his/her arms have been extended above the head, alternately opens and closes both hands. **RULING:** B1 may be penalized in both (a) and (b). The official must judge whether the act distracts the free thrower. If the official judges the act in either (a) or (b) to be disconcerting, it shall be penalized. The free thrower is entitled to protection from being distracted. It is the opponent's responsibility to avoid disconcerting the free thrower (9-1-3c Penalty 2).

9.1.3 SITUATION E: After A1 starts the free-throw motion, B1 commits a common foul on A2 along the lane before the bonus rule is in effect. **RULING:** Even if the foul occurs before the ball is in flight, the throw counts if successful. No substitute try is awarded if the throw is missed. In either case, whether the throw is made or missed, the ball is awarded to Team A at the out-of-bounds spot nearest to where the foul occurred. If, in the opinion of the official, A1 has been disconcerted, a substitute throw shall be awarded if the try is unsuccessful (4-11; 9-1-3c Penalty 2).

9.**1**.3 SITUATION F: A1 steps on the free-throw line before releasing the ball in an attempt, after which B1 disconcerts. **RULING:** The ball became dead when A1 violated by stepping on the line, therefore, the action of B1 is not a violation. The ball is awarded to Team B out of bounds at the spot nearest the violation (7-5-2; 9-1-3e Penalty 1).

9.**1**.3 SITUATION G: As A1 starts the free-throwing motion, B1 hurriedly raises his/her arms. In the judgment of the official, the action of B1 disconcerts A1 and causes the attempt to miss the basket ring. **RULING:** As soon as the ball misses the ring, it becomes dead. Since free thrower A1 violated following disconcertion, a substitute free throw is awarded (9-1-3a Penalty 4c).

9.**1**.3 SITUATION H: While A1 is attempting a final free throw, (a) B1 enters the lane too soon followed by A2, both of whom are in marked lane spaces; or (b) B1, in a marked lane space enters the lane too soon, then shooter A1 steps on the free-throw line while releasing the throw. **RULING:** In (a), the violation by A2 is ignored and, if the try is successful, the goal shall count and the violation by B1 shall be ignored. If the try is unsuccessful, the ball shall become dead when the free throw ends and a substitute free throw shall be attempted by A1 under the same conditions as those for the original free throw. In (b), a double violation is called and the ball is put in play using the alternating-possession procedure (9-1 Penalty).

COMMENT: Anytime the defense violates first, followed by a violation by the free-throw shooter, the officials should consider the possibility of disconcertion.

9.**1**.3 SITUATION I: During a free throw by A1, B1 pushes A2, then B2, who is in a marked lane space, is in the lane too soon: (a) before A1 has started a free-throwing motion; or (b) after A1 has started a throwing motion. **RULING:** In (a), the foul by B1 causes the ball to become dead immediately, therefore the act, by B2 is not a violation. A1 is permitted the specified number of free throws, after which the foul is penalized. In (b), the foul does not cause the ball to become dead immediately, so there are two infractions. Even though the foul occurred first, the violation is the first to be penalized if A1's try is unsuccessful (4-11; 6-7 Exception c; 9-1 Penalty 2).

9.**1**.3 SITUATION J: The official administering a free throw awarded to A1 places the ball at his/her disposal. A1, who is inside the free-throw semicircle leaves the semicircle to confer with a teammate. **RULING:** Violation. After the ball has been placed at the disposal of the free thrower, he/she is not permitted to leave or enter the free-throw semicircle without violating, until restrictions have ended (9-1-3e Penalty 1).

9.1.3 SITUATION K: During a free throw by A1, B1 is positioned just behind the three-point line at the top of the semicircle. Is B1's position legal and what restrictions are in effect on B1? **RULING:** The position of B1 is legal. B1 may move freely but may not break the vertical plane of the three-point line and the free-throw line extended with either foot until after the ball touches the ring or the backboard or until the free throw has ended (9-1-4).

*9.1.3 SITUATION L: Before the ball touches the ring or backboard on a free-throw attempt by A1, B1 in a marked lane space: (a) with a foot, breaks the vertical plane of the side edge of the area between lane space one and lane space two; (b) steps on the outside edge of the lane-line boundary; (c) loses his or her balance and touches the inside of the lane with both hands; or (d) extends arms over the area between the lane spaces. **RULING:** Violation in (a), (b) and (c). Legal in (d), if there is no contact. While only the area 8 inches by 12 inches is painted on the court, the neutral zone is 12 inches wide and extends away from the nearer free-throw lane boundary for 36 inches. Likewise, each 2-inch wide lane space extends 36 inches back from the nearer free-throw lane boundary. Stepping on or breaking (with a foot) the plane of any boundary of either the neutral zone or spaces along the lane or around the three-point line are violations until restrictions end (9-1-3d and g; 1-5).

9.1.3 SITUATION M: B1 illegally steps into the lane before A1's final free throw hits the rim, (a) B1 then commits basket interference; or (b), A2 then steps into the lane prematurely and commits basket interference. **RULING:** The first infraction by the defensive player B1 does not end the free throw and is a "delayed" free-throw violation; the ball is still live. In (a), the ball becomes dead when the basket interference occurs. Score the free throw for A1. Since the free throw is successful, the lane violation by B1 is ignored. Team B will have a throw-in from any point outside the end line. In (b), when A2 enters the lane prematurely, the violation is ignored, since B1 violated first. But when A2 commits basket interference, the ball becomes dead immediately and ends the free throw and no point can be scored. Therefore, the free throw is unsuccessful and A1 would be given a substitute throw. Play is resumed from the free-throw situation (9-1-3g Penalty 2a, b, 4; 9-11 Penalty 1; 6-7-9; 4-20-3).

Topic:
Goaltending Violation

Goaltending occurs when a player touches the ball during a field-goal try or tap while it is in its downward flight entirely above the basket ring level and has the possibility of entering the basket in flight, or an opponent of the free thrower touches the ball outside the cylinder during a free-throw attempt (4-22). A player shall not commit goaltending (9-12).

Goaltending Violation: Penalty

If the violation is at the opponent's basket, the opponents are awarded one point if during a free throw, three points if during a three-point try and two points in any other case. The crediting of the score and subsequent procedure are the same as if the awarded score had resulted from the ball having gone through the basket, except that the official shall hand or bounce the ball to a player of the team entitled to the throw-in.

If the violation is at a team's own basket, no points can be scored, and the ball is awarded to the opponents for a throw-in from the designated out-of-bounds spot nearest the violation.

If the violation results from touching the ball while it is in the basket after entering from below, no points are scored and the ball is awarded to the opponents for a throw-in from the designated out-of-bounds spot nearest the violation.

If there is a violation by both teams, play shall be resumed by the team entitled to the alternating-possession throw-in at the out-of-bounds spot nearest to where the simultaneous violations occurred.

> ## In Simple Terms
>
> For a goaltending violation, three items must occur:
>
> 1. The ball has to be blocked off an attempt for a goal..
> 2. The ball must have a legitimate chance to enter the basket..
> 3. The ball must be on its downward flight toward the basket outside of the cylinder when the touching occurs.

Goaltending Violation: Caseplays

4.41.4 SITUATION A: While the ball is in flight on a try for goal by A1: (a) B1 touches the ball and then time expires; or (b) time expires and then B1 touches the ball. The ball continues in flight and enters Team

A's basket. **RULING:** The goal is scored in both (a) and (b), as B1's touching did not cause the try to end. However, in both (a) and (b), if B1's touching is either goaltending or basket interference, the ball becomes dead and two points will be awarded (6-7 Exception a; 9-11, 12).

9.12 SITUATION C: B1 touches A1's try for field goal: (a) just after its release and while the ball is still in upward flight; or (b) while the ball is in downward flight outside the cylinder and above ring level. **RULING:** In (a), the legal touching does not end the try and the ball remains live. In (b), the defensive goaltending causes the ball to become dead immediately and two points are awarded to Team A (4-22; 6-7-9).

Goaltending Violation During Free Throw

A player shall not goaltend during a free throw (10-3-10).

Goaltending Violation During Free Throw: Penalty

Technical foul assessed to the offending player with two free throws plus ball for division line throw-in.

Goaltending Violation During Free Throw: Caseplays

9.12 SITUATION A: On the first free throw by A1 in a bonus situation: B1 leaps above the lane and touches the ball but it falls in the basket anyway. **RULING:** Delayed lane violation on B1; the ball is still live. The goaltending violation causes an immediate dead ball and an automatic point for A1; B1 is assessed a technical foul. A1 is awarded the bonus free throw. Following the free throws for the technical foul, it is A's ball for a division line throw-in opposite the table (4-22; 6-7-9; 10-3-9).

9.12 SITUATION B: On the second of two free-throw attempts by A1, the ball is touched outside the cylinder by A2. **RULING:** The ball became dead immediately when A2 moved into the lane prematurely. Therefore, the goaltending is ignored. The lane violation cancels the free throw and Team B will throw-in from a designated spot outside the end line (9-1 Penalty 1).

Topic:
Held Ball Violation

A held ball occurs when opponents have their hands so firmly on the ball that control cannot be obtained without undue roughness (4-25-1), or an opponent places his/her hand(s) on the ball and prevents an airborne player from throwing the ball or releasing it on a try (4-25-2).

If a held ball or violation occurs so near the expiration of time that the clock is not stopped before time expires, the quarter or extra period ends with the held ball or violation (5-6-2 Exception 2).

Held Ball Violation: Penalty

The ball is awarded out of bounds after a held ball if the alternating-possession procedure has been established (7-4-7). The throw-in shall be from the out-of-bounds spot nearest to where the ball was located when the held ball occurs (6-4-3a).

If a held ball occurs immediately after the jump ball and the alternating-possession procedure has not been established, the jump ball shall be between the two players involved in the held ball (6-4 Note).

Held Ball Violation: Caseplays

4.25.2 SITUATION: A1 jumps to try for goal or to pass the ball. B1 leaps or reaches and is able to put his/her hands on the ball and keep A1 from releasing it. A1: (a) returns to the floor with the ball; or (b) is unable to control the ball and it drops to the floor. **RULING:** A held ball results immediately in (a) and (b) when airborne A1 is prevented from releasing the ball to pass or try for goal.

6.4.5 SITUATION B: During an alternating-possession throw-in, thrower A1 holds the ball through the end-line plane and B1 grabs it, resulting in a held ball. **RULING:** Since the throw-in had not ended and no violation occurred, it is still A's ball for an alternating-possession throw-in (4-42-5).

Topic:
Illegal Dribble Violation

Dribble

A dribble is ball movement caused by a player in control who bats (intentionally strikes the ball with the hand(s)) or pushes the ball to the floor once or several times (4-15-1). During a dribble the ball may be batted into the air provided it is permitted to strike the floor before the ball is touched again with the hand(s) (4-15-2).

The dribble may be started by pushing, throwing or batting the ball to the floor before the pivot foot is lifted (4-15-3).

The dribble ends when:

• The dribbler catches or causes the ball to come to rest in one or both hands (4-15-4a);

• The dribbler palms/carries the ball by allowing it to come to rest in one or both hands (4-15-4b);

• The dribbler simultaneously touches the ball with both hands (4-15-4c);

• The ball touches or is touched by an opponent and causes the dribbler to lose control (4-15-4d);

• The ball becomes dead (4-15-4e).

A ball which touches the front faces or edges of the backboard is treated the same as touching the floor inbounds, except that when the ball touches the thrower's backboard it does not constitute a part of a dribble (4-4-5).

 COMMENT: It is not possible for a player to travel during a dribble. A player is not dribbling while slapping the ball during a jump, when a pass rebounds from his/her hand, when he/she fumbles, or when he/she bats a rebound or pass away from other players who are attempting to get to it. The player is not in control under these conditions. It is a dribble when a player stands still and bounces the ball. It is not a dribble when a player stands still and holds the ball and touches it to the floor once or more than once.

Interrupted Dribble

An interrupted dribble occurs when the ball is loose after deflecting off the dribbler or after it momentarily gets away from the dribbler. There is no player control during an interrupted dribble (4-15-5).

During an interrupted dribble: a closely guarded count shall not be started or shall be terminated (4-15-6a); a player-control foul cannot be committed (4-15-6b); a time-out request shall not be granted (4-15-6c); an out-of-bounds violation does not apply on the player involved in the interrupted dribble (4-15-5d).

Illegal Dribble Violation

A player shall not dribble a second time after his/her first dribble has ended, unless it is after he/she has lost control because of: a try for field goal (9-5-1), a touch by an opponent (9-5-2); or a pass or fumble which has then touched, or been touched by, another player (9-5-3).

Illegal Dribble Violation: Penalty

The ball is dead when the violation occurs and is awarded to the opponents for a throw-in from the designated out-of-bounds spot nearest the violation.

Illegal Dribble Violation: Caseplays

4.4.5 SITUATION: A1 attempts a pass to A2 during pressing action in A's backcourt. The ball hits B's backboard and deflects directly back to A1 who catches the ball and: (a) passes the ball to A2; or (b) starts a dribble. **RULING:** The pass against B's backboard was the start of a dribble which ended when A1 caught the ball. In (a), the pass is legal action. In (b), it is a violation for a second dribble (9-5).

4.15.1 SITUATION A: While rebounding, A1 touches the ball while trying to gain control, after which: (a) A1 allows the ball to strike the floor to begin a dribble; or (b) A1 catches the ball and then pushes the ball to the floor to begin a dribble. **RULING:** Legal in both (a) and (b). The dribble does not begin until A1 has gained control.

4.15.1 SITUATION B: A1's throw-in pass is beyond A2. (a) A2 reaches out and slaps the ball toward A's basket; or (b) A2 muffs the pass. In both situations. A2 then gains control and dribbles to the basket and scores. **RULING:** No violation in either (a) or (b).

4.15.4 SITUATION A: As dribbler A1 attempts to change directions to avoid guard B1, he/she allows the ball to come to rest in one hand in bringing the ball from the right to the left side of the body. A1 pushes the ball to the floor in an attempt to continue the dribble. **RULING:** When A1 palmed/carried the ball, the dribble ended and when he/she pushed the ball to the floor a violation occurred (9-5).

4.15.4 SITUATION B: A1, while advancing the ball by dribbling, manages to keep a hand in contact with the ball until it reaches its maximum height. A1 maintains such contact as the ball descends, pushing it to the floor at the last moment; however, after six or seven bounces, A1's hand is in contact with the ball and the palm of the hand on this particular dribble is skyward so that the ball is resting on top of the hand. **RULING:** The dribble has ended and a violation occurs if A1 dribbles again. The dribble ended when the ball came to rest in the palm of A1's hand (9-5).

4.15.4 SITUATION C: After dribbling and coming to a stop, A1 throws the ball: (a) against the opponent's backboard and catches the rebound; (b) against an official, immediately recovers the ball and dribbles again; or (c) against his/her own backboard in an attempt to score (try), catches the rebound and dribbles again. **RULING:** A1 has violated in both (a) and (b). Throwing the ball against the opponent's backboard or an official constitutes another dribble, provided A1 is first to touch the ball after it strikes the official or the board. In (c), the action is legal. Once the ball is released on the try, there is no player or team control, therefore, A1 can recover the rebound and begin a dribble.

4.15.4 SITUATION D: While dribbling: (a) A1 bats the ball over the head of an opponent, runs around the opponent, bats the ball to the floor and continues to dribble; (b) the ball bounces away but A1 is able to get to it and continues to dribble; (c) the ball hits A1's foot and bounces away but A1 is able to overtake and pick it up; or (d) A1 fumbles the ball in ending the dribble so that A1 must run to recover it. **RULING:** Violation in (a), because the ball was touched twice by A1's hand(s) during a dribble, before it touched the floor. In (b), even though the dribble was interrupted it has not ended and A1 may continue the dribble. In (c), the dribble ended when A1 caught the ball; and it ended in (d) when it was fumbled. Even though the dribble has ended in (c) and (d), A1 may recover the ball but may not dribble again (9-5).

4.15.4 SITUATION E: While A1 is dribbling in A's backcourt, the ball legally touches B1's leg, causing it to bounce away from A1. A1 quickly recovers the ball with two hands and then starts another dribble. **RULING:** Legal. The touch by B1 ended the original dribble and A1 could then recover and dribble again. However, the touch by B1 did not end team control and the 10-second backcourt count continues (9-5-2).

☑ Rationale

The definition of when a dribble ends was changed to when the loss of control by the dribbler is caused by the opponent touching, or being touched by the ball, rather than an intentional batting of the ball. The illegal dribble violation was also edited to reflect this rules change. The rules were changed because a long-standing interpretation had been that any touching of a dribble by a defender (intentional or otherwise, by the hand of otherwise) ends the dribble. The way the rule was previously written implied that the touching must be by the hand and must be intentional. The new rule is now consistent with that long-standing interpretation and current enforcement.

9.5 SITUATION: A1 dribbles and comes to a stop after which he/she throws the ball against the opponent's backboard or an official and catches the rebound. **RULING:** A1 has violated. Throwing the ball against an opponent's backboard or an official constitutes another dribble, provided A1 is first to touch the ball after it strikes the official or the board (4-15-2; Fundamental 19).

9.5.1 SITUATION: A1 ends a dribble and then jumps and releases the ball on a try for goal. B1 partially blocks the shot, but A1 secures control again while still in the air. A1 returns to the floor and dribbles to the basket and scores. **RULING:** Legal maneuver. Both player control and team control ended when A1 released the ball. When A1 recovered he/she could dribble again similar to dribbling after catching a pass or rebound.

9.5.3 SITUATION: A1 is dribbling in backcourt and ends the dribble, but defensive pressure prevents a pass to A2. A1 then passes the ball so it touches B1. A1 recovers the loose ball in backcourt and dribbles again. **RULING:** No violation. When A1's pass was touched by, or touched, another player, he/she may start a new dribble. The 10-second backcourt count continues.

Topic:
Jump Ball Violation

For any jump ball, each jumper shall have both feet within that half of the center restraining circle which is farther from his/her basket (6-3-1).

When the referee is ready and until the ball is tossed, nonjumpers shall not move onto the center restraining circle or change position around the center restraining circle (6-3-2).

Teammates may not occupy adjacent positions around the center restraining circle if an opponent indicates a desire for one of these positions before the referee is ready to toss the ball (6-3-3).

The referee shall then toss the ball upward between the jumpers in a plane at right angles to the sidelines. The toss shall be to a height greater than either of them can jump so that it will drop between them (6-3-4).

Until the tossed ball is touched by one or both jumpers, nonjumpers shall not have either foot break the plane of the center restraining circle cylinder or take a position in any occupied space (6-3-5).

The tossed ball must be touched by one or both of the jumpers after it reaches its highest point. If the ball contacts the floor without being touched by at least one of the jumpers, the referee shall toss it again (6-3-6).

Neither jumper shall touch the tossed ball before it reaches its highest point (6-3-7a); leave the center restraining circle until the ball has been touched (6-3-7b); catch the jump ball (6-3-7c); or touch the ball more than twice (6-3-7d).

The jump ball and these restrictions end when the touched ball contacts one of the eight nonjumpers, the floor, a basket or backboard.

During a jump ball, a jumper is not required to face his/her own basket, provided he/she is in the proper half of the center restraining circle. The jumper is also not required to jump and attempt to touch the tossed ball. However, if neither jumper touches the ball it should be tossed again with both jumpers being ordered to jump and try to touch the ball.

A player shall not violate any provision of the jump ball. If both teams simultaneously commit violations during the jump ball or if the referee makes a bad toss, the toss shall be repeated (9-6).

Jump Ball Violation: Penalty

The ball is dead when the violation occurs and is awarded to the opponents for a throw-in from the designated out-of-bounds spot nearest the violation.

Jump Ball Violation: Caseplays

6.3.2 SITUATION: The referee is ready to toss the ball to start the game. (a) A1 who was on the center restraining circle backs off; (b) B1 moves onto the restraining circle into an unoccupied spot; (c) B2 moves off the circle and goes behind A2 and is within 3 feet of the circle; or (d) B3 moves off the circle about 5 feet and moves around behind A3 and A4 who are occupying spaces on the circle. **RULING:** Legal in (a) and (d), but a violation in both (b) and (c). Moving off the restraining circle in (a), and around the circle when more than 3 feet away as in (d), is permissible. It is a violation to move onto the circle as in (b), until the ball leaves the official's hand, or into an occupied space as in (c), until the ball is touched. The violation by B results in a throw-in for Team A (4-3).

6.3.7 SITUATION: During a jump: (a) jumper A1 touches the ball simultaneously with both hands and then with one hand followed with one hand again; or (b) jumpers A1 and B1 do not touch the ball until one or both have returned to the floor. **RULING:** In (a), simultaneous touching counts as one, but the second separate touch causes a violation by A1 for touching the ball more than twice. In (b), it is legal; however, if the tossed ball contacts the floor without being touched, the referee shall toss it again.

Prohibiting the use of the fist for the purpose of batting the ball is one of the original rules of basketball.

6.4.1 SITUATION C: Following the jump between A1 and B1 to start the first quarter, the jump ball: (a) is touched by A2 and it then goes out of bounds; (b) is touched simultaneously by A2 and B2 and it then goes out of bounds; (c) is simultaneously controlled by A2 and B2; or (d) is caught by A1. **RULING:** In (a), Team B will have a throw-in. The alternating-possession procedure is established and the arrow is set toward A's basket when a player of Team B has the ball for the throw-in. Team A will have the first opportunity to throw-in when the procedure is used. In (b) and (c), A2 and B2 will jump in the center restraining circle regardless of where the ball went out or where the held ball occurred. In (d), Team B will have a throw-in because of the violation and the arrow for the alternating-possession will be pointed towards Team A's basket (4-12-1; 4-28-1).

Topic:
Kick/Fist Violation

Kicking the ball is intentionally striking it with any part of the leg or foot (4-29).

A player shall not intentionally kick the ball, strike it with the fist or cause it to enter and pass through the basket from below (9-4).

Kicking the ball is a violation only when it is an intentional act; accidentally striking the ball with the foot or leg is not a violation.

Kick/Fist/Ball Enters Basket From Below Violation: Penalty

The ball is dead when the violation occurs and is awarded to the opponents for a throw-in from the designated out-of-bounds spot nearest the violation.

Kick/Fist/Ball Enters Basket From Below Violation: Caseplays

4.29 SITUATION: During A1's attempt to pass to A2, B1 (a) intentionally uses his/her thigh to deflect the pass; (b) intentionally kicks the ball with his/her foot; or (c) has the ball accidentally hit his/her lower leg. **RULING:** In (a) and (b), there is a kicking violation and Team A will receive the ball out of bounds nearest the violation. In (c), the ball remains live and there is no violation (9-4).

9.4 SITUATION: At A's basket, the ball enters the net from below and passes through the basket: (a) The officials do not know whether a player of Team A or Team B was responsible; (b) the ball entered the basket after A1's pass was deflected by B1; or (c) A1 and B1 touched the ball simultaneously before it entered the basket. **RULING:** The ball becomes dead when it enters from below and passes through. In (a) and (c), a throw-in will follow by the team entitled to it under the alternating-possession procedure. In (b), it is A's ball for a throw-in, as B1 caused the violation.

Topic:
Leaving the Court Violation

A player shall not leave the floor for an unauthorized reason (9-3-3).

◹ Rationale

Leaving the court was changed to a violation from a technical foul with the hopes that the likelihood of the infraction would be called more often to help eliminate this tremendous advantage.

Leaving the Court Violation: Penalty

The ball is dead when the violation occurs and is awarded to the opponents for a throw-in from the designated out-of-bounds spot nearest to the violation.

The ball does not become dead until the try or tap ends, or until the airborne shooter returns to the floor, when the violation occurs by an opponent (6-7-9 Exception d).

Leaving the Court Violation: Caseplays

9.3.3 SITUATION A: A1 receives a pass while in the restricted area of the lane. A1 passes the ball to A2 outside the three-point line. In order to get the three-second count stopped, A1 steps directly out of bounds under A's basket. **RULING:** A1 is charged with a violation for leaving the court for an unauthorized reason (9-7).

9.3.3 SITUATION B: A1 and A2 set a double screen near the end line. A3 intentionally goes out of bounds outside the end line to have his/her defender detained by the double screen. **RULING:** The official shall call a violation on A3 as soon as he/she steps out of bounds. The ball is awarded to Team B at a designated spot nearest to where the violation occurred.

9.3.3 SITUATION C: A1 and A2 set a double screen near the end line. B3 intentionally goes out of bounds outside the end line to avoid being detained by A1 and A2. Just as B3 goes out of bounds, A3's try is in flight. **RULING:** B3 is called for a leaving-the-floor violation. Team A will receive the ball out of bounds at a spot nearest to where the violation occurred. Since the violation is on the defense, the ball does not become dead until the try has ended. If the try is successful, it will count (6-7-9 Exception d).

9.3.3 SITUATION D: The score is tied 60-60 with four seconds remaining in the game. A1 has a fast break and is near the free-throw line on his/her way to an uncontested lay-up. B5 running down the court near the sideline, intentionally runs out of bounds in the hopes of getting a leaving-the-floor violation called. **RULING:** B5's intentional violation should be ignored and A1's activity should continue without interruption.

COMMENT: Non-contact, away from the ball, illegal defensive violations (i.e. excessively swinging the elbows, leaving the floor for an unauthorized reason) specifically designed to stop the clock near the end of a period or take away a clear advantageous position by the offense should be temporarily ignored. The defensive team should not benefit from the tactic. If time is not a factor, the defense should be penalized with the violation or a technical foul for unsporting behavior (10-1-8).

Topic:
Out of Bounds Violation

A player shall not cause the ball to go out of bounds (9-3-1). No player shall be out of bounds when he/she touches or is touched by the ball after it has been released on a throw-in pass (9-3-2).

A player is out of bounds when he/she touches the floor, or any object other than a player/person, on or outside a boundary (7-1-1).

In Simple Terms

A player that steps on the boundary line while dribbling the ball is considered out of bounds even if the hand was not in contact with the ball when the touching of the boundary line occurred.

The ball is out of bounds when it touches or is touched by: a player who is out of bounds (7-1-2a); any other person, the floor, or any object on or outside a boundary (7-1-2b); the supports or back of the backboard (7-1-2c) or the ceiling, overhead equipment or supports (7-1-2d).

When a rectangular backboard is used, the ball is out of bounds if it passes over the backboard (7-2-2b).

The ball is caused to go out of bounds by the last player in bounds to touch it or be touched by it, unless the ball touches a player who is out of bounds prior to touching something out of bounds other than a player (7-2-1).

If the ball is out of bounds because of touching or being touched by a player who is on or outside a boundary line, such player causes it to go out (7-2-2).

The location of a player or nonplayer is determined by where the player is touching the floor as far as being inbounds or out of bounds (4-35-1a).

When a player is touching the out of bounds line, the player is located out of bounds (4-35-2). The dribbler has committed a violation if he/she steps on or outside a boundary, even though he/she is not touching the ball while he/she is out of bounds.

The location of an airborne player with reference to the out of bounds line is the same as at the time such player was last in contact with the floor or an extension of the floor, such as a bleacher (4-35-3).

Simultaneous Out of Bounds Violation

If the ball goes out of bounds and was last touched simultaneously by two opponents, both of whom are inbounds or out of bounds, or if the official is in doubt as to who last touched the ball or if the officials disagree, play shall be resumed by the team entitled to the alternating-possession throw-in at the spot out of bounds nearest to where the simultaneous violation occurred (7-3-1). If the alternating-possession procedure has not been established, play shall be resumed by a jump ball between the two players involved in the center restraining circle (7-3-2).

Out of Bounds Violation: Penalty

The ball is dead when the violation occurs and is awarded to the opponents for a throw-in from the designated out-of-bounds spot nearest the violation.

Out of Bounds Violation: Caseplays

4.35.2 SITUATION: Thrower A1 inbounds the ball to A2. A2 immediately throws the ball back to A1. When A1 touches the pass, he/she has: (a) both feet touching inbounds; (b) one foot touching inbounds and one out of bounds; or (c) one foot touching inbounds and the other not touching the floor. **RULING:** The ball remains live in (a) and (c), but A1 has caused the ball to be out of bounds in (b) (4-4-4).

7.1.1 SITUATION A: A1, while holding the ball inbounds near the sideline, touches (a) player B1; (b) a photographer; (c) a coach; (d) an official, all of whom are out of bounds. **RULING:** A1 is not out of bounds in (a), (b), (c) or (d). To be out of bounds, A1 must touch the floor or some object on or outside a boundary line. People are not considered to be objects and play continues. Inadvertently touching someone who is out of bounds, without gaining an advantage, is not considered a violation.

7.1.1 SITUATION B: A1 blocks a pass near the end line. The ball falls to the floor inbounds, but A1, who is off balance, steps off the court. A1 returns inbounds, secures control of the ball and dribbles. **RULING:** Legal. A1 did not leave the court voluntarily and did not have control of the ball when he/she did. This situation is similar to one in which A1 makes a try from under the basket and momentum carries A1 off the court. If the try is unsuccessful, A1 may come back onto the court and regain control since A1 did not leave the court voluntarily and did not have control of the ball when he/she did.

7.1.1 SITUATION C: A1 blocks a pass near the sideline and the ball goes into A1's front court. A1's momentum carries him/her out of bounds. He/she immediately returns inbounds, secures control of the ball, dribbles, shoots, and scores. **RULING:** Legal (4-35-1a; 7-1-2; 9-3).

7.1.1 SITUATION D: A1 jumps from inbounds to retrieve an errant pass near a boundary line. A1 catches the ball while in the air and tosses it back to the court. A1 lands out of bounds and (a) is the first to touch the ball after returning inbounds; (b) returns inbounds and immediately dribbles the ball; or (c) picks up the ball after returning to the court and then begins a dribble. **RULING:** Legal in (a) and (b). Illegal in (c) as the controlled toss of the ball to the court by A1 constitutes the start of a dribble, dribbling a second time after picking up the ball is an illegal dribble violation (4-15-5; 4-15-6d; 4-35; 9-5).

7.1.2 SITUATION A: The ball strikes the side edge or top edge of the backboard or passes over the top of the backboard and the ball: (a) came from a throw-in from behind the plane of the backboard; or (b) from a pass or try from the front or back of the plane of the backboard. The ball does not touch any supporting brace. **RULING:** If a fan-shaped backboard is being used in (a) and in (b), the ball remains live. If a rectangular backboard is used in (a), the ball remains live after touching the side edge, but it is a violation if it passes directly over the backboard. In (b), the ball remains live if it touches a side edge or the top edge if it rebounds and comes down in front of the backboard. The ball becomes dead if it passes over the top of a rectangular backboard regardless of the action which causes it to pass over or whether it comes from the front or back of the plane.

7.1.2 SITUATION B: A1, while dribbling, touches: (a) B1 who is standing on a sideline; or (b) a nearby chair or scorer's table while A1's feet are inbounds. **RULING:** (a) A1 is inbounds. However, if the ball in control of A1 touches B1, the ball is out of bounds and is awarded to Team A at that spot. In (b), A1 is out of bounds and, therefore, the ball is considered to have gone out of bounds (7-2).

7.1.2 SITUATION C: A1 is dribbling in Team A's backcourt when the ball is deflected by B1. The ball gets away and contacts a child who is (a) walking inbounds (on the playing court); or (b) walking out of bounds. The official sounds the whistle. **RULING:** In (a), the ball is not out of bounds since the person contacted, the child, was inbounds. However, for safety reasons the official should stop play and resume from the point of interruption. Team A, the team last in control, will be awarded a throw-in at a spot nearest to where the ball was located when play was interrupted. B1 has committed an out-of-bounds violation in (b) (4-36; 7-2-1).

7.2.1 SITUATION: A1 holds the ball near a sideline. B1 is inbounds and bats the ball from the hands of A1 causing it to go out of bounds. **RULING:** The ball is awarded to Team A as B1 caused it to go out of bounds.

7.2.2 SITUATION: A throw-in by A1 (a) strikes B1 who is inbounds and rebounds in flight directly from B1 and then strikes A1 who is still out of bounds; (b) is batted by B1, who is inbounds and the ball is next touched by A1 who is still out of bounds. **RULING:** A1 caused the ball to go out of bounds and it is awarded to Team B at that spot for a throw-in for both (a) and (b).

7.4 SITUATION: What and where is the violation when: (a) A1 grabs a rebound at Team A's basket and passes the ball across the division line after which it is touched by A2 in the backcourt; (b) A1, in a corner near B's end line, throws a long pass which crosses the sideline in flight at the division line and touches in the bleachers near A's end-line extended; (c) A1 makes a throw-in at the division line and is first to touch the throw-in near B's basket; or (d) a throw-in by A1 from near the division line goes through A's basket before touching another player on the court? **RULING:** In (a), the violation is not for causing the ball to go into the backcourt, but for A2 touching it first after it went there. The throw-in for Team B is at a spot out of bounds nearest to the spot where A2 touched the ball. In (b), the violation is for causing the ball to be out of bounds, but since the ball is not out of bounds until it touches something, the violation occurs when the ball touches the bleachers and the throw-in by B is at the out-of-bounds spot nearest such touching. In (c), the violation is by A1 for not throwing the ball so that it touches or is touched by another player inbounds or out of bounds before going out of bounds untouched. In (d), the violation is by A1 for throwing the ball so that it enters the basket before touching another player on the court. The throw-in by B in (c) and (d) is from the spot of A1's throw-in (9-2-2, 6; 9-9-1).

Topic:
Palming/Carrying the Ball Violation

The dribble ends when the dribbler palms/carries the ball by allowing it to come to rest in one or both hands (4-15-4b).

A player shall not dribble a second time after his/her first dribble has ended (9-5).

Palming/Carrying the Ball Violation: Penalty

The ball is dead when the violation occurs and is awarded to the opponents for a throw-in from the designated out-of-bounds spot nearest the violation.

Palming/Carrying the Ball Violation: Caseplays

4.15.4 SITUATION A: As dribbler A1 attempts to change directions to avoid guard B1, he/she allows the ball to come to rest in one hand in bringing the ball from the right to the left side of the body. A1 pushes the ball to the floor in an attempt to continue the dribble. **RULING:** When A1 palmed/carried the ball, the dribble ended and when he/she pushed the ball to the floor a violation occurred (9-5).

4.15.4 SITUATION B: A1, while advancing the ball by dribbling, manages to keep a hand in contact with the ball until it reaches its maximum height. A1 maintains such contact as the ball descends, pushing it to the floor at the last moment; however, after six or seven bounces, A1's hand is in contact with the ball and the palm of the hand on this particular dribble is skyward so that the ball is resting on top of the hand. **RULING:** The dribble has ended and a violation occurs if A1 dribbles again. The dribble ended when the ball came to rest in the palm of A1's hand (9-5).

Topic:
Ten-Second Violation

A player shall not be, nor may his/her team be, in continuous control of a ball which is in his/her backcourt for 10 seconds (9-8).

Ten-Second Violation: Penalty

The ball is dead when the violation occurs and is awarded to the opponents for a throw-in from the designated out-of-bounds spot nearest the violation.

Ten-Second Violation: Caseplays

9.8 SITUATION A: A1 is in A's backcourt and has dribbled for nine seconds and then passes the ball forward towards A2 in the frontcourt. While the ball is in the air traveling from backcourt to frontcourt, the 10-second count is reached. **RULING:** Violation by Team A as the ball has not gained frontcourt location. It is B's ball for a throw-in from the out-of-bounds spot closest to where A1 released the ball on the pass toward A2 (4-3; 7-5-2).

9.8 SITUATION B: Team A has control of the ball for eight seconds in A's backcourt when A1 passes the ball toward Team A's frontcourt. The official's count continues. The ball strikes the floor in A's frontcourt and stays there without being touched by any player. Should the count continue after the ball touches in frontcourt? **RULING:** No. The backcourt count should be terminated as soon as the ball has frontcourt location by touching the floor in Team A's frontcourt (4-4-1; 4-4-2).

9.8 SITUATION C: After A1 has dribbled for nine seconds in A's backcourt: (a) A1 requests a time-out; or (b) B1 deflects the ball out of bounds. **RULING:** In both (a) and (b), Team A will have 10 seconds to advance the ball to frontcourt following the throw-in if a player of Team A gains control in A's backcourt.

9.8 SITUATION D: Team A is in control in its backcourt for seven seconds. A1 throws the ball toward A2 in the frontcourt. B1 jumps from Team A's: (a) frontcourt; or (b) backcourt and while in the air bats the ball back to A1 in A's backcourt. Does this give Team A 10 more seconds to get the ball to the frontcourt? **RULING:** Yes, in (a), a new count starts because B1 had frontcourt location when touching the ball thus giving the ball frontcourt location. In (b), the original count continues as Team A is still in control and the ball has not gone to frontcourt (4-4-2; 4-3; 4-35-1).

Topic:
Three-Second Violation

A player shall not remain for three seconds in that part of his/her free-throw lane between the end line and the farther edge of the free-throw line while the ball is in control of his/her team in his/her frontcourt (9-7-1).

The three-second restriction applies to a player who has only one foot touching the lane boundary. The line is part of the lane. All lines designating the free-throw lane, but not lane-space marks and neutral-zone marks, are part of the lane (9-7-2).

Allowance shall be made for a player who, having been in the restricted area for less than three seconds, dribbles in or moves immediately to try for goal (9-7-3).

Rationale

The three-second violation was developed to force offensive players to move without the ball and reduce congestion within the lane area.

Three-Seconds Violation: Penalty

The ball is dead when the violation occurs and is awarded to the opponents for a throw-in from the designated out-of-bounds spot nearest the violation.

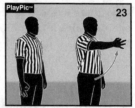

Three-Seconds Violation: Caseplays

9.7.1 SITUATION: A1 rebounds the ball off Team B's backboard. A2 is in Team A's three-second restricted area when the rebound occurs and A2 remains there while A1 is dribbling in Team A's backcourt. Three seconds expire without the ball being in the frontcourt of Team A. **RULING:** This is not a violation. The three-second lane restriction is not in effect until Team A is in control of the ball in Team A's frontcourt.

9.7.2 SITUATION: A1 is standing with one foot inside and the other outside the three-second restricted area. A1 lifts the foot from the restricted area and returns it there without touching it first to the nonrestricted area. **RULING:** Violation. This action does not terminate the three-second count. The count goes on since merely lifting the foot from the restricted space is interpreted as an attempt to evade the rule and avoid its purpose. However, there is no three-second count during rebounding action or during a throw-in. The count on a player in the restricted area is suspended when that player begins a try for goal.

Topic:
Throw-in Violations

The thrower is the player who attempts to make a throw-in (4-42-1). A throw-in is a method of putting the ball in play from out of bounds

(4-42-2). The throw-in and the throw-in count begin when the ball is at the disposal of a player of the team entitled to it (4-42-3). The throw-in count ends when the ball is released by the thrower so the passed ball goes directly into the court (4-42-4). The throw-in ends when the passed ball touches, or is legally touched by, another player who is either inbounds or out of bounds (4-42-5). The designated throw-in spot is 3 feet wide with no depth limitation and is established by the official prior to putting the ball at the thrower's disposal (4-42-6). The thrower must keep one foot on or over the spot until the ball is released. Pivot-foot restrictions and the traveling rule are not in effect for a throw-in.

Throw-in Provisions

The thrower shall not leave the designated throw-in spot until the ball has been released on a throw-in pass (9-2-1).

The ball shall be passed by the thrower directly into the court from out-of-bounds so it touches or is touched by another player (inbounds or out of bounds) on the court before going out of bounds untouched (9-2-2).

The thrown ball shall not be touched by a teammate of the thrower while the ball is on the out-of-bounds side of the throw-in boundary-line plane (9-2-3). After a goal or awarded goal, the team not credited with the score shall make the throw-in from the end of the court where the goal was made and from any point outside the end line. A team retains this privilege if the scoring team commits a violation or common foul (before the throw-in ends and before the bonus is in effect) and the ensuing throw-in spot would have been on the end line. Any player of the team may make a direct throw-in or he/she may pass the ball along the end line to a teammate(s) outside the boundary line (7-5-7).

Once the throw-in starts, the ball shall be released on a pass directly into the court before five seconds have elapsed (9-2-4).

The thrower shall not carry the ball onto the court (9-2-5).

The thrown ball shall not touch the thrower in the court before it touches or is touched by another player (9-2-6).

The thrown ball shall not enter the basket before it touches or is touched by another player (9-2-7).

The thrown ball shall not become lodged between the backboard and ring or come to rest on the flange before it touches or is touched by another player (9-2-8).

The thrower shall not be replaced by a teammate after the ball is at the thrower's disposal (9-2-9).

No teammate of the thrower shall be out of bounds after a designated-spot throw-in begins (9-2-11).

Throw-in Violation: Penalty

The ball becomes dead when the violation occurs. Following a violation, the ball is awarded to the opponents for a throw-in at the original throw-in spot.

Throw-in Violation: Caseplays

7.6.2 SITUATION: During a throw-in, A1 passes the ball over the braces supporting a rectangular backboard. The ball does not touch any of the braces and is subsequently controlled by A2, who throws the ball in Team A's basket. The ball did not pass over any part of the rectangular backboard. **RULING:** The ball was live and the throw-in ended when it was touched by A2, thus A2 scored a field goal. This play is somewhat different than those most frequently used to bring out the point that the ball becomes dead when it passes over a rectangular board. The rules do not identify the supports as being part of the backboard (5-1; 7-1-2 Note).

7.6.3 SITUATION: A1 is out of bounds for a designated-spot throw-in. The administering official has designated the spot and put the ball at A1's disposal. In order to avoid some of the defensive pressure near the throw-in spot, A1 takes several steps directly backward, but keeps one foot on or over the designated area prior to releasing the ball on a throw-in pass. **RULING:** Legal throw-in. It is permissible for the thrower to move backward or forward within the 3-foot-wide designated area without violating and he/she may move laterally if at least one foot is kept on or over the designated area until the ball is released. The thrower may also jump vertically and pass from the designated throw-in spot.

 COMMENT: Pivot-foot restrictions and the traveling rule are not in effect for a throw-in. The thrower must keep one foot on or over the spot until the ball is released.

9.2.2 SITUATION A: Thrower A1 (a) causes the ball to carom from the wall behind him/her, or from the floor out of bounds and then into the court; (b) caroms the ball from the back of the backboard to a player in the court; or (c) throws the ball against the side or the front face of the backboard, after which it rebounds into the hands of A2. **RULING:** Violation in (a) and (b), since the throw touched an object out of bounds. The throw-in in (c) is legal. The side and front face of the backboard are inbounds and, in this specific situation, are treated the same as the floor inbounds.

9.2.2 SITUATION B: The throw-in by A1 is: (a) first touched in the court by A1; or (b) touched or caught by A2 whose hand(s) is on the out-of-bounds side of the throw-in boundary plane. **RULING:** Violation in both (a) and (b), B's ball at the spot of the throw-in (9-2-3; 9-2-6).

9.2.2 SITUATION C: A1 scores a basket. After the ball goes through the net, B1 grabs it and makes a move toward the end line as though preparing to make a throw-in. However, B1 never legally steps out of bounds, both feet remain inbounds. B1 immediately passes the ball up the court to a fast-breaking teammate, who scores a basket. **RULING:** Cancel Team B's goal, throw-in violation on B1. The ball was at B1's disposal after the made basket to make a throw-in. B1 must be out of bounds to make a legal throw-in (7-4-3; 7-5-7).

9.2.2 SITUATION D: A1 dribbles the ball on floor on the out-of-bounds area before making a throw-in. **RULING:** Legal, a player may bounce the ball on the out-of-bounds area prior to making a throw-in.

9.2.5 SITUATION: Thrower A1 inadvertently steps onto the court inbounds. A1 immediately steps back into normal out-of-bounds throw-in position. The contact with the court was during a situation: (a) with; or (b) without defensive pressure on the throw-in team. **RULING:** A violation in both (a) and (b).

 COMMENT: Whether or not there was defensive pressure or whether or not stepping on the court was inadvertent, it is a violation and no judgment is required in making the call.

9.2.8 SITUATION: Team A is awarded an alternating-possession throw-in. A1 lobs the throw-in pass toward A2 who is breaking to the basket. The throw-in pass is too high and lodges between the ring and backboard. **RULING:** Violation by A1 for lodging the untouched throw-in pass. Team B's ball at the throw-in spot. Since A1 violated during an alternating-possession throw-in, Team A has lost the arrow. Team B will have the arrow for the next alternating-possession throw-in (6-4-5).

9.2.9 SITUATION: Following a violation, the official has properly signaled and awarded a throw-in to Team A at a designated spot. No Team A player comes to the spot even though the official has allowed ample time for them to respond. The official then places the ball on the floor and begins the five-second count (a) Both A1 and A2 step out of bounds and A1 picks up the ball; or (b) both A1 and A2 step out of bounds and A1 picks up the ball and hands it to A2. **RULING:** In (a), A2 must immediately return inbounds. In (b), it is a throw-in violation when A1 hands the ball to A2 (9-2-12).

Topic:
Traveling Violation

Traveling (running with the ball) is moving a foot or feet in any direction in excess of prescribed limits while holding the ball. The limits on foot movements are as follows:

A player who catches the ball with both feet on the floor, may pivot, using either foot. When one foot is lifted, the other is the pivot foot (4-44-1).

> ### Fundamental #5
>
> Neither the dribble nor traveling rule operates during the jump ball, throw-in or free throw.

A player, who catches the ball while moving or dribbling, may stop, and establish a pivot foot (4-44-2).

If both feet are off the floor and the player lands: simultaneously on both feet, either foot may be the pivot (4-44-2a-1); on one foot followed by the other, the first foot to touch is the pivot (4-44-2a-2); or on one foot, the player may jump off that foot and simultaneously land on both. Neither foot can be a pivot in this case (4-44-2a-3).

If one foot is on the floor it is the pivot when the other foot touches in a step (4-44-2b-1) The player may jump off that foot and simultaneously land on both. Neither foot can be a pivot in this case (4-44-2b-2).

After coming to a stop and establishing a pivot foot, the pivot foot may be lifted, but not returned to the floor, before the ball is released on a pass or try for goal (4-44-3a). If the player jumps, neither foot may be returned to the floor before the ball is released on a pass or try for goal (4-44-3b). The pivot foot may not be lifted before the ball is released to start a dribble (4-44-3c).

After coming to a stop when neither foot can be a pivot, one or both feet may be lifted, but may not be returned to the floor before the ball is released on a pass or try for goal (4-44-4a). Neither foot may be lifted before the ball is released to start a dribble (4-44-4b).

> ### Fundamental #6
>
> It is not possible for a player to travel during a dribble.

A player holding the ball may not touch the floor with a knee or any other part of the body other than hand or foot (4-44-5a). After gaining control while on the floor and touching with other than hand or foot, a player may not attempt to get up or stand (4-44-5b).

A player shall not travel with the ball (9-4).

Traveling Violation: Penalty

The ball is dead when the violation occurs and is awarded to the opponents for a throw-in from the designated out-of-bounds spot nearest the violation.

Traveling Violation: Caseplays

4.33 SITUATION: A1 catches the ball while both feet are off the floor, alights on one foot, jumps off that foot and comes to a stop with both feet simultaneously hitting the floor. A1 then lifts one foot and throws for a goal or passes. **RULING:** Legal. A1 may lift either foot in passing or trying for a goal in this situation. However, A1 may not pivot; that is, A1 may not lift one foot from the floor and then step (touch the floor) with that foot before the ball has left the hand(s). By rule, a pivot means a player "steps once or more than once with the same foot..." (4-44-4a).

4.44 SITUATION A: A1 attempts to catch the ball while running rapidly. A1 muffs the ball, but succeeds in securing it before it strikes the floor. A1 then begins a dribble, taking several steps between the time the ball was first touched until it was caught. **RULING:** There has been no violation provided A1, after catching the ball, released the ball to start the dribble before the pivot foot was lifted from the floor (4-15).

4.44 SITUATION B: A1 attempts a try after ending the dribble. The try does not touch the backboard, the rim or any other player. A1 runs and is able to catch the ball before it strikes the floor. Is this traveling? **RULING:** No. When A1 recovered his/her own try, A1 could either dribble, pass or try again. There was no team control after the ball was released on a try (4-12; 4-41).

4.44.2 SITUATION A: Dribbler A1 catches the ball with the right foot touching the floor and then jumps off that foot and alights on both feet simultaneously: (a) with feet parallel; or (b) with one foot in advance. **RULING:** The position of the feet has no significance, but they must come to the floor simultaneously. In both (a) and (b), it is a violation if A1 pivots on either foot.

The original rules of basketball mandated that a player could not run with the ball. The player must throw it from the spot at which it was caught. An allowance was to be made for a player who catches the ball while running at a good rate of speed, commonly known as a pivot foot today.

4.44.2 SITUATION B: Airborne A1 and A2 jointly grab the rebound and each alights simultaneously on both feet. A1 and A2 each move one foot in attempting to wrestle the ball from each other before realizing they are teammates. A1 lets go and A2 dribbles away. **RULING:** Legal. There has been no violation as neither A1 or A2 moved their pivot foot while they were in joint control.

4.44.3 SITUATION A: A1 jumps to try for goal. B1 also jumps and: (a) slaps the ball out of A1's hands; (b) touches the ball but does not prevent A1 from releasing the ball; (c) touches the ball and A1 returns to the floor holding the ball; or (d) touches the ball and A1 drops it to the floor and touches it first after it bounces. **RULING:** In (a) and (b), the ball remains live. In (c), a traveling violation. In (d), a violation for starting a dribble with the pivot foot off the floor. Since the touching did not prevent the pass or try in (b), (c) and (d), the ball remains live and subsequent action is covered by rules which apply to the situation.

4.44.3 SITUATION B: A1 receives the ball with both feet off the floor and he/she lands simultaneously on both feet without establishing a pivot foot. A1 then jumps off both feet in an attempt to try for goal, but realizing the shot may be blocked, A1 drops the ball to the floor and dribbles. **RULING:** A1 has traveled as one foot must be considered to be the pivot and must be on the floor when the ball is released to start a dribble. The fact that no pivot foot had been established does not alter this ruling.

4.44.3 SITUATION C: A1 receives a pass and establishes the right foot as the pivot. While faking a pass or try, A1 lifts the pivot foot and stands on the left foot alone while undecided as to what to do. Has A1 traveled? **RULING:** No. Traveling would occur only if A1 begins a dribble or returns the pivot foot to the floor. While in this position A1 may pass, try for goal or call a time-out.

4.44.3 SITUATION D: (a) A1 tosses the ball from one hand to the other while keeping his/her pivot foot in contact with the floor; or (b) A1 throws the ball over the head of B1 and then takes several steps before catching it. **RULING:** Legal in (a), but a traveling violation in (b). In (b), since the ball did not touch the floor, the tossing and subsequent catch is illegal (9-4).

4.44.5 SITUATION A: Is it traveling if A1 falls to the floor: (a) while holding the ball; or (b) after being airborne to catch a pass or control a rebound? **RULING:** Yes in both (a) and (b).

4.44.5 SITUATION B: A1 dives for a loose ball and slides after gaining control. A1 is in a position either on his/her back or stomach. What can A1 do without violating? **RULING:** A1 may pass, shoot, start a dribble or call a time-out. Once A1 has the ball and is no longer sliding, he/she may not roll over. If flat on his/her back, A1 may sit up without violating. Any attempt to get to the feet is traveling unless A1 is dribbling. It is also traveling if A1 puts the ball on the floor, then rises and is first to touch the ball (4-44-5b).

4.44.5 SITUATION C: A1 is dribbling when he/she: (a) drops to a position with a knee on the floor and then ends the dribble; or (b) drops one knee to the floor and then stands again while continuing the dribble. **RULING:** The action in both (a) and (b) is legal. However, if A1 touches a knee to the floor while holding the ball, it would be traveling as A1 has touched the floor with something other than a hand or foot.

4.44.5 SITUATION D: A1 secures possession of the ball with one knee in contact with the floor. May A1 assume a standing position without committing a traveling violation? **RULING:** It depends on what A1 does. If A1 attempts to stand up while holding the ball, a traveling violation occurs. However, if A1 starts a dribble and then rises, no violation has occurred. Also, A1 could pass, try for goal or call a time-out from that position.

Topic 11

Classifications of Fouls

Key Terms

A foul is an infraction of the rules which is charged and is penalized (4-19). The ball becomes dead, or remains dead when a foul, other than player-control or team-control, occurs (6-7-7).

The ball does not become dead until the try or tap ends, or until the airborne shooter returns to the floor, when: a foul occurs while a try or tap for a field goal is in flight (6-7-7 exception a); a foul occurs while a try for a free throw is in flight (6-7-7 exception b); or a foul, other than player-control or team-control, is committed by any opponent of a player who has started a try or tap for goal (and is in the act of shooting) before the foul occurred, provided time did not expire before the ball was in flight (6-7-7 exception c).

A team foul is any personal foul or technical foul (except indirect technical fouls) which is charged to either team. All team fouls are counted to reach the bonus free throw (4-19-13).

An unsporting foul is a noncontact technical foul which consists of unfair, unethical, dishonorable conduct or any behavior not in accordance with the spirit of fair play (4-19-14).

When a foul occurs, an official shall signal the timer to stop the clock. The official shall designate the offender to the scorer and indicate with finger(s) the number of free throws (2-9-1).

Point of interruption is a method of resuming play after a double personal, double technical or simultaneous foul (4-36-1). Play shall be resumed by a throw-in to the team that was in control at a spot nearest to where the ball was located when the stoppage occurred (4-36-2a); a free throw or a throw-in when the stoppage occurred during this activity or if a team is entitled to such (4-36-2b); or an alternating-possession throw-in when the point of interruption is such that neither team is in control and no goal, infraction, nor end of quarter/extra period is involved (4-36-2c).

Topic:
Classifications of Fouls

Personal Foul

A personal foul is a player foul which involves illegal contact with an opponent while the ball is live, which hinders an opponent from performing normal defensive and offensive movements. A personal foul also includes contact by or on an airborne shooter when the ball is dead (4-19-1).

Personal Foul: Penalty

Offender is charged with one foul, and if it is her/her fifth foul (personal and technical) or if it is flagrant, he/she is disqualified (10-6 Penalty).

Common Foul

A common foul is a personal foul which is neither flagrant nor intentional nor committed against a player trying or tapping for a field goal nor a part of a double, simultaneous or multiple foul (4-19-2).

Common Foul: Penalty

No free throws for each common foul prior to the bonus rule being in effect. Any player of the offended team shall make the throw-in from the designated out-of-bounds spot nearest the foul (7-5-4a).

Bonus free throw for seventh, eighth and ninth team foul each half, if the first free throw is successful (10 Penalties 3a). Bonus free throw beginning with the 10th team foul of each half whether or not first free throw is successful (10 Penalties 3b).

Common Fouls: Caseplay

4.41.1 SITUATION: B1 commits a common foul by holding A1 during a field-goal try, but after A1 has completed the act of shooting. The foul occurs before the bonus rule applies. The attempt is: (a) successful; or (b) unsuccessful. RULING: A personal foul is charged to B1 in both (a) and (b), but no free throw is awarded to A1 in either case. In both (a) and (b), the ball is awarded to Team A at the spot out of bounds nearest where the foul occurred (7-5-4a).

Technical Foul

A technical foul is:

• A foul by a nonplayer (4-19-5a).

• A noncontact foul by a player (4-19-5b).

• An intentional or flagrant contact foul while the ball is dead, except a foul by an airborne shooter (4-19-5c).

• A direct technical, charged to the head coach because of his/her actions or for permitting a player to participate after having been disqualified (4-19-5d).

• An indirect technical, charged to the head coach as a result of a bench technical foul being assessed to team bench personnel (4-19-5e).

• A technical foul being assessed to a team member for dunking or grasping the ring during pregame warm-up or at intermission (4-19-5e).

Technical Foul: Penalty

Two free throws for the offended team (10 Penalties). After a technical foul, any player of the team to whom the free throws have been awarded shall make the throw-in from out of bounds at the division line on the side of the court opposite the scorer's and timer's table (7-5-6a).

COMMENT: If a technical foul occurs after the ball has become dead to end a quarter, the next quarter is started by administering the free throws. This applies even when the foul occurs after the first half has ended. It also applies when the foul occurs after the second half has ended, provided the score is tied. If the score is not tied, the free throws are administered unless the outcome of the game will not be affected. If the outcome is not already decided, the free throws are attempted immediately as if the foul had been a part of the fourth quarter. In this case, if any overtime period is necessary, it will start with a jump ball. The division line throw-in following the technical foul cannot be carried over to the overtime as the fourth quarter ended with the last free throw (5-6-4).

Intentional Foul

An intentional foul is a personal or technical foul which neutralizes an opponent's obvious advantageous position. Contact away from the ball or when not making a legitimate attempt to play the ball or a player, specifically designed to stop or keep the clock from starting, shall be intentional. Intentional fouls may or may not be premeditated and are not based solely on the severity of the act. A foul also shall be ruled intentional if while playing the ball a player causes excessive contact with an opponent (4-19-3).

Intentional Foul: Penalty

Two free throws plus ball for throw-in (10 Penalties 4). After an intentional personal foul, any player of the team to whom the free throws have been awarded shall make the throw-in from the out-of-bounds spot nearest the foul (7-5-4b).

Flagrant Foul

A flagrant foul may be a personal or technical foul of a violent or savage nature, or a technical noncontact foul which displays unacceptable conduct. It may or may not be intentional. If personal, it involves, but is not limited to violent contact such as: striking, kicking and kneeing. If technical, it involves dead-ball contact or noncontact at any time which is extreme or persistent, vulgar or abusive conduct. Fighting is a flagrant act (4-19-4).

Flagrant Foul: Penalty

Two free throws if flagrant, plus ball for throw-in (10 Penalties 4). Any player who commits a flagrant foul is disqualified. After a flagrant personal foul, any player of the team to whom the free throws have been awarded shall make the throw-in from the out-of-bounds spot nearest the foul (7-5-4b).

Rationale

A flagrant foul is always unsporting and may or may not be intentional. The term "flagrant" implies that the infraction is so bad it cannot escape notice, it cannot be condoned and, in general, it exceeds any reasonable limit.

Flagrant Foul: Caseplays

4.19.6 SITUATION B: Is it possible for airborne shooter A1 to commit a foul which would not be player control? **RULING:** Yes. The airborne shooter could be charged with an intentional or flagrant personal foul or with a technical foul (4-19-2, 3, 4).

5.6.4 SITUATION A: Following the final horn in a game which has Team A leading 62-60, the coach of Team A sprints after the game officials and shouts profanity at the referee who has just left the playing court outside the end line. **RULING:** The referee shall charge the coach with a flagrant technical foul and the results of the two free throws will determine whether an extra period will be necessary. The jurisdiction of the officials had not ended as the referee was still within the visual confines of the playing area (2-2-4).

5.6.4 SITUATION C: Team A is leading 61-60. B1 fouls A1 in the act of shooting as time expires. As the officials approach the scorer's table, the Team A coach rushes the floor and begins screaming obscenities at the officials. **RULING:** A flagrant technical foul is assessed to the Team A coach. The foul at the expiration of time is no longer ignored. The flagrant technical foul on the Team A coach created a false double foul situation, which may affect the outcome of the game. The penalties are administered in the order in which they occurred. With the lane cleared,

A1 shoots two free throws for being fouled in the act of shooting. If both are successful, the game is over. If one or both are missed, an eligible player from Team B shoots the two technical foul free throws. The free throws will determine the outcome of the game or an extra period will be played (4-9-19; 5-6-3 exception; 10-4-1c).

 COMMENT: Jurisdiction of the officials is terminated when all officials leave the visual confines of the playing area. While the preferred action would be for all officials to immediately leave the playing area, such an observable action by the coach should be penalized as unsporting or flagrant.

10.5 SITUATION: A1 commits a flagrant technical foul against B1. **RULING:** The flagrant technical foul disqualifies A1 from further participation in the contest. A disqualified team member or student bench personnel shall go to or remain on the bench. However, in an unusual situation, an official has the authority to require that these individuals who have committed a flagrant technical foul must leave the vicinity of the court. This action is necessary when permitting such offenders to remain at courtside would tend to incite the crowd, to incite the opponents, or to subject the officials, opponents or others administering the game, to unsporting harassment. In such circumstances, the official should require the individual who has committed a flagrant foul to leave the vicinity of the court with an adult supervisor. It must be emphasized that an official does have this authority, when the circumstances resulting from any flagrant foul warrant it (10-5 Note 2).

Player-Control Foul

A player-control foul is a common foul committed by a player while he/she is in control of the ball or by an airborne shooter (4-19-6).

Player-Control Foul: Penalty

No free throws for a player-control foul (10 Penalties 1b). After a player-control foul, any player of the offended team shall make the throw-in from the designated out-of-bounds spot nearest the foul (7-5-4a).

Team-Control Foul

A team-control foul is a common foul committed by a member of the team that has team control (4-19-7).

Team-Control Foul: Penalty

No free throws for a team-control foul (10 Penalties 1b). After a team-control foul, any player of the offended team shall make the throw-in from the designated out-of-bounds spot nearest the foul (7-5-4a).

Team-Control Foul: Caseplays

4.12.1 SITUATION B: A1 is dribbling in A's backcourt when the ball accidentally strikes his/her ankle and bounces away. During the interrupted dribble, A1 fouls B1 in attempting to continue the dribble. **RULING:** A team-control foul is charged to A1. It is not a player-control foul as the contact occurred during an interrupted dribble (4-19-7).

4.19.7 SITUATION A: A1 is dribbling the ball in the frontcourt when A2 sets an illegal screen against B2. Team B is in the bonus. **RULING:** No free throws are awarded as this is a team-control foul. Award the ball to Team B at a designated spot out of bounds closest to where the foul occurred (4-12-2; 7-5-4a).

4.19.7 SITUATION B: A1 is passing the ball to A2 in the team's frontcourt when B2 deflects the pass. As A2 and B2 are attempting to retrieve the loose ball, A2 illegally pushes B2 from behind and is called for a foul. Team B is in the bonus. **RULING:** No free throws are awarded as this is a team-control foul. Award the ball to Team B at a designated spot out of bounds closest to where the foul occurred (4-12-2; 4-12-3b; 7-5-4a).

*4.19.7 SITUATION C: A1 has the ball for a throw-in. The throw-in pass deflects off of A2. As A2 and B2 are attempting to retrieve the loose throw-in pass, A2 illegally pushes B2 from behind and is called for a foul. Team B is in the bonus. **RULING:** This is not a team-control foul since team control had not been established. B2 is awarded a bonus free-throw situation (4-12-6).

4.19.7 SITUATION D: A1 ends the dribble and passes the ball to A2: (a) while the ball is in the air; or (b) after A2 has control, A1 charges into B2. **RULING:** The foul on A1 in both (a) and (b) is a team-control foul. Team B is awarded the ball for a designated spot nearest to where the foul occurred (4-12-2).

Double Personal Foul

A double personal foul is a situation in which two opponents commit personal fouls against each other at approximately the same time (4-19-8a).

Double Personal Foul: Penalty

No free throws for a double personal foul (10 Penalties 1c). After a double personal foul, play shall be resumed at the point of interruption (7-5-3b).

Double Personal Foul: Caseplays

4.19.8 SITUATION A: A1 and B1 foul one another at approximately the same time. The contact occurs during: (a) a live-ball situation; or (b) a dead-ball situation. **RULING:** In (a), it is a double personal foul and in (b), it is a double technical foul. No free throws are awarded in (a) or (b) and play resumes at the point of interruption (4-36).

4.19.8 SITUATION B: While the ball is being dribbled near the division line, A1 and B1 are engaged in extremely rough play in the low post area and the covering official calls a double personal foul. After the whistle, A1 and B1 use profanity directed at each other and the covering official calls a double technical foul. **RULING:** The double personal foul during the live ball results in no free throws. The dead-ball profanity results in a double technical foul, again with no free throws. A1 and B1 have each accumulated two fouls toward their five for disqualification. Play is resumed at the point of interruption (4-36).

*4.19.8 SITUATION C: A1 drives for a try and jumps and releases the ball. Contact occurs between A1 and B1 after the release and before airborne shooter A1 returns one foot to the floor. One official calls a blocking foul on B1 and the other official calls a charging foul on A1. The try is (a) successful, or (b) not successful. **RULING:** Even though airborne shooter A1 committed a charging foul, it is not a player-control foul because the two fouls result in a double personal foul. The double foul does not cause the ball to become dead on the try. In (a), the goal is scored; play is resumed at the point of interruption, which is a throw-in for Team B from anywhere along the end line. In (b), the point of interruption is a try in flight; therefore the alternating-possession procedure is used (4-36).

4.19.8 SITUATION D: A1 has possession of the ball and is about to attempt the first of a one-and-one free-throw situation when A4 and B4 are whistled for a double foul. **RULING:** A4 and B4 are charged with personal fouls and play shall resume from the point of interruption. A1 receives the ball to attempt the one-and-one free throw with the lane spaces properly occupied (4-36-2b; 7-5-3b).

4.19.8 SITUATION E: A1 has control of the ball in Team A's frontcourt. Post players A5 and B5 are pushing each other in an attempt to gain a more advantageous position on the block while (a) A1 is dribbling the ball; (b) the ball is in the air on a pass from A1 to A2; or (c) the ball is in the air on an unsuccessful try for goal by A1. An official calls a double personal foul on A5 and B5. **RULING:** In (a) and (b), Team A had control of the ball when the double foul occurred, and thus play will be resumed at the point of interruption. Team A will have a designated spot throw-in nearest the location where the ball was located when the double foul occurred. In (c), no team has control while a try for goal is in flight, and since the try was unsuccessful, there is no obvious point of interruption. Play will be resumed with an alternating possession throw-in nearest the location where the ball was located when the double foul occurred. Had the try been successful, the point of interruption would have been a throw-in for Team B from anywhere along the end line (4-36; 6-4-3g; 7-5-3b).

Double Technical Foul

A double technical foul is a situation in which two opponents commit technical fouls against each other at approximately the same time (4-19-8b).

Double Technical Foul: Penalty

No free throws for a double technical foul (10 Penalties 1c). After a double technical foul, play shall be resumed at the point of interruption (7-5-3b).

Double Technical Foul: Caseplays

4.19.8 SITUATION A: A1 and B1 foul one another at approximately the same time. The contact occurs during: (a) a live-ball situation; or (b) a dead-ball situation. **RULING:** In (a), it is a double personal foul and in (b), it is a double technical foul. No free throws are awarded in (a) or (b) and play resumes at the point of interruption (4-36).

*4.19.8 SITUATION B: A1 and B1 are engaged in extremely rough play in the low post area and the covering official calls a double personal foul. After the whistle, A1 and B1 use profanity directed at each other and the covering official calls a double technical foul. **RULING:** The double personal foul during the live ball results in no free throws. The dead-ball profanity results in a double technical foul, again with no free throws. A1 and B1 have each accumulated two fouls toward their five for disqualification. Play is resumed at the point of interruption (4-36).

False Double Foul

A false double foul is a situation in which there are fouls by both teams, the second of which occurs before the clock is started following the first, and such that at least one of the attributes of a double foul is absent (4-19-9).

False Double Foul: Penalty

In case of a false double foul, each foul carries its own penalty (10 Penalty 7).

False Double Foul: Caseplays

4.19.9 SITUATION A: A1 leaps high and is fouled by B1 as he/she taps the ball which subsequently goes through A's basket. A1 fouls B2 in returning to the floor. **RULING:** This is a false double foul. The foul by B1 does not cause the ball to become dead. However, the player-control foul by A1 does cause the ball to become dead and also dictates that no goal can be scored. Since the goal is not scored, A1 is awarded two free throws for the foul by B1. No players are allowed along the lane as Team B will be awarded the ball following the last free throw. If the last throw is successful, the throw-in is from anywhere along the end line. If the last throw is unsuccessful, the throw-in is from a designated spot nearest the foul (4-1; 4-11; 4-41-1; 6-7-7 Exception c: 6-7-4; 7-5-4a).

4.19.9 SITUATION B: B1 holds A1, whose team is in the bonus. A1 is successful in both free-throw attempts. While B1 is making the throw-in from behind the end line, A1 pushes B2 near midcourt. Team B is or is not in the bonus situation. **RULING:** If Team B is in the bonus, B2 is either awarded a one-and-one and the ball remains in play if either free-throw attempt touches the basket ring but is not successful, or is awarded two free throws and the ball remains in play if the second is unsuccessful. If the last free-throw attempt by B2 is successful, Team A shall put the ball in play from out of bounds anywhere along the end line by B's basket. If Team B is not in the bonus, it is awarded the ball for a throw-in from a designated spot out of bounds nearest to where the foul occurred. Penalties are administered in the order in which the fouls occurred (7-5-4a).

4.19.9 SITUATION C: A1 has a breakaway lay-up. B1 commits a hard foul against A1 from behind and is called for an intentional foul. The Team A head coach protests, feeling the foul should have been a flagrant foul and is assessed a technical foul. **RULING:** Award A1's goal if successful. A1 shall receive two free throws with the lane spaces cleared. Any Team B player is then awarded two free throws for the technical foul. Team B will be awarded the ball for a throw-in at the division line opposite the scorer's table.

Simultaneous Foul

A simultaneous foul (personal or technical) by opponents is a situation in which there is a foul by both teams which occurs at approximately the same time, but are not committed by opponents against each other (4-19-10).

Simultaneous Foul: Penalty

No free throws for a simultaneous foul by opponents (10 Penalties d). After a simultaneous foul, play shall be resumed at the point of interruption (7-5-3b).

Simultaneous Foul: Caseplays

4.19.10 SITUATION: B1 fouls dribbling A1 near the division line. At approximately the same time, A2 fouls B2 in the lane near Team A's basket. **RULING:** This is a simultaneous personal foul. B1 and A2 are charged with personal fouls. The ball shall be put back in play at the point of interruption. Team A is awarded a throw-in on the sideline nearest to where the ball was located when the fouls occurred (7-5-3b; 4-36).

Multiple Foul

A multiple foul is a situation in which two or more teammates commit personal fouls against the same opponent at approximately the same time (4-19-11).

Multiple Foul: Penalty

One free throw for each foul with no try involved, a successful or unsuccessful two-point try or tap or a successful three-point try or tap (10 Penalties 6a). Two free throws for each foul that is intentional or flagrant, or an unsuccessful three-point try or tap. Ball is awarded for a throw-in if one of the fouls is intentional or flagrant (10 Penalties 2b). If one or both fouls of a multiple foul are flagrant, two free throws are awarded for each flagrant foul.

Multiple Foul: Caseplay

4.19.11 SITUATION: B1 and B2 foul A1 at the same time while A1 is: (a) driving down the lane; (b) in the act of shooting a successful or unsuccessful two-point try; (c) a successful three-point try; or (d) an unsuccessful three-point try. **RULING:** One free throw for each foul in (a), (b) and (c) and two free throws for each in (d) (10 Penalty 6).

False Multiple Foul

A false multiple foul is a situation in which there are two or more fouls by the same team and the last foul is committed before the clock is started following the first, and at least one of the attributes of a multiple foul is absent (4-19-12).

False Multiple Foul: Penalty

In case of a false multiple foul, each foul carries its own penalty (10 Penalty 7).

False Multiple Foul: Caseplay

4.19.12 SITUATION: B1 fouls airborne A1 who is in the act of shooting. Before airborne shooter A1 returns one foot to the floor, he/she is fouled by B2 who has moved into A1's landing area. The ball: (a) does; or (b) does not, enter the basket. **RULING:** This is a false multiple foul and each foul carries its own penalty. In (a), the goal is counted and A1 is awarded one free throw for each foul. In (b), A1 is awarded two free throws for each foul (10 Penalty 6, 7).

Topic 12

Contact Fouls

PlayPic™

Key Terms

Rebounding is an attempt by any player to secure possession of the ball following a try or tap for goal (4-37-1).

A screen is legal action by a player who, without causing contact, delays or prevents an opponent from reaching a desired position (4-40-1).

Guarding is the act of legally placing the body in the path of an offensive opponent (4-23-1).

An airborne shooter is a player who has released the ball on a try for a goal and has tapped the ball and not returned to the floor (4-1-1). The airborne shooter is considered to be in the act of shooting (4-1-2).

The act of shooting begins simultaneously with the start of the try or tap and ends when the ball is clearly in flight (4-41-1).

Verticality applies to a legal position by a player (4-45).

Contact

A player shall not hold, push, charge, trip; nor impede the progress of an opponent by extending an arm, shoulder, hip or knee, or by bending the body into other than a normal position; nor use any rough tactics (10-6-1). A player shall not contact an opponent with his/her hand unless such contact is only with the opponent's hand while it is on the ball and is incidental to an attempt to play the ball (10-6-2). A player shall not use his/her hands on an opponent in any way that inhibits the freedom of movement of the opponent or acts as an aid to a player in starting or stopping (10-6-3). A player shall not extend the arm(s) fully or partially other than vertically so that freedom of movement of an opponent is hindered when contact with the arms occurs. A player may hold his/her hand(s) and arm(s) in front of his or her own face or body for protection and to absorb force from an imminent charge by an opponent (10-6-4). A player shall not use the forearm and/or hand to prevent an opponent from attacking the ball during a dribble or when throwing for goal (10-6-5). Contact caused by a defensive player who approaches from behind is pushing; contact caused by the momentum of a player who has thrown for a goal is a form of charging (10-6-6). A player shall adhere to the rules pertaining to illegal contact as related to guarding (4-23), rebounding (4-37), screening (4-40) and verticality (4-45).

Incidental Contact

Incidental contact is contact with an opponent which is permitted and which does not constitute a foul (4-27).

The mere fact that contact occurs does not constitute a foul. When 10 players are moving rapidly in a limited area, some contact is certain to occur (4-27-1).

Contact which may result when opponents are in equally favorable positions to perform normal defensive or offensive movements, should not be considered illegal, even though the contact may be severe (4-27-2).

Similarly, contact which does not hinder the opponent from participating in normal defensive or offensive movements should be considered incidental (4-27-3).

A player who is screened within his/her visual field is expected to avoid contact with the screener by stopping or going around the screener. In cases of screens outside the visual field, the opponent may make inadvertent contact with the screener, and such contact is to be ruled incidental contact, provided the screener is not displaced if he/she has the ball (4-27-4).

If, however, a player approaches an opponent from behind or from a position from which he/she has no reasonable chance to play the ball without making contact with the opponent, the responsibility is on the player in the unfavorable position (4-27-5).

Every player is entitled to a spot on the playing court, provided the player gets there first without illegally contacting an opponent (4-37-3).

Verticality

Verticality applies to a legal position. The basic components of the principle of verticality are:

• A legal guarding position must be obtained initially and movement thereafter must be legal (4-45-1).

• From this position, the defender may rise or jump vertically and occupy the space within his/her vertical plane (4-45-2).

• The hands and arms of the defender may be raised within his/her vertical plane while on the floor or in the air (4-45-3).

• The defender should not be penalized for leaving the floor vertically or having his/her hands and arms extended within his/her vertical plane (4-45-4).

• The offensive player whether on the floor or airborne, may not "clear out" or cause contact within the defender's vertical plane which is a foul (4-45-5).

• The defender may not "belly up" or use the lower part of the body or arms to cause contact outside his/her vertical plane which is a foul (4-45-6).

• The player with the ball is to be given no more protection or consideration than the defender in judging which player has violated the rules (4-45-7).

Topic:
Blocking Foul

Blocking is illegal personal contact which impedes the progress of an opponent with or without the ball (4-7-1).

A dribbler shall neither charge into nor contact an opponent in his/her path no attempt to dribble between to opponents or between an opponent and a boundary, unless the space is such as to provide a reasonable chance for him/her to go through without contact (10-6-7).

When a dribbler, without contact, sufficiently passes an opponent to have head and shoulders in advance of that opponent, the greater responsibility for that subsequent contact is on the opponent (10-6-8). A player may hold the hands and arms in front of his/her face or body for protection and to absorb force from an imminent charge by an opponent (10-6-4).

Blocking Foul: Caseplays

4.23.3 SITUATION B: A1 is dribbling near the sideline when B1 obtains legal guarding position. B1 stays in the path of A1 but in doing so has (a) one foot touching the sideline. **RULING:** In (a), B1 is called for a blocking foul because a player may not be out of bounds and obtain or maintain legal guarding position (4-23-2; 4-23-3a).

10.6.1 SITUATION C: B1 is standing behind the plane of the backboard before A1 jumps for a lay-up shot. The forward momentum causes airborne shooter A1 to charge into B1. **RULING:** B1 is entitled to the position obtained legally before A1 left the floor. If the ball goes through the basket before or after the contact occurs, the player-control foul cancels the goal. However, if B1 moves into the path of A1 after A1 has left the floor, the foul is on B1. B1's foul on the airborne shooter is a foul during the act of shooting. If the shot is successful, one free throw is awarded and if it is unsuccessful, two free throws result (4-19-1, 6; 6-7-4; 10 Penalty 2, 5a).

Topic:
Charging Foul

Charging is illegal personal contact caused by pushing or moving into an opponent's torso (4-7-2).

A player who is moving with the ball is required to stop or change direction to avoid contact if a defensive player has obtained a legal guarding position in his/her path (4-7-2a).

If a guard has obtained a legal guarding position, the player with the ball must get his/her head and shoulders past the torso of the defensive player. If contact occurs on the torso of the defensive player, the dribbler is responsible for the contact (4-7-2b).

In Simple Terms

A charging foul will most often occur by an offensive player without the ball.

There must be reasonable space between two defensive players or a defensive player and a boundary line to allow the dribbler to continue in his/her path. If there is less than 3 feet of space, the dribbler has the greater responsibility for the contact (4-7-2c).

The player with the ball may not push the torso of the guard to gain an advantage to pass, shoot or dribble (4-7-2c).

It is legal to hold the hands and arms in front of the face or body for protection and to absorb force from an imminent charge by an opponent (4-24-3).

A dribbler shall not charge into nor contact an opponent in his/her path nor attempt to dribble between two opponents or between an opponent and a boundary, unless the space is such as to provide a reasonable chance for him or her to go through without contact (10-6-7). If a dribbler, without contact, sufficiently passes an opponent to have head and shoulders in advance of that opponent, the greater responsibility for subsequent contact is on the opponent (10-6-8). If a dribbler in his/her progress is moving in a straight-line path, he/she may not be crowded out of that path, but if an opponent is able to legally obtain a defensive position in that path, the dribbler must avoid contact by changing direction or ending his/her dribble (10-6-9). The dribbler should not be permitted additional rights in executing a jump try for goal, pivoting, feinting or in starting a dribble (10-6-10).

To obtain or maintain a legal rebounding position, a player may not charge an opponent (4-37-2a) or extend shoulders, hips, knees or extend the arms or elbows fully or partially in a position other than vertical so that the freedom of movement of an opponent is hindered when contact with the arms or elbows occurs (4-37-2b).

Charging Foul: Caseplays

10.6.1 SITUATION A: B1 takes a certain spot on the court before A1 jumps in the air to catch a pass: (a) A1 lands on B1; or (b) B1 moves to a new spot while A1 is airborne. A1 lands on one foot and then charges into B1. **RULING:** In (a) and (b), the foul is on A1 (4-23-5d).

10.6.1 SITUATION B: The bonus is in effect and while the ball is in flight during a try for a field goal by A1, A2 charges into B1. Following this there is a basket-interference violation by: (a) B2 or (b) A3. **RULING:** In (a), both the foul by A2 and the violation by B2 are penalized, but in the reverse order of occurrence. Two points are first awarded to Team A because of the violation by B2. B1 is then awarded a one-and-one. Had the bonus not been in effect in (a), B would have been awarded the ball out of bounds at its end line where the basket was awarded. In (b), there are no rule complications. The violation by A3 caused the ball to become dead. Ordinarily, the ball would go to B out-of-bounds at the spot nearest the violation. However, this penalty is ignored because of the penalty enforcement for the foul by A2 (7-5-7; 9-11 Penalty).

Topic:
Hand Check Foul

It is not legal to use hands on an opponent which in any way inhibits the freedom of movement of the opponent or acts as an aid to a player in starting or stopping (4-24-5). A player shall not contact an opponent with his/her hand unless such contact is only with the opponent's hand while it is on the ball and is incidental to an attempt to play the ball (10-6-2).

Hand Check Foul: Caseplay

10.6.9 SITUATION: A1 begins a drive toward the basket with a quick dribble and step to evade B1. B1 momentarily hand checks A1 and forces A1 to take a wider approach. **RULING:** A hand-checking foul on B1. Even though the contact was only momentary it did give B1 an opportunity to get into better position and forced A1 to take a different route toward the basket.

Topic:
Holding Foul

Holding is illegal personal contact with an opponent which interferes with his/her freedom of movement (4-26).

It is not legal to hold the screener in order to maintain a guarding position relative to his/her opponent (4-24-4).

To obtain a legal rebounding position, a player may not bend his/her body in an abnormal position to hold or displace an opponent (4-37-2c).

A player shall not hold nor impede the progress of an opponent by extending an arm, shoulder, hip or knee, or by bending the body into other than a normal position (10-6-1).

Topic:
Illegal Use of Hands Foul

It is legal to extend the arms vertically above the shoulders and need not be lowered to avoid contact with an opponent when the action of the opponent causes contact. This legal use of the arms and hands usually occurs when guarding the player making a throw-in, the player with the ball in pressing tactics and a player with the ball who is maneuvering to try for goal by pivoting, jumping, etc (4-24-1).

It is legal use of hands to reach to block or slap the ball controlled by a dribbler or a player throwing for goal or a player holding it and accidentally hitting the hand of the opponent when it is in contact with the ball (4-24-2).

It is legal to hold the hands and arms in front of the face or body for protection and to absorb force from an imminent charge by an opponent. This same protective use of the arms and hands occurs when a player who has set a screen outside the opponent's visual field is about to be run into by the player being screened. The action, however, should be a recoil action rather than a pushing action (4-24-3).

It is not legal to use hands on an opponent which in any way inhibits the freedom of movement of the opponent or acts as an aid to a player in starting or stopping (4-24-5).

It is not legal to extend the arms fully or partially in a position other than vertical so that the freedom of movement of an opponent is hindered when contact with the arms occurs. The extension of the elbows when the hands are on the hips or when the hands are held near the chest or when the arms are held more or less horizontally are examples of the illegal positions used (4-24-6).

A player shall not contact an opponent with his/her hand unless such contact is only with the opponent's hand while it is on the ball and is incidental to an attempt to play the ball (10-6-2).

Topic:
Player-Control Foul

A player-control foul is a common foul committed by a player while he/she is in control of the ball or by an airborne shooter (4-19-6).

An airborne shooter is a player who has released the ball on a try for a goal or has tapped the ball and has not returned to the floor (4-1-1). The airborne shooter is considered to be in the act of shooting (4-1-2).

It is not legal to extend the arms fully or partially in a position other than vertical so that the freedom of movement of an opponent is hindered when contact with the arms occurs. The extension of the elbows when the hands are on the hips or when the hands are held near the chest or when the arms are held more or less horizontally are examples of the illegal positions used (4-24-6).

> ## In Simple Terms
> A basket can never count when a player-control foul occurs.

It is not legal to use the hand and/or forearm to prevent an opponent from attacking the ball during a dribble or when throwing for goal (4-24-7).

A dribbler shall not charge into nor contact an opponent in his/her path nor attempt to dribble between two opponents or between an opponent and a boundary, unless the space is such as to provide a reasonable chance for him or her to go through without contact (10-6-7).

If a dribbler, without contact, sufficiently passes an opponent to have head and shoulders in advance of that opponent, the greater responsibility for subsequent contact is on the opponent (10-6-8). If a dribbler in his/her progress is moving in a straight-line path, he/she may not be crowded out of that path, but if an opponent is able to legally obtain a defensive position in that path, the dribbler must avoid contact by changing direction or ending his/her dribble (10-6-9). The dribbler should not be permitted additional rights in executing a jump try for goal, pivoting, feinting or in starting a dribble (10-6-10).

Fundamental #13

A live-ball foul by the offense (team in control, or last in control if the ball is loose), or the expiration of time for a quarter or extra period, causes the ball to become dead immediately, unless the ball is in flight during a try or tap for goal. The ball also becomes dead when the airborne shooter fouls.

When a guard moves into the path of a dribbler and contact occurs, either player may be responsible for the contact, but the greater responsibility is that of the dribbler if the guard conforms to the following principles, which officials use in reaching a decision. The guard is assumed to have obtained a guarding position if he/she is in the dribbler's path facing him/her. If he/she jumps into position, both feet must return to the floor after the jump before he/she has obtained a guarding position. No specific stance or distance is required. It is assumed the guard may shift to maintain his/her position in the path of the dribbler, provided he/she does not charge into the dribbler nor otherwise cause contact. The responsibility of the dribbler for contact is not shifted merely because the guard turns or ducks to absorb shock when contact by the dribbler is imminent. The guard may not cause contact by moving under or in front of a passer or thrower after he or she is in the air with both feet off the floor (4-23).

Player-Control Foul: Caseplays

4.12.1 SITUATION A: A1 drives toward the lane and goes up in the air for a jump shot. Before A1 becomes airborne, B1 obtains a legal position on the court that is directly in line with A1's drive (a) Before; or (b) after releasing the ball, A1 illegally contacts B1. In both cases, the ball goes through the basket. **RULING:** A1 has committed a player-control foul in both (a) and (b). There is no goal in either case. Player-control foul provisions in (b) continue until airborne shooter A1 returns one foot to the floor. Team B is awarded the ball for a throw-in at the out-of-bounds spot nearest the foul (7-5-3a).

4.19.6 SITUATION A: B1 obtains a legal position in A1's path before A1 becomes airborne. A1 jumps and releases the ball on a try for goal. Before returning to the floor, airborne shooter A1 charges into B1 (a) Before the foul by A1, B2 commits basket interference; or (b) after the foul on A1, B2 slaps the ball on its downward flight. **RULING:** In (a), both the violation and the foul are penalized. The basket interference by B2 causes the ball to become dead immediately. The violation is penalized by awarding the two points. The player-control foul on A1 is also charged. Team B is awarded the ball for a throw-in anywhere along the end line. A defensive-goaltending or basket-interference violation committed prior to a player-control foul does not contradict the general statement that when a player-control foul occurs that player cannot score. In the case of a defensive violation, it is the violation which results in awarding the score. In (b), the ball becomes dead and the try ends immediately when the player-control foul on A1 occurs. The action of B2 is ignored as goaltending cannot occur after the try has ended. The ball is awarded to Team B for a throw-in from a designated spot out of bounds closest to where the foul occurred (4-12-1; 6-7-4; 6-7-9 Exception; 7-5-4a; 9-11).

4.23.2 SITUATION: B1 jumps in front of dribbler A1 and obtains a legal guarding position with both feet touching the court and facing A1. Dribbler A1 contacts B1's torso. **RULING:** Player control foul on A1 (4-7-2).

4.23.3 SITUATION A: B1 has obtained a legal guarding position on A1 and moves to maintain it. A1 moves laterally and contacts defender B1 but does not get his/her head and shoulders past the torso of B1. Contact occurs on the side of B1's torso. **RULING:** Player-control foul by A1 (4-7-2).

4.23.3 SITUATION B: A1 is dribbling near the sideline when B1 obtains legal guarding position. B1 stays in the path of A1 but in doing

In Simple Terms

A player must be in player control or be an airborne shooter when a player-control foul occurs.

so has (b) one foot in the air over the out-of-bounds area when A1 contacts B1 in the torso. **RULING:** In (b), A1 is called for a player-control foul because B2 had obtained and maintained legal guarding position (4-23-2; 4-23-3a).

10.6.1 SITUATION C: B1 is standing behind the plane of the backboard before A1 jumps for a lay-up shot. The forward momentum causes airborne shooter A1 to charge into B1. **RULING:** B1 is entitled to the position obtained legally before A1 left the floor. If the ball goes through the basket before or after the contact occurs, the player-control foul cancels the goal. However, if B1 moves into the path of A1 after A1 has left the floor, the foul is on B1. B1's foul on the airborne shooter is a foul during the act of shooting. If the shot is successful, one free throw is awarded and if it is unsuccessful, two free throws result (4-19-1, 6; 6-7-4; 10 Penalty 2, 5a).

10.6.7 SITUATION: During congested play in the free-throw semicircle, B1 and B2 are less than 3 feet apart when dribbler A1 fakes to one side and then causes contact in attempting to dribble between them. **RULING:** Unless one of the defensive players is faked out of position to permit adequate space for the dribbler to go between without making contact, it is a player-control foul on A1.

 COMMENT: Screening principles apply to the dribbler who attempts to cut off an opponent who is approaching in a different path from the rear. In this case, the dribbler must allow such opponent a maximum of tow steps or an opportunity to stop or avoid contact. When both the dribbler and the opponent are moving in exactly the same path and direction, the player behind is responsible for contact which results if the player in front slows down or stops.

Topic:
Pushing Foul

It is not legal for a player to use hands and arms or hips and shoulders to force his/her way through a screen and then to push him/her aside in order to maintain a guarding position relative to his/her opponent (4-24-4).

To obtain or maintain a legal rebounding position, a player may not displace or push an opponent (4-37-2a).

A player shall not push nor impede the progress of an opponent by extending an arm, shoulder, hip or knee, or by bending the body into other than a normal position nor use any rough tactics (10-6-1).

Pushing Foul: Caseplay

4.37.1 SITUATION: While A1's try or tap is in flight, A2 and B2 legally obtain potential rebounding positions. B2's position has his/her back to A2 and is directly between A2 and the basket. As the unsuccessful try or tap rebounds from the ring: (a) B2 moves backward and pushes/displaces A2 from his/her legal position; or (b) A2 "beats" B2, getting his/her head and shoulders past the front of B2's torso. B2 then moves laterally and pushes/displaces A2. **RULING:** A foul on B2 in both (a) and (b) (4-7-1; 4-19-1).

Topic:
Screening Foul

A screen is legal action by a player who, without causing contact, delays or prevents an opponent from reaching a desired position (4-40-1).

To establish a legal screening position: the screener may face any direction (4-40-2a); time and distance are relevant (4-40-2b); the screener must be stationary, except when both are moving in the same path and the same direction (4-40-2c) and the screener must stay within his/her vertical plane with a stance approximately shoulder width apart (4-40-2d).

When screening a stationary opponent from the front or side, the screener may be anywhere short of contact (4-40-3).

When screening a stationary opponent from behind, the screener must allow the opponent one normal step backward without contact (4-40-4).

When screening a moving opponent, the screener must allow the opponent time and distance to avoid contact. The distance need not be more than two strides (4-40-5).

When screening an opponent who is moving in the same path and direction as the screener is moving, the opponent is responsible for contact if the screener slows up or stops (4-40-6).

It is legal to hold the hands and arms in front of the face or body for

The original rules of basketball prohibited shouldering, holding, pushing, tripping or striking an opponent in any way. The first penalty counted as a foul and the second disqualified the individual until the next goal was made.

protection and to absorb force from an imminent charge by an opponent. This same protective use of the arms and hands occurs when a player who has set a screen outside the opponent's visual field is about to be run into by the player being screened. The action, however, should be a recoil action rather than a pushing action (4-24-3).

It is not legal to use hands and arms or hips and shoulders to force his/her way through a screen or to hold the screener and then to push him/her aside in order to maintain a guarding position on an opponent (4-40-8).

It is not legal to lock arms or grasp a teammate(s) in an effort to restrict the movement of an opponent (4-24-9).

A player who is screened within his/her visual field is expected to avoid contact with the screener by stopping or going around the screener. In cases of screens outside the visual field, the opponent may make inadvertent contact with the screener and if the opponent is running rapidly, the contact may be severe. Such a case is to be ruled as incidental contact provided the opponent stops or attempts to stop on contact and moves around the screen, and provided the screener is not displaced if he/she has the ball (4-40-7). If, however, a player approaches an opponent from behind or from a position from which he/she has no reasonable chance to play the ball without making contact with the opponent, the responsibility is on the player in the unfavorable position (4-27-5).

A player who screens shall not:

• When he/she is outside the visual field of a stationary opponent, take a position closer than a normal step from the opponent (4-40-3).

• Take a position within his/her vertical plane with a stance that is greater than approximately shoulder width apart (4-40-2d).

• When screening a stationary opponent from behind (outside the visual field), the screener must allow the opponent one normal step backward without contact (4-40-4).

• When screening a moving opponent, the screener must allow the opponent time and distance to avoid contact by stopping or changing direction. The speed of the player to be screened will determine where the screener may take his/her stationary position. The position will vary and may be one or two normal steps or strides from the opponent (4-40-5).

• When screening an opponent who is moving in the same path and direction as the screener, the player behind is responsible if contact made because the player in front slows up or stops and the player behind overruns his/her opponent (4-40-6).

• If the screener violates any of these provisions and contact results, he/she has committed a personal foul (10-6-11 Penalty).

A player who is screened within his/her visual field is expected to avoid contact by going around the screener. In cases of screens outside the visual field, the opponent may make inadvertent contact with the screener and if the opponent is running rapidly, the contact may be severe. Such a case is to be ruled as incidental contact provided the opponent stops or attempts to stop on contact and moves around the screen, and provided the screener is not displaced if he/she has the ball (4-40-7). A player may not use the arms, hands, hips or shoulders to force his/her way through a screen or to hold the screener and then push the screener aside in order to maintain a guarding position on an opponent (4-40-8).

Screening Foul: Caseplays

10.6.11 SITUATION A: A1 holds the ball near the center of the court. A2 is on the right side of the basket and closely guarded by B1. A3 moves to a position behind B1, after which A2 circles B1 and receives a pass on the left side of the basket and scores. **RULING:** Legal goal unless there was contact and responsibility for it is charged to A3. This will depend on whether A3 took a position at such distance as to permit B1 one step space for normal movement without making contact (4-40).

10.6.11 SITUATION B: A1, in attempting to screen, takes a stationary position in the path of moving B1. The position of A1: (a) is so close that B1 cannot avoid A1 and contact results; or (b) is far enough away so that B1, who is aware of the position of A1, has an opportunity to avoid A1 but contact still results. **RULING:** In (a), the foul is on A1 for blocking. In (b), B1 did not use the opportunity to avoid A1 and, therefore, is responsible for the contact and is charged with the foul (4-40).

10.6.11 SITUATION C: A defensive player takes a position in front of the post player A1 to prevent A1 from receiving the ball. A high pass is made over the head and out of reach of the defensive player. The post player A1 moves toward the basket to catch the pass and try for goal. As the pass is made, a teammate of the defensive player moves into the path of A1, in a guarding position. What are the rights of the pivot player A1 and the defensive player who moves into A1's path? **RULING:** The defensive player has switched to guard a player who does not have the ball. Therefore, the switching player must assume a position one or two strides in advance of the post player (depending upon the speed of movement of such player) to make the action legal. If the defensive player moves into the path of the post player A1 after A1 has control of the ball (provided the post player is not in the air at the time), the play becomes a guarding situation on a player with the ball and no distance or time limit is involved (4-40).

10.6.11 SITUATION D: A1 is running toward A's goal but is looking back to receive a pass. B1 takes a position in the path of A1 while A1 is 10 feet away from B1 (a) A1 runs into B1 before receiving the ball; or (b) A1 receives the ball and before taking a step contacts B1. **RULING:** In both (a) and (b), A1 is responsible for contact. In (a), B1's position is legal if A1 has been given two strides prior to contact. In (b), since the position of B1 is legal when A1 has the ball, the contact is charging by A1 (4-40).

Topic:
Intentional Foul

An intentional foul is a personal or technical foul which neutralizes an opponent's obvious advantageous position. Contact away from the ball or when not making a legitimate attempt to play the ball or a player, specifically designed to stop or keep the clock from starting, shall be intentional. Intentional fouls may or may not be premeditated and are not based solely on the severity of the act. A foul also shall be ruled intentional if while playing the ball a player causes excessive contact with an opponent (4-19-3).

Contact after the ball has become dead that cannot be ignored is considered an intentional technical foul (4-19-5c).

If an opponent of the thrower reaches through the throw-in boundary-line plane and fouls the thrower, an intentional personal foul shall be charged to the offender. No warning for delay required (9-2-11 Penalty 4).

 The original language of an intentional foul claimed any evidence of intent to injure another person was punishable. The offender was disqualified for the whole game and no substitute was allowed to take his/her place.

Rationale

Fouling is an accepted coaching strategy, however there is a right way and a wrong way to foul. Officiating philosophies should not change because of the time remaining in the game or the score differential. When a foul meets the criteria, an intentional foul shall be called.

Intentional Foul: Caseplays

4.19.3 SITUATION A: B1 is charged with an intentional foul on A1 who is in the act of shooting: (a) a successful two-point or three-point try; (b) an unsuccessful two-point try; or (c) an unsuccessful three-point try. **RULING:** In (a) and (b), A1 is awarded two free throws. In (c), A1 is awarded three free throws. In all situations following the free throws, Team A is awarded a throw-in at the out-of-bounds spot nearest the foul.

4.19.3 SITUATION B: A1 drives to the basket with B1 in pursuit. As A1 begins the act of shooting, B1 gets a hand on the ball from behind and the subsequent contact takes A1 forcefully to the floor and out of bounds. **RULING:** An intentional foul shall be charged when the contact is judged to be excessive, even though the opponent is playing the ball (4-11).

4.19.3 SITUATION C: Team A leads by three points with four seconds remaining in the fourth quarter. Team A is to throw-in from a spot out of bounds on the end line. Players begin jockeying for positions just after the official has handed the ball to A1. B1, while trying to deny a pass from A1 to A2: (a) grabs A2's jersey; or (b) pushes A2 from behind. **RULING:** In (a) and (b), it is an intentional personal foul designed to keep the clock from starting or to neutralize an opponent's obvious advantageous position.

4.19.3 SITUATION D: Late in the fourth quarter Team B is trailing by six points. Team B's head coach begins to yell to his or her players to "foul, foul, foul!" B1 responds by (a) grabbing A1 from behind, or (b) reaching for the ball but illegally contacting A1 on the arm. **RULING:** In (a), an intentional foul shall be called. In (b), a common foul shall be called as B1 was making a legitimate attempt to "play the ball."

4.19.6 SITUATION B: Is it possible for airborne shooter A1 to commit a foul which would not be player control? **RULING:** Yes. The airborne shooter could be charged with an intentional or flagrant personal foul or with a technical foul (4-19-2, 3, 4).

Topic:
Shooting Foul

The act of shooting begins simultaneously with the start of the try or tap and ends when the ball is clearly in flight, and includes the airborne shooter (4-41-1).

A try for field goal is an attempt by a player to score two or three points by throwing the ball into a team's own basket. A player is trying for goal when the player has the ball and in the official's judgment is throwing or attempting to throw for goal. It is not essential that the ball leave the player's hand as a foul could prevent release of the ball (4-41-2).

Fundamental #17

Continuous motion applies both to tries for field goals and free throws, but it has no significance unless there is a foul by the defense during the interval which begins when the habitual throwing movement starts, and ends when the ball is clearly in flight.

A tap for goal is the contacting of the ball with any part of a player's hand(s) in an attempt to direct the ball into his/her basket (4-41-5). A tap shall be considered the same as a try for field goal, except when play is resumed with a throw-in or free throw and three-tenths (.3) of a second or less remain on the clock (4-41-5). The tap starts when the player's hand(s) touches the ball (4-41-7) and ends in exactly the same manner as a try (4-41-8).

Continuous motion applies to a try or tap for field goals and free throws, but it has no significance unless there is a foul by any defensive player during the interval which begins when the habitual throwing movement starts a try or with the touching on a tap and ends when the ball is clearly in flight (4-11-1).

If an opponent fouls after a player has started a try for goal, he/she is permitted to complete the customary arm movement, and if pivoting or stepping when fouled, may complete the usual foot or body movement in any activity while holding the ball. These privileges are granted only when the usual throwing motion has started before the foul occurs and before the ball is in flight (4-11-2).

Continuous motion does not apply if a teammate fouls after a player has started a try for a goal and before the ball is in flight. The ball becomes dead immediately (4-11-3).

COMMENT: If an opponent fouls after A1 has started to throw for goal, A1 is permitted to complete the customary arm movement; and, if A1 is pivoting or stepping when A1 or a teammate is fouled, A1 may complete the usual foot or body movement in any activity, as long as A1 is still holding the ball. If A1 starts a dribble, the "continuous motion" immediately ends. These privileges are granted only when the usual throwing motion has started before the foul occurs. The continuous-motion rule applies to a free-throw try as well as to a field-goal try or tap for goal. However, in a tap for goal, the motion does not begin until the ball is touched.

The "continuous-motion" provision does not apply to batting or tipping the ball during rebounding or a jump ball. In these cases, A1 is not considered as being in the act of trying or tapping for goal. If an opponent commits a foul during this type of action before the ball is in flight, the foul causes the ball to become dead immediately. In rebounding, the ball is not always batted. It might be caught in one hand and then thrown into the basket with a snap of the wrist or fingers or touched and tapped toward the basket. Under these circumstances, an official is justified in ruling that it is a try or tap instead of a bat.

Continuous motion is of significance only when there is a personal or technical foul by B after the trying or tapping motion by A1 is started and before the ball is in flight. It includes any body, foot or arm motion normally used in trying for a field goal or free throw, and it ends when the ball leaves the hand(s) on the try or tap.

Shooting Foul: Caseplays

*4.1.1 SITUATION: A1 is high in the air on a jump shot in the lane. A1 releases the ball on a try and is then fouled by B1 who has also jumped in an unsuccessful attempt to block the shot. A1's try is: (a) successful; or (b) unsuccessful. **RULING:** A1 is an airborne shooter when the ball is released until one foot returns to the floor. An airborne shooter is in the act of shooting. B1 has fouled A1 in the act of shooting. A1 is awarded one free throw in (a), and two in (b) (4-41-1).

4.41.2 SITUATION: A1 becomes confused and throws the ball at the wrong basket. A1 is fouled by B1 and the ball goes into the basket. Is this a successful basket? If A1 missed, would A1 be awarded two free throws for the foul by B1? **RULING:** No goal. The ball became dead when the foul occurred. When a player throws at the opponent's basket, it is not a try. If the team is in the bonus when B1 fouled A1, A1 is given either a one-and-one attempt or two free throws at Team A's basket. If Team A was not in the bonus, then the ball is awarded to Team A for a throw-in at the out-of-bounds spot nearest the foul (7-5-4a).

6.7 SITUATION C: Under what circumstances does the ball remain live when a foul occurs just prior to the ball being in flight during a try or tap? **RULING:** The ball would ordinarily become dead at once, but it remains live if the foul is by the defense, and this foul occurs after A1 has started the try or tap for goal and time does not expire before the ball is in flight. The foul by the defense may be either personal or technical and the exception to the rule applies to field goal tries and taps and free-throw tries (4-11; 4-41-1).

6.7 SITUATION D: A1 has started a try for a goal (is in the act of shooting), but the ball is not yet in flight when the official blows the whistle for B2 fouling A2. A1's try is successful. **RULING:** Score the goal by A1. If Team A is in the bonus, A2 will shoot free throws. If not, Team A will have a designated spot throw-in nearest to where the foul occurred (6-7 exception c).

 COMMENT: The foul by the defense need not be on the player in the act of shooting for continuous motion principles to apply.

6.7 SITUATION E: Prior to the bonus and after A1 starts the free-throwing motion: B5 fouls A5. **RULING:** The "continuous motion" rule applies and A1 may release the ball and if the throw is successful, the point counts. Award Team A the ball out-of-bounds at the spot nearest to where B5 fouled A5 (4-19-12).

6.7.4 SITUATION: Airborne A1 is fouled by B1 during a field-goal try or tap. After the ball is in flight, A1 illegally contacts B2 in returning to the floor. The ball goes through the basket. **RULING:** The foul by B1 did not cause the ball to become dead since A1 had started the trying or tapping motion. However, airborne shooter A1's foul is a player-control foul which does cause the ball to become dead immediately. No goal can be scored even if the ball had already gone through the basket before the foul. Since the goal is unsuccessful, A1 is awarded two free throws for the foul by B1. No players are allowed in the lane spaces as Team B will be awarded the ball following the last free throw. If the last throw is successful, the throw-in is from anywhere along the end line. If the last throw is unsuccessful, the throw-in is from a designated spot nearest the foul. The situation is a false double foul (4-11; 4-19-6, 9).

6.7.7 SITUATION: As the hand of A1 contacts the ball to tap it toward Team A's basket, B1 fouls A1. The ball definitely is not airborne from the hand of A1 when the contact occurs, but the tapped ball goes into the basket. **RULING:** The foul does not cause the ball to become dead immediately. The subsequent tap of the ball results in a goal, the same as a try for goal. The foul is penalized the same as being fouled in the act of shooting. Continuous motion does apply to a tap (4-11; 4-41-2, 5).

6.7.9 SITUATION: A1 is fouled in the act of shooting by B1. While the ball is in the cylinder above the basket, A2 touches the ball. **RULING:** The basket interference by A2 causes the ball to become dead and no goal can be scored. However, A1 is awarded two free throws for being fouled in the act of shooting an unsuccessful try. Players must occupy lane spaces as required and play continues as per rule when the last free throw is made or missed (9-11).

Topic:
Contact Team Technical Foul

A team technical foul is charged when players lock arms or grasp a teammate(s) in an effort to restrict the movement of the opponent (10-1-11).

Topic:
Contact Player Technical Foul

A player shall not intentionally or flagrantly contact an opponent when the ball is dead and such contact is not a personal foul (10-3-8) or be charged with fighting (10-3-9).

Contact Player Technical Foul: Caseplays

4.19.5 SITUATION: A1 is fouled by B1. A1 subsequently pushes B1. **RULING:** If a foul is called on A1, it must be either an intentional or flagrant technical. If it is ruled flagrant, A1 must be disqualified. If A1's contact during a dead ball was neither intentional nor flagrant, it should have been ignored (4-19-1 Note; 10-3-9).

10.3.8 SITUATION: B1 fouls A1 during an unsuccessful try. While the calling official is reporting the foul, A1 pushes B1 into another player. **RULING:** Intentional contact while the ball is dead constitutes an intentional technical foul. If other dead-ball contact is not intentional or flagrant, it should be ignored. The foul by A1 creates a false double-foul situation.

Topic:
Fighting

Fighting is a flagrant act and can occur when the ball is dead or live. Fighting includes, but is not limited to combative acts such as:

• An attempt to strike, punch or kick by using a fist, hands, arms, legs or feet regardless of whether contact is made (4-18-1).

• An attempt to instigate a fight by committing an unsporting act that causes a person to retaliate by fighting (4-18-2).

Players on the Court Fighting

If there are a corresponding number of players from each team, double flagrant fouls are awarded, all participants are disqualified, no free throws are awarded and ball is put in play at the point of interruption (10 Pen 8-a-1). If the number of players are not corresponding, flagrant fouls are assessed and disqualification for all participants. Two free throws are awarded for the offended team for each additional player and the offended team is awarded a division-line throw-in (10 Pen 8-a-2).

Rationale

There is simply no justification for fighting as part of an educational program in which all participants are representing their school. Officials must enforce the rules consistently and record those offenders in order to disqualify all who violate the rule.

Players on the Court Fighting: Caseplays

4.18.2 SITUATION: A1 dunks over B1 and then taunts B1. B1 retaliates and punches A1. **RULING:** Both A1 and B1 are charged with a flagrant technical foul for fighting and are disqualified. A1's action is defined as fighting when the taunting caused B1 to retaliate by fighting (10-3; 10-3-6c; 10-3-8).

10.4.5 SITUATION B: A fight breaks out between A1 and B1 during a dead-ball and clock-stopped situation. The head coach of Team A rushes onto the court. **RULING:** A1 and B1 are charged with flagrant technical fouls and are disqualified. No free throws are awarded for the double technical foul by A1 and B1. Since the coach was not beckoned onto the court by an official, he/she is charged with a flagrant technical foul and is disqualified. Team B is awarded two free throws and the ball for a throw-in at the division line opposite the table.

Players Leave Bench During Fight

If bench personnel leave the team bench during a fight or when a fight may break out and do not participate in the fight, non-participants are assessed flagrant fouls and disqualified. The head coach is assessed a maximum of one indirect technical foul (regardless of the number leaving the bench). If the number of each team's offenders is corresponding, no free throws are awarded and the ball is put in play at the point of interruption. If the number of each team's offenders is unequal, a maximum of two free throws are awarded to the offended team, followed by a division-line throw-in opposite the table (10 Pen 8-b-1).

If bench personnel leave the team bench during a fight or when a fight may break out and participate in the fight, all participants are assessed flagrant fouls and disqualified. The head coach is assessed one indirect technical foul for each bench player participating in the fight. If the number of each team's participants is corresponding, no free throws are awarded and the ball is put in play at the point of interruption. If the number of each team's participants is unequal, two free throws are awarded to the offended team for each additional player, followed by a division-line throw-in opposite the table (10 Pen 8-b-2).

Players Leave Bench During Fight: Caseplays

4.19.13 SITUATION: Three substitutes of Team B leave their bench and come onto the court during a fight. **RULING:** The three substitutes are each charged with a flagrant technical foul and are disqualified. The Team B head coach is also charged indirectly with a technical foul. Team A is awarded two free throws plus the ball for a throw-in for this multiple infraction. Team B is charged with three fouls for reaching the bonus. In addition, the proper fouls are charged and penalties are assessed for the players who were fighting (10-4-5 Penalty).

10.4.5 SITUATION A: Post-players A1 and B1 begin punching each other and play is stopped. Two substitutes from each team leave the bench area and come onto the court. The four substitutes: (a) do not become involved in the fight; (b) all become involved in the fight; or (c) substitutes A6, A7, and B6 do not participate in the fight, but B7 becomes involved in the fight. **RULING:** A1 and B1 are charged with flagrant fouls and are disqualified, but no free throws result from the double personal flagrant fouls. The four substitutes are charged with flagrant technical fouls and are disqualified. No free throws are awarded for the simultaneous technical fouls as the number committed and the penalties are the same for both teams. In (a), one technical foul is also charged indirectly to the head coach of each team. In (b), each head coach is charged indirectly with two technical fouls (one for each bench player leaving the bench and becoming involved in the fight). In (c), the Team A head coach is charged indirectly with one technical foul and the Team B head coach is indirectly charged with two technical fouls (one for substitutes B6 and B7 leaving the bench, and one for B7 becoming involved in the fight). In all situations, the ball is put in play at the point of interruption (4-36; 7-5-3b).

10.4.5 SITUATION C: Substitutes A6, A7 and A8 enter the floor and fight with substitutes B6, B7 and B8. **RULING:** A6, A7, A8, B6, B7 and B8 are charged with flagrant fouls and disqualified. Each head coach is charged with three indirect technical fouls and disqualified and must leave the vicinity or the playing area and have no further contact with the team. Because the substitute's fouls were offsetting, no free throws will be awarded. Charge each team with three fouls toward the bonus and resume play at the point of interruption.

10.4.5 SITUATION D: A1 and B1 begin to fight during a dead-ball period. Two substitutes from Team A and one from Team B leave their bench area and enter the court to be near the action. **RULING:** A1, B1 and the three substitutes are all disqualified and each is charged with a flagrant technical foul. Each coach is also charged indirectly with a technical foul. No free throws are awarded for the double technical foul by A1 and B1. The free throws for one substitute's foul by each team are canceled as the penalties offset. However, Team B is awarded two free throws and the ball for a division-line throw-in opposite the table for the second substitute's foul, which does not have a corresponding simultaneous technical foul by an opponent.

10.4.5 SITUATION E: A1 and B1 begin fighting and play is stopped. Substitute A6 leaves the bench area and enters the court to observe. B6 also enters the court at the same time, but B6 actually participates in the fight. **RULING:** A1, B1, A6 and B6 are all disqualified. No free throws result from the double flagrant foul by A1 and B1 or from the simultaneous technical fouls by A6 and B6. Each head coach is charged with one indirect technical foul. Play resumes at the point of interruption (4-36; 10-3-9).

10.4.5 SITUATION F: It appears a fight may occur on the playing court when (a) A6 and A7; or (b) A6 and B6 leave their respective benches. **RULING:** In (a) and (b), all players leaving the bench are assessed flagrant fouls and disqualified. The respective head coach is assessed a maximum of one indirect technical foul (regardless of the number of players leaving the bench). In (a), Team B is awarded two free throws and the ball for a division line throw-in. In (b), no free throws are awarded and the ball is put into play at the point of interruption (4-36).

Topic 13

Technical Fouls

PlayPic™

Topic:
Team Technical Foul

A team technical foul shall be charged with the penalty of two free three throws plus the ball for a division-line throw-in when a team:

Fails to Supply Starters

A team fails to supply the scorer with the name and number of each team member who may participate and designate the five starting players at least 10 minutes before the scheduled starting time (10-1-1). One foul for both requirements, penalized when it occurs.

 Rationale

In Simple Terms

A team technical foul is not charged directly to any individual, but does count toward the number of fouls eligible to reach the bonus.

The 10-minute time limit before the game was enacted in order for teams to be able to prepare a game plan for the opposing team's starters. It was also put into place to help alleviate scorebook errors.

After the 10-minute time limit specified in 10-1-1 (only one foul per team regardless of the number of infractions), the following five infractions apply:

1. Coach Changes Designated Starter

The coach changes a designated starter unless necessitated by illness, injury, illegal equipment or apparel, etc., or to attempt a technical foul free throw (10-1-2a).

2. Coach Adds Name in Scorebook

The coach adds a name to the team member list (10-1-2b). Penalized when it occurs.

Coach Adds Name in Scorebook: Caseplay

10.1.2 SITUATION: (a) Three minutes prior to the start of the game; or (b) during a time-out in the second quarter of play, the Team B coach requests the scorer to add a name to the team list. When is the penalty invoked for this administrative infraction? **RULING:** The infraction occurs when the scorer is advised to add to or change the scorebook. The foul must be charged when it occurs and enforced when the ball next becomes live. Once the ball has become live, it is too late to penalize.

3. Coach Changes Number in Scorebook

The coach requires the scorer to change a team member's or player's number in the scorebook (10-1-2c). Penalized when it occurs.

Coach Changes Number in Scorebook: Caseplay

10.1.2 SITUATION: (a) Three minutes prior to the start of the game; or (b) during a time-out in the second quarter of play, the Team B coach requests the scorer to change a team member's number in the scorebook. When is the penalty invoked for this administrative infraction? **RULING:** The infraction occurs when the scorer is advised to add to or change the scorebook. The foul must be charged when it occurs and enforced when the ball next becomes live. Once the ball has become live, it is too late to penalize.

4. Player Changes Number

The team requires a player to change to the number in the scorebook (10-1-2d).

5. Identical Numbers

The team has identical numbers on team members and/or players (10-1-2e). Penalized when discovered.

Uses Illegal Equipment

Uses television monitoring or replay equipment or computers (other than for statistics) for coaching purposes during the game or any intermission or use a megaphone or any mechanical sounding device or any electronic transmission device at courtside for coaching purposes, or electronic equipment for voice communication with players (10-1-3).

Uses Illegal Equipment: Caseplays

10.1.3 SITUATION A: Team A's coach: (a) uses a megaphone or an electronic amplifier to shout instructions to players; (b) is in contact with an assistant coach in the press box via a headset; or (c) is in direct contact with one or more players via electronic voice communication. **RULING:** A team technical is charged in (a), (b) and (c). The team technical counts toward reaching the bonus, but is not charged to the head coach. In (a), the use of a rolled up program would be legal.

10.1.3 SITUATION B: The home team: (a) has a television monitor in the press box or the dressing room and is relaying information to the player's bench; or (b) uses a replay of the first half during the intermission for use by the coach in preparation for the second half.

RULING: Illegal in both (a) and (b). A technical foul is charged to the home team in both cases. The prohibition does not affect the filming, televising or taping of a game if it is not used for coaching purposes during that particular game.

Fails To Occupy Bench

The team fails to occupy the team member's bench to which it is assigned (10-1-4).

Delays the Game

The team allows the game to develop into an actionless contest, this includes the following and similar acts:

• When the clock is not running consuming a full minute through not being ready when it is time to start either half (10-1-5a).

• Delay the game by preventing the ball from being made promptly live or from being put in play (10-1-5b).

• Commit a violation of the throw-in boundary-line plane after any team warning for delay (10-1-5c).

• Contact with the free thrower or a huddle of two or more players by either team prior to a free throw following the team warning for this delay (10-1-5d).

• Interfering with the ball following a goal after any team warning for delay (10-1-5e).

• Not having the court ready for play following any time-out after any team warning for delay (10-1-5f).

Delays the Game: Caseplays

10.1.5 SITUATION A: A1 is fouled by B1 during an unsuccessful try and is awarded two free throws. Team B requests and is granted a charged 60-second time-out. Team B disregards the 15-second warning signal and the signal ending the time-out and is still huddling with their coach at the end of the charged time-out. **RULING:** The official shall administer the first free throw using the resumption-of-play procedure and a violation occurs if it is missed. If two B players are not in the required position when the official is ready to put the ball in play for the substitute throw, a delay of game technical foul will be assessed. If the first attempt is good, the same procedure is used for the second (9-1-2; 10-1-5b).

10.1.5 SITUATION B: The calling official has reported the foul and is ready to administer the free throw. Free thrower A1 is: (a) huddling with teammates by the team bench area; or (b) is in the semicircle, but teammates are huddling in the lane area. **RULING:** A technical foul for delay by A1 in (a). In (b), Team A is warned for delay. In (b), if Team A had been warned previously for any delay-of-game situation, a team technical foul would be charged (10-1-5d; 10-3-5c).

10.1.5 SITUATION C: The calling official has reported the foul and proceeds to his/her proper position for the first of two free throws awarded to A1. B1 and B2 are: (a) huddling in the lane; or (b) two B players are not occupying the first two marked spaces next to the end line as required. **RULING:** In (a), if the huddle delays the officials' administration, Team B is warned. The warning is recorded by the scorer and reported to the head coach. If Team B had been previously warned for delay, a technical foul shall be charged. In (b), Team B will be directed to occupy the required spaces. If there is delay, a team technical foul shall be charged to Team B (4-47).

10.1.5 SITUATION D: Immediately following a goal by A1, A3 slaps the ball away so that Team B is unable to make a quick throw-in. **RULING:** The official shall sound his/her whistle and go to the table to have the scorer record a team warning for delay. The warning shall then be reported to the head coach of Team A. Any subsequent similar delay by Team A shall result in a team technical foul charged to Team A (4-47-3).

Too Many Players Participating

The team has more than five team members participating simultaneously (10-1-6). Penalized if discovered while being violated.

Too Many Players Participating: Caseplay

10.1.6 SITUATION: With Team A leading 51 to 50, a held ball is called. A6 properly reports and enters the game. Time is then called by Team A. The clock shows two seconds remaining in the game. After play is resumed by a throw-in, the officials: (a) recognize that A has six players competing, but cannot get the clock stopped; or (b) do not notice Team A has six players on the court. Following the throw-in, time expires. Team B now reports to the officials that Team A had six players on the court. **RULING:** In (a), since one of the officials had knowledge that Team A had six players participating simultaneously and this was detected prior to time expiring, a technical foul is assessed against Team A. In (b), since it was not recognized by either official, but was called to their attention after time had expired, it is too late to assess any penalty.

Requests an Excess Time-out

The team requests an excess time-out (10-1-7). Penalized when discovered.

Requests an Excess Time-out: Caseplays

10.1.7 SITUATION: A1 requests and Team A is granted a time-out late in the fourth quarter. Team A had already used its three 60-second time-outs and its two 30-second time-outs. **RULING:** Team A is granted the time-out and is charged with a technical foul. No indirect foul is charged to the head coach.

Before 1978, an official was instructed to ignore a time-out request by a team when it was excessive.  **Did You Know?**

Commits an Unsporting Foul

A team shall not commit an unsporting foul (10-1-8). An unsporting foul is a noncontact technical foul which consists of unfair, unethical, dishonorable conduct or any behavior not in accordance with the spirit of fair play (4-19-14).

Commits an Unsporting Foul: Caseplays

10.1.8 SITUATION: Immediately following a goal or free throw by Team A, A1 inbounds the ball to A2 and A2 subsequently throws the ball through A's basket. **RULING:** The following procedure has been adopted to handle this specific situation if it is recognized before the opponents gain control or before the next throw-in begins: (a) charge Team A with an unsporting technical foul; (b) assess a delay-of-game warning for interfering with the ball after a goal; (c) cancel the field goal; (d) cancel any common foul(s) committed and any non-flagrant foul against A2 in the act of shooting; and (e) put "consumed" time back on the clock.

 COMMENT: If there is no doubt the throw-in was a result of confusion, the entire procedure would be followed except no unsporting team technical foul would be charged. A team technical would be assessed if the team had received a previous delay warning. This procedure shall not be used in any other throw-in situation in which a mistake allows the wrong team to inbound the ball. (4-47-3; 10-1-5d)

All Players Fail to Return to the Court

The team fails to have all players return to the court at approximately the same time following a time-out or intermission (10-1-9).

All Players Fail to Return to the Court: Caseplay

10.1.9 SITUATION: Following a charged time-out Team B is still with their coach on the sideline when the official sounds the whistle to indicate play will resume. Four players of B return to the court just in time to play defense as A1 attempts an unsuccessful three-pointer. B1 rebounds and throws a long pass to B5 who enters the court just in time to catch the pass. **RULING:** A technical foul is immediately charged to Team B for failing to have all players return to the court at approximately the same time following a time-out or intermission. While it is true the entire team may be off the court while the procedure is being used, once a team responds, all players must enter the court at approximately the same time.

 COMMENT: The resumption-of-play procedure is in effect to start the second half unless either team is not on the court. In that case regular delay provisions are in force.

Violates Throw-in Boundary Plane

Following a team warning for delay, a team commits a violation of the throw-in boundary-line plane (10-1-3c).

Violates Throw-in Boundary Plane: Caseplay

10.1.10 SITUATION: Team B is warned in the first half when B1 reaches through the inbounds side of the throw-in boundary plane. Early in the fourth quarter: (a) B1; or (b) B2 does the same thing. **RULING:** The technical foul in both (a) and (b) is charged to Team B. A team will only receive one of the four delay-of-game warnings during a game. Thereafter, any delay-of-game situation by a member of that same team results in a technical foul (9-2-10).

Players Lock Arms

A team allows players to lock arms or grasp a teammate(s) in an effort to restrict the movement of an opponent (10-1-10).

Topic:
Substitution Technical Foul

A substitute shall not enter the court without reporting to the scorer (10-2-1) or without being beckoned by an official, except between quarters (10-2-2).

A single flagrant technical foul or the second technical foul charged to a substitute results in disqualification of the offender to the team bench (10-2 note).

Substitution Technical Foul Penalty

Two free throws plus ball for division-line throw-in. One foul each for either not reporting or entering without being beckoned. Penalized if discovered before the ball becomes live.

Substitution Technical Foul: Caseplays

10.2.1 SITUATION A: Substitute A1 enters the court without reporting to the scorer. The infraction is discovered: (a) before the ball becomes live; or (b) after the ball becomes live. **RULING:** In (a), a technical foul is charged to A1. In (b), it is too late to penalize A1.

10.2.1 SITUATION B: Team A substitute No. 24: (a) reports to the scorer, but enters the court without being beckoned; or (b) goes directly from the bench and onto the court without being beckoned. **RULING:** One technical foul is charged to No. 24 in (a) and (b). In (b), even though No. 24 failed to comply with both requirements, only one foul is charged.

10.2.2 SITUATION: During a live ball and with the clock running, substitute A6 enters the court. **RULING:** A technical foul is charged if recognized by an official before the ball becomes live following the first dead ball.

Topic:
Player Technical Foul

A player shall not commit a technical foul.

Player Technical Foul Penalty

Two free throws plus the ball for division-line throw-in.

Player Participates After Changing Number

A player shall not participate after changing his/her number without reporting it to the scorer and an official (10-3-1). It should be penalized if discovered while being violated and is considered a flagrant foul.

Player Delays Returning from Out of Bounds

A player shall not purposely and/or deceitfully delay returning after being out of bounds (10-3-2). Penalize when the infraction occurs.

Player Delays Returning from Out of Bounds: Caseplays

10.3.2 SITUATION A: A1 has the ball out of bounds for a throw-in. A1 completes the throw-in to A2 and then purposefully delays his/her return by taking four or five steps along the end line prior to coming inbounds behind a screen set by A3 and A4. A1 gets a return pass from A2 and takes an unchallenged try for goal. **RULING:** A1 is charged with a technical foul for purposefully delaying his/her return to the court following the throw-in. A1's movement out of bounds along the end line was to take advantage of the screen and return to the court in a more advantageous position.

10.3.2 SITUATION B: After a lengthy substitution process involving multiple substitutions for both Team A and Team B, A5 goes to the bench and remains there, mistakenly believing he/she has been replaced. The ball is put in play even though Team A has only four players on the court. Team A is bringing the ball into A's frontcourt when the coach of Team A realizes they have only four players. The coach yells for A5 to return and he/she sprints directly onto the court and catches up with the play. **RULING:** No technical foul is charged to A5. A5's return to the court was not deceitful, nor did it provide A5 an unfair positioning advantage on the court.

Player Hangs on Rim/Pregame or Halftime Dunk

A player shall not grasp either basket during the time of the officials' jurisdiction, dunk or stuff, or attempt to dunk or stuff a dead ball prior to or during the game or during any intermission until jurisdiction of all officials has ended. This applies to all team members. A player may grasp the basket to prevent injury (10-3-3). For dunking or grasping during pregame or intermission, the foul is also charged indirectly to the head coach.

Player Hangs on Rim/Pregame or Halftime Dunk: Caseplays

6.4.1 SITUATION A: Twelve minutes before the game is scheduled to start, team member A1 dunks the ball and is charged with a technical foul. B1 is discovered to be wearing an illegal shirt, as the players prepare for the start of the game. **RULING:** The game will be started by awarding Team B two free throws for A1's technical foul. Team A will then be given two free throws and the ball for a division-line throw-in for B1's infraction. When the thrower of Team A has the ball for the throw-in, they have control for purposes of establishing the procedure and the arrow is immediately set toward B's basket. Team B will have the first opportunity for an alternating-possession throw-in (4-3).

10.3.3 SITUATION A: A1 is dribbling rapidly toward A's basket and appears to have an uncontested opportunity to score. B1 comes in quickly from the side and violently undercuts A1 who is in the act of shooting. A1 momentarily grasps the ring to regain balance and avoid injury. **RULING:** A1 is not penalized for grasping the ring, as it clearly was done to prevent possible injury. B1 is charged with a flagrant personal foul and is disqualified. Whether the try was successful or not, A1 is awarded two free throws with no players along the lane. Following the last throw, Team A is awarded the ball for a throw-in at the out-of-bounds spot nearest to where the foul occurred.

10.3.3 SITUATION B: A1 jumps for a try near the basket but loses his/her balance after releasing the ball. A1 grasps the basket to prevent injury. The ball: (a) is; or (b) is not, in the basket or on the ring while A1 is hanging on the ring. **RULING:** In (a), it is basket interference by A1 which causes the ball to become dead and no goal can be scored. In (b), there is no violation unless A1 is still hanging on the ring when the ball touches the basket or goes into the basket. In both (a) and (b), A1's grasping is not penalized if it is judged there was a possibility of injury had he/she not grasped the basket (9-1).

10.3.3 SITUATION C: Fifteen minutes before the game is scheduled to start, team member A1 dunks. Two minutes later A2 dunks. **RULING:** A1 and A2 are both charged with a technical foul. In addition, the head coach is charged indirectly with a technical foul for each act. The two fouls are team fouls for purpose of reaching the bonus. When dunking occurs during the pregame practice period the official notifies the team member and the head coach, but does not sound the whistle. If the game is played in a state which utilizes the optional coaching box, the coach should be informed that he/she has lost the privilege of using the coaching box for the entire game.

In Simple Terms

Any player involved in the play may grasp the basket to prevent possible injury.

10.3.3 SITUATION D: A1 dunks the ball, then grasps the ring: (a) to avoid possible injury as he/she has lost his/her balance; or (b) because A2 or B1 is lying on the floor directly under the basket. **RULING:** Grasping the ring to prevent injury as in (a) or (b), is permitted without penalty.

Player Intentionally Slaps Backboard

A player shall not place a hand on the backboard or ring to gain an advantage (10-3-4a), or while a try or tap is in flight, intentionally slap or strike backboard or cause the ring to vibrate (10-3-4b).

In Simple Terms

A player who follows through on a blocked shot and contacts the backboard in the normal course of action shall not be assessed a technical foul.

Player Intentionally Slaps Backboard: Caseplays

10.3.4 SITUATION: A1 tries for a goal, and (a) B1 jumps and attempts to block the shot but instead slaps or strikes the backboard and the ball goes into the basket; or (b) B1 vibrates the ring as a result of pulling on the net and the ball does not enter the basket. **RULING:** In (a) legal and the basket counts; and (b) a technical foul is charged to B1 and there is no basket.

COMMENT: The purpose of the rule is to penalize intentional contact with the backboard while a shot or try is involved or placing a hand on the backboard to gain an advantage. A player who strikes either backboard so forcefully it cannot be ignored because it is an attempt to draw attention to the player, or a means of venting frustration may be assessed a technical foul pursuant to Rule 10-3-6.

Player Delays Action

A player shall not delay the game by acts such as:

• Preventing the ball from being made live promptly or from being put in play (10-3-5a).

• Failing when in possession, to immediately pass the ball to the nearer official when a whistle blows (10-3-5b).

• The free thrower fails to be in the free-throw semicircle when the official is ready to administer the free throw unless the resumption-of-play procedure is in effect following a time-out or intermission (10-3-5c).

• Committing repeated violations of the throw-in (10-3-5d).

Player Delays Action: Caseplay

10.3.5 SITUATION: The calling official has reported the foul and has given directions to players along the lane. The official is ready to put the ball at free thrower A1's disposal, but A1 is at the sideline talking to the coach. **RULING:** A technical foul for delay is charged to A1. No warning is authorized in this situation (10-3-5c).

Player Commits Unsporting Foul

A player shall not commit an unsporting foul, which includes but is not limited to acts such as:

• Disrespectfully addressing or contacting an official or gesturing in such a manner to indicate resentment (10-3-6a).

• Using profane or inappropriate language or obscene gestures (10-3-6b); baiting or taunting an opponent (10-3-6c).

• Purposely obstructing an opponent's vision by waving or placing hand(s) near his/her eyes (10-3-6d).

• Climbing on or lifting a teammate to secure greater height (10-3-6e).

• Faking being fouled, knowingly attempting a free throw or accepting a foul to which the player was not entitled (10-3-6f).

• Use tobacco or smokeless tobacco (10-3-6g).

• Removing the jersey and or pants/skirt within the visual confines of the playing area (10-3-6h).

Player Commits Unsporting Foul: Caseplays

10.3.6 SITUATION A: Does holding or moving a hand or hands in front of the face of a player who has the ball, by an opponent who is in a legal guarding position, constitute unsporting tactics? **RULING:** Yes. The described action is illegal. It is unsporting for a guard to take a position behind a post player, or to take a position facing an opponent, or to take a position with his/her back to the ball and facing the opponent and then in either case, wave or hold the hands in front of the opponent's eyes so that the opponent cannot see. Holding or waving hands near the eye for the ostensible purpose of obstructing an opponent's vision is unsporting (10-3-6c).

10.3.6 SITUATION B: A1 has the ball out of bounds for a designated spot throw-in. B1 is putting great pressure on and the count is at four seconds when A1 throws the ball and it strikes B1's face. The ball rebounds from B1's face directly out of bounds. **RULING:** The administering official will have to make a decision based upon a number of observations. Was the throw-in to B1's face purely accidental or was it a voluntary, planned act? Was the ball contact caused by the movement of the defender? Was the act of a an unsporting nature? The administering official must be aware that players often react negatively in situations where they are frustrated or are retaliating for something which happened earlier in the game.

Player Goaltends During Free Throw

A player shall not goaltend during a free throw (10-3-9).

Player Dislodges Ball on Throw-in

A player shall not reach through the boundary-line plane and touch or dislodge the ball during a throw-in (10-3-10).

Player Dislodges Ball on Throw-in: Caseplay

10.3.11 SITUATION A: After a field goal, A1 has the ball out of bounds for a throw-in. Thrower A1 holds the ball: (a) B2 crosses the boundary line and fouls A1; or (b) B2 reaches through the out-of-bounds plane and touches the ball while in the hands of A1. RULING: It is an intentional personal foul in (a), and a technical foul in (b). In (a), such a contact foul with the thrower during a throw-in shall be considered intentional, or if it is violent, it should be ruled flagrant.

 COMMENT: Either act is a foul and it should be called whenever it occurs during a game without regard to time or score or whether the team had or had not been warned for a throw-in plane violation. If the player making the throw-in (A1) reaches through the out-of-bounds plane into the court and B1 then slaps the ball from the hand of A1, no violation has occurred. B1 has merely slapped a live ball from the hands of A1 (4-19-3, 4; 9-2-10 Penalty 3, 4).

10.3.11 SITUATION B: After a field goal, the score is A-55, B-54. A1 has the ball out of bounds for a throw-in with two seconds remaining in the game. A1 throws the ball toward A2 who also is out of bounds along the end line. B2 reaches across the end line and grabs or slaps the ball while it is in flight. Time expires close to the moment the official indicates the infraction. **RULING:** A technical foul is charged against B2. The remaining time or whether Team B had been previously warned for a delay-of-game situation is not a factor. No free throws are awarded as the winner of the game has been determined (9-2-10 Penalty 3, 4).

 In 1972, a player who committed a foul had to raise one hand only and lower it in a sporting manner. A player who failed to comply with this stipulation was assessed a technical foul. The rule was rescinded before the 1974 season.

10.3.11 SITUATION C: Team A scores near the end of the fourth quarter and is trailing by one point. B1 has the ball and is moving along the end line to make the throw-in. A2 steps out of bounds and fouls B1. Is the foul personal or technical? **RULING:** This is an intentional personal foul. The time remaining to be played or whether Team A had been previously warned for a delay-of-game situation is not a factor. If the team had not been warned, the foul constitutes the warning (4-19-1; 9-2-10 Penalty 4).

*10.3.11 SITUATION D: A1 is out of bounds for a throw-in. B1 reaches through the boundary plane and knocks the ball out of A1's hands. Earlier in the game, Team B had received a team warning for delay. **RULING:** Even though Team B had already been issued a warning for team delay, when B1breaks the plane and subsequently contacts the ball in the thrower's hand, it is considered all the same act and the end result is penalized. A player technical foul is assessed to B1; two free throws and a division line throw-in for Team A will follow. The previous warning for team delay still applies with any subsequent team delay resulting in a team technical foul (4-47; 9-2-10 Penalty 3; 10-1-10).

Player Contacts Opponent During Dead Ball

A player shall not intentionally or flagrantly contact an opponent when the ball is dead and such contact is not a personal foul (10-3-7) or be charged with fighting (10-3-8).

Player Contacts Opponent During Dead Ball: Caseplays

4.19.5 SITUATION: A1 is fouled by B1. A1 subsequently pushes B1. **RULING:** If a foul is called on A1, it must be either an intentional or flagrant technical. If it is ruled flagrant, A1 must be disqualified. If A1's contact during a dead ball was neither intentional nor flagrant, it should have been ignored (4-19-1 Note; 10-3-8).

10.3.7 SITUATION: B1 fouls A1 during an unsuccessful try. While the calling official is reporting the foul, A1 pushes B1 into another player. **RULING:** Intentional contact while the ball is dead constitutes an intentional technical foul. If other dead-ball contact is not intentional or flagrant, it should be ignored. The foul by A1 creates a false double-foul situation.

Topic:
Bench Technical Foul

The head coach is responsible for his/her own conduct and behavior, as well as substitutes, disqualified team members and all other bench personnel. Bench personnel, including the head coach, shall not commit an unsporting foul.

Bench Technical Foul Penalty

Two free throws plus ball for division-line throw-in. If the head coach is the offender, the foul is charged directly to him/her. The foul is charged to the offender (if not the head coach) and also charged indirectly to the head coach.

Disrespectfully Address an Official

Bench personnel shall not disrespectfully address an official (10-4-1a).

Disrespectfully Address an Official: Caseplays

10.4.1 SITUATION A: A technical foul is charged to: (a) a Team A substitute; (b) Team B's manager; (c) Team A's trainer; or (d) Team B's assistant coach. In all cases, the foul is charged because of uncomplimentary remarks addressed to an official. **RULING:** The individuals in (a), (b), (c) and (d) are all considered to be bench personnel and have violated the rules governing conduct while on the "bench." A second technical charged to any of these individuals results in disqualification. In addition to charging a technical to the individuals in all cases, the technical foul is also charged indirectly to the head coach. A second technical foul charged directly, or the third technical foul (direct or indirect) charged to the head coach results in similar disqualification and ejection (10-4-1a).

10.4.1 SITUATION B: At halftime, as the teams, coaches, and officials are making their way through a hallway to the dressing room, a Team A member verbally abuses one of the officials. **RULING:** A technical foul is charged to the team member and is also charged indirectly to the head coach. During intermission all team members are bench personnel and are penalized accordingly. If the conduct is flagrant, the team member shall be disqualified. The third quarter will begin with two Team B free throws and the ball awarded at half court. The alternating-possession arrow is unaffected. Team A will also have one foul toward the team-foul count (10-4-1a).

Influence an Official's Decision

Bench personnel shall not attempt to influence an official's decision (10-4-1b).

Use Inappropriate Language

Bench personnel shall not use profane or inappropriate language or obscene gestures (10-1-4c).

Use Inappropriate Language: Caseplays

4.34.3 SITUATION: Substitute A6 reports to the scorer to replace player A1 and awaits entry to the game. The U2 beckons A6 onto the court, and A1 swears at the official while heading to the bench. **RULING:** A6 became a player upon being beckoned by the official and entering the court. A1, now bench personnel, is penalized with a technical foul, which is added to the team-foul total and also charged as an indirect technical foul to the head coach.

10.4.1 SITUATION E: A1 is driving toward the basket for an apparent goal when the official, while trailing the play advancing in the direction in which the ball is being advanced, is cursed by the head coach or bench personnel of Team B. How should the official handle this situation? **RULING:** The official shall withhold blowing the whistle until A1 has either made or missed the shot. The official shall then sound the whistle and assess the Team B head coach or bench personnel with a technical foul. If the official judges the act to be flagrant, the offender shall be ejected. If A's coach or bench personnel was the offender, the whistle shall be sounded immediately when the unsporting act occurs (10-4-1a).

Bait or Taunt Opponent

Bench personnel shall not disrespectfully address, bait or taunt an opponent (10-1-4d).

Standing or Using Gestures

Bench personnel shall not object to an official's decision by rising from the bench or using gestures (10-1-4e).

Standing or Using Gestures: Caseplay

4.34.2 SITUATION: The third quarter ends and as the teams are heading to their respective benches, team members A1 and B1 verbally taunt one another. **RULING:** Double technical foul charged to A1 and B1. During the intermission between quarters, all team members are bench personnel. Both head coaches are indirectly charged with technical fouls and lose their coaching box privileges. Play will resume at the point of interruption, which is an alternating-possession arrow throw-in, to begin the fourth quarter (10-4-1c Penalty; 10-5-1a).

Incite Crowd

Bench personnel shall not incite undesirable crowd reactions (10-1-4f).

Remove Jersey

Bench personnel shall not remove the jersey and/or pants/skirt within the visual confines of the playing area (10-3-6h).

Remove Jersey: Caseplay

10.4.4 SITUATION C: After the horn sounds to end the first half, A1 removes his/her jersey near the team bench. **RULING:** A technical foul is charged to A1 and an indirect technical foul is charged to the head coach; A1 is considered bench personnel in this situation (10-4-1h).

10.4.4 SITUATION B: A1 commits his/her fifth foul and is disqualified. On the way to the team bench, A1 removes his/her shirt or pulls it over their face: (a) before the coach is notified; or (b) after the coach is notified. **RULING:** In (a) and (b), a technical foul is charged to A1. In (b), an indirect technical foul is also charged to the head as A1 is considered to be bench personnel. (10-4-1h)

Enter the Court

Bench personnel shall not enter the court unless by permission of an official to attend an injured player (10-4-2).

Use Tobacco

Bench personnel shall not use tobacco or smokeless tobacco (10-4-3).

Standing

Bench personnel are not permitted to stand at the team bench while the clock is running or is stopped, and must remain seated, except:

• The head coach with states that utilize the coaching box (10-4-4a).

• When a team member is reporting to the scorer's table (10-4-4b).

• During a charged time-out or the intermission between quarters and extra periods (10-4-4c).

• To spontaneously react to an outstanding play by a team member or to acknowledge a replaced player(s), but must immediately return to his/her seat (10-4-4d).

Standing: Caseplays

10.4.4 SITUATION A: Late in the game, A1 has been replaced and returns to the bench (a) Some team members of Team A rise to applaud A1; or (b) the coach of Team A rises and shakes hands with A1 as A1 leaves the court. In both cases the individuals are immediately seated. **RULING:** There has been no violation of the bench conduct rule as it is specifically indicated that bench personnel may rise to acknowledge a replaced player. Displays of sporting behavior and fair play are to be encouraged and are clearly identifiable as such. If the state has adopted the optional coaching box, the head coach may remain standing (10-4-4d; 10-5-1).

Topic:
Fighting

Fighting is considered a flagrant act (4-19-4).

Players on the Court Fighting

If there are a corresponding number of players from each team, double flagrant fouls are awarded, all participants are disqualified, no free throws are awarded and ball is put in play at the point of interruption (10 Pen 8-a-1). If the number of players are not corresponding, flagrant fouls are assessed and disqualification for all participants. Two free throws are awarded for the offended team for each additional player and the offended team is awarded a division-line throw-in (10 Pen 8-a-2).

Players on the Court Fighting: Caseplays

4.18.2 SITUATION: A1 dunks over B1 and then taunts B1. B1 retaliates and punches A1. **RULING:** Both A1 and B1 are charged with a flagrant technical foul for fighting and are disqualified. A1's action is defined as fighting when the taunting caused B1 to retaliate by fighting (10-3; 10-3-7c; 10-3-9).

10.4.5 SITUATION B: A fight breaks out between A1 and B1 during a dead-ball and clock-stopped situation. The head coach of Team A rushes onto the court. **RULING:** A1 and B1 are charged with flagrant technical fouls and are disqualified. No free throws are awarded for the double technical foul by A1 and B1. Since the coach was not beckoned onto the court by an official, he/she is charged with a flagrant technical foul and is disqualified. Team B is awarded two free throws and the ball for a throw-in at the division line opposite the table.

Players Leave Bench During Fight

If bench personnel leave the team bench during a fight or when a fight may break out and do not participate in the fight, all players leaving the bench are assessed flagrant fouls and disqualified, and the head coach is assessed a maximum of one indirect technical foul (regardless of the number leaving the bench). If the number of each team's offenders is corresponding, no free throws are awarded and the ball is put in play at the point of interruption. If the number of each team's offenders is unequal, a maximum of two free throws are awarded to the offended team, followed by a division-line throw-in opposite the table (10 Pen 8-b-1).

If bench personnel leave the team bench during a fight or when a fight may break out and participate in the fight, all participants are assessed flagrant fouls and disqualified. The head coach is assessed one indirect technical foul for each bench player participating in the fight. If the number of each team's participants is corresponding, no free throws are awarded and the ball is put in play at the point of interruption. If the number of each team's participants is unequal, two free throws are awarded to the offended team for each additional player, followed by a division-line throw-in opposite the table (10 Pen 8-b-2).

Players Leave Bench During Fight: Caseplays

4.19.13 SITUATION: Three substitutes of Team B leave their bench and come onto the court during a fight. RULING: The three substitutes are each charged with a flagrant technical foul and are disqualified. The Team B head coach is also charged indirectly with a technical foul. Team A is awarded two free throws plus the ball for a throw-in for this multiple infraction. Team B is charged with three fouls for reaching the bonus. In addition, the proper fouls are charged and penalties are assessed for the players who were fighting (10-4-5 Penalty).

10.4.5 SITUATION A: Post-players A1 and B1 begin punching each other and play is stopped. Two substitutes from each team leave the bench area and come onto the court. The four substitutes: (a) do not become involved in the fight; (b) all become involved in the fight; or (c) substitutes A6, A7, and B6 do not participate in the fight, but B7 becomes involved in the fight. **RULING:** A1 and B1 are charged with flagrant fouls and are disqualified, but no free throws result from the double personal foul. The four substitutes are charged with flagrant technical fouls and are disqualified. No free throws are awarded for the simultaneous technical fouls as the number of bench personnel leaving the bench and the penalties are the same for both teams. In (a), one technical foul is also charged indirectly to the head coach of each team. In (b), each head coach is charged indirectly with two technical fouls (one for each bench player leaving the bench and becoming involved in the fight). In (c), the Team A head coach is charged indirectly with one technical foul and the Team B head coach is indirectly charged with two technical fouls (one for substitutes B6 and B7 leaving the bench, and one for B7 becoming involved in the fight). In all situations, the ball is put in play at the point of interruption (4-36; 7-5-3b).

10.4.5 SITUATION C: Substitutes A6, A7 and A8 enter the floor and fight with substitutes B6, B7 and B8. **RULING:** A6, A7, A8, B6, B7 and B8 are charged with flagrant fouls and disqualified. Each head coach is charged with three indirect technical fouls and disqualified and must leave the vicinity or the playing area and have no further contact with the team. Because the substitute's fouls were offsetting, no free throws will be awarded. Charge each team with three fouls toward the bonus and resume play at the point of interruption.

10.4.5 SITUATION D: A1 and B1 begin to fight during a dead-ball period. Two substitutes from Team A and one from Team B leave their bench area and enter the court to be near the action. **RULING:** A1, B1 and the three substitutes are all disqualified and each is charged with a flagrant technical foul. Each coach is also charged indirectly with a technical foul. No free throws are awarded for the double technical foul by A1 and B1. The free throws for one substitute's foul by each team are canceled as the penalties offset. However, Team B is awarded two free throws and the ball for a division-line throw-in opposite the table for the second substitute's foul, which does not have a corresponding simultaneous technical foul by an opponent.

10.4.5 SITUATION E: A1 and B1 begin fighting and play is stopped. Substitute A6 leaves the bench area and enters the court to observe. B6 also enters the court at the same time, but B6 actually participates in the fight. **RULING:** A1, B1, A6 and B6 are all disqualified. No free throws result from the double flagrant foul by A1 and B1 or from the simultaneous technical fouls by A6 and B6. Each head coach is charged with one indirect technical foul. Play resumes at the point of interruption (4-36; 10-3-8).

10.4.5 SITUATION F: It appears a fight may occur on the playing court when (a) A6 and A7; or (b) A6 and B6 leave their respective benches. **RULING:** In (a) and (b), all players leaving the bench are assessed flagrant fouls and disqualified. The respective head coach is assessed a maximum of one indirect technical foul (regardless of the number of players leaving the bench). In (a), Team B is awarded two free throws and the ball for a division line throw-in. In (b), no free throws are awarded and the ball is put into play at the point of interruption (4-36).

Topic 14

Warnings and Delays

Key Terms

A warning to a team for delay is an administrative procedure by an official which is recorded in the scorebook by the scorer and reported to the coach (4-47). A warning shall be issued in the following cases:

- Throw-in plane violations (4-47-1).

- Huddle by either team and contact with the free thrower (4-47-2).

- Interfering with the ball following a goal (4-47-3).

- Failure to have the court ready for play following a time-out (4-47-4).

A delay is any act that allows the game to develop into an actionless contest (10-1-5).

Topic:
Throw-in Plane Violation
Warning

The opponent(s) of the thrower shall not have any part of his/her person through the inbounds side of the throw-in boundary-line plane until the ball has been released on a throw-in pass (9-2-11). The thrower may penetrate the plane provided he/she does not touch the inbounds area before the ball is released on the throw-in pass. The opponent in this situation may legally touch or grasp the ball.

The thrower shall have a minimum of 3 feet horizontally (1-2-2).

 ## Rationale

Since the warning is issued to the team, the penalty should be too. Since a technical foul on a player counts toward disqualification, the impact of the act on the game did not justify charging it to a player.

Throw-in Plane Violation Warning: Penalty

The first violation of the throw-in boundary-line plane by an opponent(s) of the thrower shall result in a team warning for delay being given (one warning per team per game). The warning does not result in the loss of the opportunity to move along the end line when and if applicable.

The second or additional violations will result in a technical foul assessed to the offending team.

If an opponent(s) of the thrower reaches through the throw-in boundary-line plane and touches or dislodges the ball while in possession of the thrower or being passed to a teammate outside the boundary line (as in 7-5-7), a technical foul shall be charged to the offender. No warning for delay required.

If an opponent(s) of the thrower reaches through the throw-in boundary-line plane and fouls the thrower, an intentional personal foul shall be charged to the offender. No warning for delay required.

The ball becomes dead when the violation (warning) or technical foul occurs. Following a violation, the ball is awarded to the opponents for a throw-in at the original throw-in spot.

Rationale

The elimination of multiple warnings for various delay-of-game situations will better assist with the flow of the game as well as the administration of the rule by officials and scorers. With new tactics of additional delay-of-game situations increasing (wiping up the floor following time-outs, etc.), the rule gives coaches and officials clear direction on limiting these situations by allowing only one warning prior to administering a team technical foul.

Throw-in Plane Violation Warning: Caseplays

7.6.4 SITUATION A: While attempting a throw-in, A1 holds the ball through the plane of the end line. B1: (a) slaps the ball from A1's hand(s); or (b) simply grabs the ball and then throws it through B's basket. **RULING:** In (a), no violation has occurred and play continues. In (b), score two points for Team B.

7.6.4 SITUATION B: During an attempted throw-in, A1: (a) holds the ball through the plane of the end line and then passes it; (b) steps through the plane (makes contact with the floor inbounds) before passing the ball to A2; or (c) holds the ball through the plane and hands it to A2. **RULING:** A legal throw-in in (a), but a throw-in violation in (b) and (c).

7.6.4 SITUATION C: A1 is attempting to make a throw-in and Team B is applying a great deal of pressure. B1 reaches through the boundary-line plane and waves his/her hand in an effort to prevent the pass. The action takes place on a court which has more than 3 feet of unobstructed space outside the boundary line. **RULING:** Team B is warned for violation of the boundary plane. The warning is reported to the scorer and to the coach and applies for the rest of the game. Any subsequent delay-of-game situation by Team B shall result in a technical foul charged to Team B (9-2-10; 10-1-10).

7.6.4 SITUATION D: The sideline is very near the spectators leaving little space out of bounds for A1 to make a throw-in. As a result, the administering official has directed B1 to move back a step to give the thrower some room: (a) as soon as the ball is handed or bounced to A1, B1 moves right back to the boundary line in front of A1; or (b) A1 attempts to complete the throw-in just inside the boundary line and B1 moves to his/her original position in order to defend. **RULING:** In (a), it is a violation by B1 and will also result in a warning for Team B which is reported to the scorer and to the head coach. Any subsequent delay-of-game situation or noncompliance with the verbal order will result in a technical foul charged to Team B. In (b), B1 is expected to stay back one step unless the throw-in is attempted between this area and the boundary line. No violation in this case as B1 is allowed to defend the area if the throw-in is attempted there (10-1-10).

7.6.4 SITUATION E: Following a goal, A1 is running the end line when B1 reaches through the plane in an attempt to prevent the throw-in. **RULING:** Team B is warned for the violation which is reported to the scorer and to the head coach. A1 may run the end line during the subsequent throw-in.

7.6.4 SITUATION F: Thrower A1 inadvertently holds the ball through the end-line plane during a throw-in. B1 is able to get his/her hands on the ball and A1 cannot pull it back. **RULING:** There is no player or team control during a throw-in, therefore a held ball is called, resulting in an alternating-possession throw-in. If the original throw-in is an alternating-possession throw-in, Team A still has the arrow following the held ball.

9.2.10 SITUATION: A1 is out of bounds for a throw-in. B1 reaches through the boundary plane and knocks the ball out of A1's hands. Team B has not been warned previously for a throw-in plane infraction. **RULING:** B1 is charged with a technical foul and it also results in the official having a team warning recorded and reported to the head coach.

COMMENT: In situations with the clock running and five or less seconds left in the game, a throw-in plane violation or interfering with the ball following a goal should be ignored if its only purpose is to stop the clock. However, if the tactic in any way interferes with the thrower's efforts to make a throw-in, a technical foul for delay shall be called even though no previous warning had been issued. In this situation, if the official stopped the clock and issued a team warning, it would allow the team to benefit from the tactic (4-47-1; 10-1-5c).

10.1.10 SITUATION: Team B is warned in the first half when B1 reaches through the inbounds side of the throw-in boundary plane. Early in the fourth quarter either: (a) B1; or (b) B2 does the same thing. **RULING:** The warning is only given once per game to each team. Thereafter, another violation by a member of that team results in a technical foul. The technical foul in both (a) and (b) is charged to Team B (9-2-10).

Topic:
Free-throw Huddle Delay Warning

A team warning for delay shall be issued for contact with the free thrower or a huddle of two or more players by either team prior to a free throw (4-47-2).

Free-Throw Huddle Delay Warning: Penalty

The first violation for contact with the free thrower or a huddle of two or more players by either team prior to a free throw results in a team warning for delay. Any additional violation results in a team technical foul which includes two free throws plus the ball for a division line throw-in (10-1-5c).

Free-throw Huddle Delay Warning: Caseplays

8.1.1 SITUATION B: B1 fouls A1 during an unsuccessful try for goal. The calling official has properly reported the foul and is in position for the free throws. The administering official has given all instructions and signals. Team B is properly occupying the required spaces, but three teammates of A1 are huddling inside the lane. **RULING:** Team A is warned for delay, the scorer records it and it

In Simple Terms

If the delay becomes so common that the normal tempo of the game has been altered, a team warning for delay shall be issued.

is reported to the head coach. If Team A commits any delay thereafter in the game, a team technical foul shall be charged (10-1-5d; 10-3-5c).

 COMMENT: Since this situation is not a throw-in or following a time-out or intermission, the resumption-of-play procedure shall not be used. If the free thrower is not in the semicircle when the administering official is ready, a technical foul is charged to the free thrower. If the free thrower is in the semicircle, but does not accept the ball, it shall be placed on the floor and the count started.

10.1.5 SITUATION C: The calling official has reported the foul and proceeds to his/her proper position for the first of two free throws awarded to A1. B1 and B2 are: (a) huddling in the lane; or (b) two B players are not occupying the first two marked spaces next to the end line as required. **RULING:** In (a), if the huddle delays the officials' administration, Team B is warned. The warning is recorded by the scorer and reported to the head coach. If Team B had been previously warned for delay, a technical foul shall be charged. In (b), Team B will be directed to occupy the required spaces. If there is delay, a team technical foul shall be charged to Team B (4-47).

Topic:
Interfering With the Ball
Following a Goal Warning

A team warning for delay shall be issued for interfering with the ball following a goal (4-47-3).

Interfering With the Ball Following a Goal Warning: Penalty

A team warning for delay shall be issued for interfering with the ball following a goal. Interfering with the ball following a goal after a team warning for delay has been issued results in a team technical foul (10-1-5d).

At one time, a lack of action warning could be issued to either the offense or defense.	

Interfering With the Ball Following a Goal Warning: Caseplay

10.1.5 SITUATION D: Immediately following a goal by A1, A3 slaps the ball away so that Team B is unable to make a quick throw-in. **RULING:** The official shall sound his/her whistle and go to the table to have the scorer record a team warning for delay. The warning shall then be reported to the head coach of Team A. Any subsequent delay by Team A shall result in a team technical foul charged to Team A (4-47-3).

Topic:
Failure to Have the Court Ready for Play Following a Time-out Warning

A warning to a team for delay shall be given for failure to have the court ready for play following any time-out (4-47-4).

Failure to Have the Court Ready for Play Following a Time-out Warning: Penalty

A team warning for delay shall be issued for failing to have the court ready for play following a time-out. After a team warning for delay has been issued, a team technical foul shall be assessed for any occurrence (10-1-5e).

In Simple Terms

A team will receive one delay warning per game for any of the four team delay actions. The next occurrence of delay will result in an immediate technical foul.

Failure to Have the Court Ready for Play Following a Time-out Warning: Caseplay

10.1.5 SITUATION: Following the second horn, indicating the time-out has ended, Team A is still wiping up water from the playing court and delays the game from resuming. **RULING:** Team A is warned for delay. If a previous warning for any type of delay had been issued, a technical foul shall be charged (10-1-5e; 4-47-4).

Topic: Delays

Other Team Delays

The resumption-of-play procedure may be used to prevent delay in putting the ball in play when a throw-in team does not make a thrower available or following a time-out or intermission (unless either team is not on the court to start the second half). The procedure results in a violation instead of a technical foul for initial delay in specific situations (4-38).

When the clock is not running, a team shall not consume a full minute through not being ready when it is time to start either half (10-1-5a).

A team shall not delay having all players return to the court at approximately the same time following a time-out or intermission (10-1-9).

Other Team Delays: Penalty

A team technical foul shall be charged in all situations. Two free throws plus ball for division-line throw-in to the offended team.

Other Team Delays: Caseplays

10.1.9 SITUATION: Following a charged time-out Team B is still with their coach on the sideline when the official sounds the whistle to indicate play will resume. Four players of B return to the court just in time to play defense as A1 attempts an unsuccessful three-pointer. B1 rebounds and throws a long pass to B5 who enters the court just in time to catch the pass. **RULING:** A technical foul is immediately charged to Team B for failing to have all players return to the court at approximately the same time following a time-out or intermission. While it is true the entire team may be off the court while the procedure is being used, once a team responds, all players must enter the court at approximately the same time.

Other Player Delays

A player shall not delay returning after legally being out of bounds (10-3-3).

A player shall not prevent the ball from being made live promptly or from being put in play (10-3-6a).

A player shall not fail when in possession, to immediately pass the ball to the nearer official when a whistle blows (10-3-6b).

The free thrower shall not fail to be in the free-throw semicircle when the official is ready to administer the free throw unless the resumption-of-play procedure is in effect following a time-out or intermission (10-3-6c).

A player shall not commit repeated violations of the throw-in (10-3-6d). This includes not replacing a teammate after the ball is at the thrower's disposal (9-2-9).

▨ Rationale

A player that fails to move directly onto the court after a throw-in shall be assessed a technical foul. It is clear in such an instance the player's actions are a definite attempt to deceive and should be dealt with accordingly.

Other Player Delays: Penalty

A technical foul shall be charged in all situations. Two free throws plus ball for division-line throw-in to the offended team.

Other Player Delays: Caseplays

10.3.2 SITUATION A: A1 has the ball out of bounds for a throw-in. A1 completes the throw-in to A2 and then purposefully delays his/her return by taking four or five steps along the end line prior to coming inbounds behind a screen set by A3 and A4. A1 gets a return pass from A2 and takes an unchallenged try for goal. **RULING:** A1 is charged with a technical foul for purposefully delaying his/her return to the court following the throw-in. A1's movement out of bounds along the end line was to take advantage of the screen and return to the court in a more advantageous position.

10.3.2 SITUATION B: After a lengthy substitution process involving multiple substitutions for both Team A and Team B, A5 goes to the bench and remains there, mistakenly believing he/she has been replaced. The ball is put in play even though Team A has only four players on the court. Team A is bringing the ball into A's frontcourt when the coach of Team A realizes they have only four players. The coach yells for A5 to return and he/she sprints directly onto the court and catches up with the play. **RULING:** No technical foul is charged to A5. A5's return to the court was not deceitful, nor did it provide A5 an unfair positioning advantage on the court.

Topic 15

Correcting Errors

Key Terms

A rule is one of a group of regulations which governs the game (4-39-1). A single infraction is not complicated by a second infraction unless so stated or implied (4-39-3).

Topic:
—— Correctable Errors ——

Officials may correct an error if a rule is inadvertently set aside, resulting in:

• The failure to award a merited free throw (2-10-1a).

• The awarding of an unmerited free throw (2-10-1b).

• Permitting a wrong player to attempt a free throw (2-10-1c).

• Attempting a free throw at the wrong basket (2-10-1d).

• Erroneously counting or canceling a score (2-10-1e).

In order to correct any of the officials' errors listed, such error must be recognized by an official no later than during the first dead ball after the clock has properly started (2-10-2).

If the error of erroneously counting or canceling a score is made while the clock is running and the ball dead, it must be recognized by an official before the second live ball (2-10-3).

In Simple Terms

Correctable errors involve mistakes which do not involve either judgment or the setting aside of a rule which may be corrected when discovered.

Correctable Errors: Caseplays

2.10.1 SITUATION A: A1 is fouled and entitled to two free throws under the double-bonus rule, however, the officials indicate a one-and-one bonus situation. The first attempt is unsuccessful; B4 rebounds the ball and passes it up to B2. The error is discovered with B2 in possession of the live ball near mid-court. **RULING:** The error is discovered within the correctable error timeframe, and shall be corrected. Team B securing the rebound and passing to a teammate constitutes no change in team possession. Therefore, A1 will receive the merited free throw with players on the lane and play resumes from the free throw (2-10-1a).

2.10.1 SITUATION B: The score is tied with three seconds remaining in the final period. A1 is fouled and is given a one-and-one. A1 misses the first free throw; B1 grabs the rebound and attempts a long shot. The try is unsuccessful and the teams prepare for overtime. Before the overtime begins, the officials are notified that A1 should have received two free throws instead of a one-and-one. **RULING:** The error is discovered within the correctable error timeframe, and shall be corrected. The second free throw is awarded, if successful, the game is over. If the free throw is missed, overtime is played (2-10-1a).

2.10.1 SITUATION C: A1 is fouled with one second remaining in the second quarter. Team A is awarded a throw-in and A1 passes the ball inbounds to A2, the horn sounds ending the quarter. As officials enter the court from the half-time intermission, the scorer informs the Referee that A1 should have been awarded one-and-one bonus situation. **RULING:** The error is discovered within the correctable error timeframe, and shall be corrected. A1 is awarded a one-and-one bonus situation with the lane cleared. Resume play from the point of interruption, which is an alternating-possession throw-in to start the third quarter (2-10-1a; 2-10-6; 5-6-2 Exception 3).

*2.10.1 SITUATION D: A1 is fouled. Team A is awarded the ball out of bounds. The foul was Team B's seventh team foul and A1 should have been awarded a one and one bonus. Team A scores on the ensuing throw-in. As the ball passes through the net, the officials are informed of the error. **RULING:** The error is discovered within the correctable error timeframe. Count the goal by A; A1 will be awarded the bonus with no players along the lane lines. There has been a change of possession and the point of interruption is the goal by Team A, therefore Team B will be awarded a throw-in anywhere along the end line (2-10-1a; 2-10-5).

*2.10.1 SITUATION E: A1 has been given the ball for a throw-in when A2 commits a foul against B2. B1 is awarded the ball for a throw-in and commits a throw-in violation by touching a foot inbounds before releasing the throw-in pass. The ball is at A1's disposal for the subsequent throw-in when the officials are informed that A2's foul was Team A's seventh team foul. **RULING:** The clock had not started and the error is discovered within the correctable error timeframe. B2 is awarded the bonus with no players along the lane lines. The point of interruption is the throw-in for Team A (2-10-1a; 2-10-6).

2.10.1 SITUATION F: A1 is fouled. The scorer informs the official that Team B has committed 10 team fouls and that the two-free-throw penalty is in effect. The official administers the free throw and states and indicates "two" throws. The first free throw is unsuccessful and the second is successful. B1 has the ball out of bounds for the throw-in. The scorer informs the official that there were only nine team fouls on Team B and that the penalty should have been one and one. **RULING:** The error is discovered within the correctable error timeframe, and shall be corrected. The second free throw is canceled and play is resumed at the point of interruption. Since "no goal" has been scored, play is resumed with an alternating-possession throw-in at a spot nearest to where the ball was located when the stoppage occurred (2-10-1b; 2-10-6; 4-36-2c).

2.10.1 SITUATION G: A1 is fouled but erroneously is not awarded two free throws even though the automatic bonus is in effect. Team A is given a throw-in, and A1 inbounds the ball to A2 who is tied up by B1 resulting in a held-ball situation. The error is discovered following the held-ball call. The possession arrow is pointing to: (a) A's; or (b) B's basket. **RULING:** In (a), the merited free throws will be awarded, and play will continue from that action, since Team A had not lost possession between the error and when the error was recognized. However, in (b), the lane is cleared for A1's merited free throws, and play resumes from the point of interruption which is an alternating-possession throw-in by Team B.

2.10.1 SITUATION H: A1 has been awarded two free throws. Erroneously, the ball is allowed to remain in play after A1 misses on the first attempt. A2 rebounds the miss and tosses the ball through the basket. B1 secures the ball and inbounds it. Play continues until a foul is called on A2 as B is passing the ball in B's frontcourt. **RULING:** The goal by A2 counts, but the error of not awarding A1 a second free throw is no longer correctable. Since the ball remained in play on the missed free throw, the clock started and the ball became dead when the goal was scored. When the ball became live on the subsequent throw-in, the time period for correction had expired.

2.10.1 SITUATION I: A1 is fouled prior to the bonus, but erroneously A1 is awarded a one-and-one. The error is discovered: (a) after A1 makes the first throw; (b) after A1 makes both; (c) after B1 has rebounded the miss on the second free throw; (d) after B1 has the ball for a throw-in after both attempts are successful; or (e) after B2 has control of the throw-in from B1 after A1's two successful throws.

RULING: In (a) and (b), the successful free throw(s) is canceled, and A1 is given the ball for a throw-in at the spot out of bounds nearest to where B1 fouled originally. In (c), (d) and (e), the successful free throw(s) are canceled and play continues with a throw-in by B as B had the ball when the game was interrupted for correction.

2.10.1 SITUATION J: A1 is fouled by B1 while in the act of shooting and the try or tap is successful. The administering official erroneously awards and announces two free throws instead of one. A1's first attempt is unsuccessful and B1 rebounds. Play continues briefly with B1 advancing the ball before the official recognizes the error and stops play. **RULING:** Since A1 has attempted the merited free throw he/she was entitled to, there is no further correction to be made. Play shall resume with a throw-in by Team B at the out-of-bounds spot nearest to where play was interrupted.

2.10.1 SITUATION K: (a) A1; or (b) B1 commits basket interference at Team A's basket. In (a), the referee erroneously counts the score; or in (b), fails to count it. In each case, the error is not discovered until the ball has become live following the dead ball during which the error occurred. **RULING:** The official's error in both (a) and (b) is still correctable.

2.10.1 SITUATION L: A1 attempts a goal from behind the three-point line: (a) but the covering official fails to give the successful signal after the ball goes through the basket, and the scorer records only two points; or (b) and the covering official gives the successful signal, but the scorer records only two points. Team B inbounds the ball and proceeds to score. The coach of Team A goes to the table and requests a 60-second time-out to discuss the error. **RULING:** In (a), the error of not awarding three points is correctable as it was detected prior to the second live ball after the error. The extra point is scored, the 60-second time-out is not charged and the game continues from the point of interruption. In (b), it is a mistake by the scorer which can be corrected any time until the final score has been approved.

2.10.1 SITUATION M: A1 jumps and releases a try for goal apparently from behind the three-point line. The try is successful. The covering official does not indicate a three-point try and does not signal three points after the goal. The Team A coach rushes to the table and requests a 60-second time-out to discuss a correctable error. It is determined neither official clearly observed A1's location before he/she jumped to try. **RULING:** No change can be made and two points are properly

scored. The 60-second time-out remains charged to Team A (5-8-4).
2.10.2 SITUATION: B1 fouls A1. Team A is in the bonus, but the official erroneously awards the ball to Team A for a throw-in. A1's throw-in is intercepted by B1 who scores a goal. A1's throw-in is controlled by A2 who dribbles into Team A's midcourt and then asks for a time-out. During the time-out, the scorer advises the referee that Team A was in the bonus when B1 fouled A1. **RULING:** It is too late to correct the error. The error could have been corrected anytime during the dead ball following the goal by B1, as this was the first dead ball after the clock started following the error.

Topic:
Coach Requesting Correction

Time-out occurs and the clock, if running, shall be stopped when an official responds to the scorer's signal to grant a coach's request that a correctable error, or a timing, scoring or alternating-possession mistake be prevented or rectified. The appeal to the official shall be presented at the scorer's table where a coach of each team may be present (5-8-4).

Coach Requesting Correction: Caseplays

5.8.4 SITUATION A: The appeal of the coach of Team A to an official, made while the ball is dead and the clock is stopped, is made when it is too late for correction of an error. **RULING:** Following the conference, the 60-second time-out remains charged to Team A and they are given the privilege of utilizing whatever time remains. The official will terminate the discussion with the coach immediately upon making a decision. If the discussion takes more than one minute, only one 60-second time-out is charged (2-10-2; 5-11-3).

5.8.4 SITUATION B: The head coach from Team A requests a 60-second time-out to rectify a timing error. The referee grants the time-out to investigate the matter, but determines that no correction can be made. The scorer then informs the referee that Team A cannot be charged a 60-second time-out as they only have one 30-second time-out remaining. **RULING:** Since they have no 60-second time-outs

In Simple Terms

A coach may request a time-out to discuss a correctable error, problem with points, timing or the alternating-possession arrow. If the error is correctable by rule and within the appropriate timeframe, no time-out shall be charged.

remaining and there was no timing correction made, Team A will be charged their remaining 30-second time-out regardless of the amount of time consumed (5-11-3).

Topic:
Free Throw Errors

If the error is a free throw by the wrong player or at the wrong basket, or the awarding of an unmerited free throw, the free throw and the activity during it, other than unsporting, flagrant, intentional or technical fouls, shall be canceled (2-10-4).

Free Throw Errors Correction: Caseplay

2.10.4 SITUATION A: A1 is fouled by B1 during a field-goal try which is successful. A2 is erroneously awarded the free throw. While A2's successful attempt is in the air: (a) B1 fouls A3; or (b) B1 intentionally fouls A3. Prior to the ball becoming live, the coach of Team B properly asks the referee to correct the error of awarding the free throw to the wrong player. **RULING:** The free throw by A2 is canceled and A1 will properly attempt the free throw which should have been awarded originally. The common foul by B1 in (a) is canceled. The intentional foul in (b) cannot be canceled. In (b), the game continues with the administration of the two free throws to A3 resulting from the intentional foul by B1. Team A will then be awarded the ball for a throw-in. If the corrected error is a free throw by the wrong player, at the wrong basket or the awarding of an unmerited free throw, the free throw and the activity during it other than unsporting, flagrant, intentional or technical fouls are canceled.

*2.10.4 SITUATION B: The officials erroneously permit A1 to shoot technical foul free throws at Team B's basket; A1 makes both free throws. When the error is discovered, the timeframe for the correctable error (a) has not passed; or (b) has passed. **RULING:** In (a), cancel the successful free throws by A1 and administer the free throws again at the correct basket. In (b), the free throws by A1 shall not be canceled and count toward Team A's point total.

Action Not Nullified

Points scored, consumed time and additional activity, which may occur prior to the recognition of an error, shall not be nullified. Errors because of free-throw attempts by the wrong player or at the wrong basket shall be corrected by administering correctly (2-10-5).

Resuming Play After Error

If an error is corrected, play shall be resumed from the point of interruption to rectify the error, unless it involves awarding a merited free throw(s) and there has been no change of team possession since the error was made, in which case play shall resume as after any free-throw attempt (2-10-6).

Play shall be resumed by a throw-in to the team that was in control at a spot nearest to where the ball was located when the stoppage occurred (4-36-2a). If the stoppage occurred during a free throw or throw-in that a team was entitled to, play shall be resumed with that (4-36-2b).

If the point of interruption is such that neither team is in control and no goal, infraction, nor end of quarter/extra period is involved, then play shall be resumed with an alternating-possession throw-in.

Resuming Play After Error: Caseplays

2.10.6 SITUATION A: A1 is fouled by B1. It is a non-shooting personal foul. It is Team B's 7th foul of the half, but the official scorer fails to notify the officials and they award Team A the ball out of bounds. After the inbound pass, Team A misses a shot and Team B secures the rebound. Team B then misses a shot at their offensive end, and A1 secures the rebound. A1 requests and is granted a time-out. During the time-out, the officials are informed that Team A should have been awarded a bonus free throw situation on its previous possession. **RULING:** The error can still be corrected. A1 shoots a bonus free throw situation with no players on the lane. Team A is then awarded the ball out of bounds nearest the spot where the time-out was requested. Since the error involves the failure to award a merited free throw(s) and there has been a change in team possession, play shall be resumed from the point at which it was interrupted, after the error has been rectified.

2.10.6 SITUATION B: A1 is fouled by B1. It is a non-shooting personal foul. It is Team B's 7th foul of the half, but the official scorer fails to notify the officials and they award Team A the ball out of bounds. After the inbound pass, Team A misses a shot and Team B secures the rebound. While Team B has the ball in its possession, B1 is charged with an illegal screen against A2. Before Team A is handed the ball for the throw-in, the officials are informed that Team A should have been awarded the automatic bonus on its previous possession. **RULING:** The error can still be corrected. A1 shoots a bonus free throw situation with no players on the lane. Team A is then awarded a throw-in for B1's team-control foul and play will continue from that point. Since the error involved the failure to award a merited free-throw(s) and there has been a change in team possession, play shall be resumed from the point at which it was interrupted after the error has been rectified.

7.5.2 SITUATION A: Team A is awarded a throw-in near the division line. The administering official by mistake, puts the ball at B1's disposal. B1 completes the throw-in and Team B subsequently scores a goal. **RULING:** No correction can be made for the mistake by the official.

Topic:
Timing Errors

The referee may correct an obvious mistake by the timer to start or stop the clock properly only when he/she has definite information relative to the time involved. The exact time observed by the official may be placed on the clock (5-10-1).

If the referee determines that the clock malfunctioned or was not started/stopped properly, or if the clock did not run, an official's count or other official information may be used to make a correction (5-10-2).

The referee shall decide matters upon which the timer and scorer disagree and correct obvious timing errors (2-5-5).

Timing Errors: Caseplays

5.10.1 SITUATION A: The score is tied with two seconds remaining in the game. A1 is awarded a bonus free throw. After the ball had been placed at the disposal of A1, B1 disconcerts A1. The free-throw attempt is missed. The timer does not hear the official's whistle sound and permits the clock to start. May the referee put the two seconds back on the clock? **RULING:** Yes. The rules provide "…the referee may correct the mistake when he/she has definite information relative to time involved." The referee not only orders the timer to put two seconds back on the clock but also awards A1 a substitute throw for the disconcertion by B1.

 Rationale

With new clock technology and the ability to observe tenths of a second, when an official has definite knowledge relative to the time involved, he/she should have the ability to put the correct time on the game clock.

5.10.1 SITUATION B: Team A leads by one point when they inbound the ball in their backcourt with 12 seconds remaining in the fourth quarter. A1's throw-in pass is to A2 who dribbles in the backcourt until the horn sounds. The trail official does not make a 10-second call because he/she "lost the count." **RULING:** The game is over. The clock may not be reset as there are no rule provisions to do this. If the count was not accurate or was not made, it cannot be corrected. There is no provision for the correction of an error made in the official's accuracy in counting seconds.

5.10.1 SITUATION C: As the official calls a three-second lane violation, he/she properly sounds the whistle and gives the signal to stop the clock. While doing this, the official is able to see the exact time remaining in the fourth quarter. The clock shows five seconds remaining. The timer stops the clock: (a) at five seconds; (b) at four seconds; (c) at three seconds; or (d) the time runs out completely. **RULING:** No correction is needed in (a). In (b), (c) and (d), the referee will order five seconds put on the clock.

5.10.1 SITUATION D: There are six seconds left on the clock in the fourth quarter and the ball is out of bounds in the possession of Team A. The throw-in by A1 touches the referee on the court and then goes across the court and out of bounds. The timer permits two seconds to run off the clock. What recourse does the coach of either team have in such situation? **RULING:** Either coach may step to the scorer's table and request a 60-second time-out and have the referee come to the table. The coach is permitted to do this under provisions of the coach's rule. The referee shall come to the sideline and confer with one or both coaches and the timer about the matter; and if the referee has definite knowledge that there were six seconds on the clock when the ball was awarded to Team A for the throw-in, it is the responsibility of the referee to have the two seconds put back on the clock. The timer and scorer and the other official(s) can be used by the referee to gain definite information. If there is no mistake or if it cannot be rectified, the requesting team will be charged with a 60-second time-out (5-11-3 Exception b; 5-8-4; 10-5-1c).

5.10.1 SITUATION E: Team A scores a goal to lead by four points with 10 seconds remaining in the fourth quarter. Team B then quickly scores with approximately five seconds remaining; now trailing by two points. Team A expects to withhold the ball out of bounds for the throw-in with the time remaining (less than five seconds). The timer mistakenly stops the clock shortly following the Team B goal; the game clock reads 4.0

seconds remaining. The official sounds the whistle, (a) immediately to address the timing mistake; (b) after reaching a throw-in count of three to address the timing mistake; or (c) upon reaching a five-second throw-in count on Team A. **RULING:** In (a) and (b), Team A will have a throw-in from anywhere along the end line with (a) no change to the game clock; and (b) the game clock corrected to display 1.0 seconds. In (c), the game is over as time has expired.

 COMMENT: An official's count may be used to correct a timing mistake (5-10-2).

5.10.2 SITUATION: Following a violation in the fourth quarter, there are five seconds on the clock as A1 is bounced the ball for a throw-in. The throw-in is completed to A2. The official properly signals the clock to start and immediately begins a closely-guarded count on A2. The official reaches a count of three seconds when B1 fouls A2. The official stops play properly and reports the foul at the table. The timer reports that he/she did not start the clock when the throw-in was touched by A2. The clock still shows five seconds. **RULING:** The referee will order the clock set at two seconds. The referee has definite knowledge of the amount of time involved in this situation by using the closely-guarded count.

Topic:
Other Errors

Inadvertent Whistle

The ball becomes dead when an official's whistle is blown unless a try or tap is in flight, a foul is committed by any opponent of a player who has started a try or tap for goal (is in the act of shooting) before the foul occurred, provided time did not expire before the ball was in flight, or a violation, as in 9-3-2 or 9-13-1, occurs by an opponent (6-7-5).

Inadvertent Whistle: Caseplay

6.7.5 SITUATION: A1 is at the free-throw line for the second of two attempts. After the ball is at A1's disposal, B1 commits a lane violation. The administering official inadvertently sounds his/her whistle: (a) before A1 starts the free-throw motion; (b) after the ball has been released; or (c) during A1's motion but before release of the ball.

RULING: Whether or not the whistle was sounded inadvertently it has the same result. In (a) and (c), the ball becomes dead immediately. In (b), the whistle does not cause the ball to become dead until the free throw ends. Because B1 violated, in all cases, a substitute throw is awarded if the free-throw attempt by A1 is unsuccessful (4-20-3).

7.5.3 SITUATION: An official sounds his/her whistle accidentally: (a) while A1 is dribbling and in player control; (b) while Team A is in control and passing among teammates; (c) while A1's unsuccessful try attempt is in flight; or (d) while A's successful try attempt is in flight. **RULING:** The ball is put in play at the point of interruption. In (a) and (b), Team A is awarded a throw-in at the nearest out-of-bounds spot to where the ball was when the whistle was accidentally sounded. In (c) and

Fundamental #16
The official's whistle seldom causes the ball to become dead (it is already dead).

(d), the ball does not become dead until the try ends. In (c), since there is no team control when the ball becomes dead, the ball is put in play by the team entitled to the throw-in using the alternating-possession procedure. In (d), since a goal has been scored by Team A, the ball is given to Team B for a throw-in anywhere along the end line. (7-4-4; 4-12-3,6; 4-36)

Officials Authority

No official has the authority to set aside or question decisions made by the other official(s) within the limits of their respective outlined duties (2-6).

 # Rationale

Although the referee and umpire(s) have clearly defined duties and responsibilities, they share concurrent responsibilities during the game. After the ball is tossed, no one should really be aware as to which official is the referee and which is the umpire(s).

Officials Authority: Caseplays

2.6 SITUATION A: The umpire observes traveling, stepping out of bounds or another violation by A1. At approximately the same time, A1 tries for a field goal or the referee observes contact by B1 on A1. **RULING:** The officials must decide definitely which act occurred first. There is no rules coverage to administer the acts as occurring simultaneously. If the violation occurred first, the ball became dead. If the ball was in flight during the try before the touching of the boundary, there was no violation. If the contact occurred after a violation was observed, it is not a foul unless the contact is intentional or flagrant.

2.6 SITUATION B: A violation and personal contact occur at about the same time. Both are observed by the same official, or the violation is observed by one official and the contact by the other. What is the proper procedure? **RULING:** The officials shall decide which occurred first. If the violation was first, it caused the ball to become dead; hence, the contact which followed was not a foul unless intentional or flagrant. If the contact occurred first, it caused the ball to become dead and no violation occurred.

5.8.3 SITUATION E: The official erroneously grants Team B a time-out in a situation when Team B cannot have one. What happens now? **RULING:** Team B is entitled to use the time-out since it was granted. The time-out once granted cannot be revoked and is charged to Team B. All privileges and rights permitted during a charged time-out are available to both teams.

Overtime-Related Corrections

Once the ball becomes live in the extra period, it will be played even though a correction in the fourth quarter score is made (5-7-4).

Overtime-Related Corrections: Caseplay

5.7.3 SITUATION: Following a violation in the first extra period, the timer beckons the referee to the table. The timer informs the referee that by mistake the period started with: (a) more; or (b) less than four minutes on the clock. **RULING:** In (a), if the mistake is discovered before the clock reaches four minutes, the clock shall be set at four minutes and play resumes. If discovered after reaching four minutes, no correction is allowed. In (b), the appropriate amount of time shall be added to reflect a four-minute period (2-5-5).

5.7.4 SITUATION: The score is tied at the end of regulation time. During the overtime period, the official scorer informs the referee that Team A had an additional point in the fourth quarter that was not counted. In (a), the referee reviews the scorebook and recognizes where a point was not properly credited to Team A; or (b) the referee does not have definite knowledge that a point was not credited to Team A. **RULING:** In (a), the referee adds a point to Team A's score. In (b), the referee does not add a point to Team A's score. In either case, the referee continues the overtime period to completion (2-11-11).

Scorebook Errors

The scorer shall compare records with the visiting scorer after each goal, each foul, each charged time-out, and end of each quarter and extra period, notifying the referee at once of any discrepancy. If the mistake cannot be found, the referee shall accept the record of the official scorebook, unless he/she has knowledge which permits him/her to decide otherwise. If the discrepancy is in the score and the mistake is not resolved, the referee shall accept the progressive team totals of the official scorebook. A bookkeeping mistake may be corrected at any time until the referee approves the final score. The scorebook of the home team shall be the official book, unless the referee rules otherwise. The official scorebook shall remain at the scorer's table throughout the game, including all intermissions (2-11-11).

Scorebook Errors: Caseplay

*2.11.11 SITUATION: Team A's scorebook is the official scorebook for the game. Team A's scorer is requested by Team A's head coach to bring the scorebook to the locker room at halftime to review several pieces of information. **RULING:** Prohibited; the scorebook shall remain at the table throughout the game, including all intermissions. There is no specific penalty for removing the scorebook; however, if the officials believe the scorebook was removed as an unsporting act, it could be penalized accordingly (10-1-8; 10-3-6; 10-4-1).

10.5.3 SITUATION: A5 has just received his/her fifth foul of the game. A5 (a) is erroneously permitted to remain in the game for another two minutes before the scorer realizes the mistake; or (b) leaves the game after the coach is notified of the disqualification. At the intermission between the third and fourth quarter, A5 reports as a substitute and subsequently enters the game. **RULING:** In (a), as soon as the error is discovered, the player is removed from the game, no penalties are assessed. In (b), A5 will not actually "participate" until the ball becomes live. If detected prior to the ball becoming live, A5 would be directed to the bench and no penalty assessed unless the official deemed it was a deliberate attempt to circumvent the rules. If detected after the ball becomes live, it is a technical foul charged directly to the head coach. The player is immediately removed from the game and Team B is awarded two free throws and the ball (2-11-5 Note 2).

Mistake in Order of Administration

Penalties for fouls are administered in the order in which the fouls occurred (8-7).

Mistake in Order of Administration: Caseplay

8.7 SITUATION B: B1 fouls A1 just as the first quarter ends and then A1 retaliates and intentionally contacts B1. A1's foul is a technical foul as it occurred during a dead ball. Team A is in the bonus. The officials by mistake administer the penalty for the technical foul before the free throw(s) by A1. **RULING:** The penalties should have been administered in the order in which the fouls occurred. However, since all merited free throws were attempted it does not constitute a correctable error situation. The second quarter will begin with an alternating-possession throw-in (4-19-5c).

Teams Going Wrong Way

If by mistake the officials permit a team to go the wrong direction, when discovered all points scored, fouls committed, and time consumed shall count as if each team had gone the proper direction. Play shall resume with each team going the proper direction based on bench location (4-5-4).

Teams Going Wrong Way: Caseplays

5.2.1 SITUATION E: During the pregame practice period, the visiting team properly uses the east goal and the home team the west goal. The officials, by mistake, allow the jumpers to face the wrong direction to start the game. A1 controls the tap by tapping the ball back to A2. A2, realizing that he/she had warmed up at the basket behind A1, dribbles to that basket and scores an uncontested basket. **RULING:** Score the basket for Team A. The officials should stop the game and emphasize to both teams the proper direction. The mistake is an official's error by allowing A1 and B1 to face the wrong direction; not a correctable error.

5.2.1 SITUATION F: During the pregame practice period, the visiting team properly uses the east goal and the home team the west goal. The officials, by mistake, allow the jumpers to face the wrong direction to start the game. Several baskets are scored before it is recognized that both teams are throwing the ball into the opponent's basket. **RULING:** All points scored count as if the teams had gone the right direction and scored in their own basket. Once the mistake is recognized, play shall continue with each team attempting to score in its own basket (4-5-4).

Topic 16

Time-outs, Halftime and Overtime

PlayPic™

Key Terms

A 60-second time-out charged to a team is a maximum of one minute in length. A 30-second time-out charged to a team is a maximum 30 seconds in length (4-43-1).

Topic:
Time-Outs

Number Allowed

Three 60-second and two 30-second time-outs may be charged to each team during a regulation game. Each team is entitled to one additional 60-second time-out during each extra period. Unused time-outs accumulate and may be used at any time (5-12-1).

State associations may determine the number of electronic media time-outs for games which are transmitted and may reduce the number of charged time-outs (5-12-1 Note).

Time-outs in excess of the allotted number may be requested and shall be granted during regulation playing time or any extra period at the expense of a technical foul for each (5-12-2).

Rationale

Thirty-second time-outs were increased from 20 seconds to give teams the equivalent of four 60-second time-outs, the original number allowed.

Number Allowed: Caseplays

5.8.4 SITUATION B: The head coach from Team A requests a 60-second time-out to rectify a timing error. The referee grants the time-out to investigate the matter, but determines that no correction can be made. The scorer then informs the referee that Team A cannot be charged a 60-second time-out as they only have one 30-second time-out remaining. **RULING:** Since they have no 60-second time-outs remaining and there was no timing correction made, Team A will be charged their remaining 30-second time-out regardless of the amount of time consumed (5-11-3).

5.12.1 SITUATION A: The state association has contractually arranged to have live telecasts of state semi-final and final games. One TV time-out each quarter will be permitted (at first dead ball closest to 3:30 remaining in quarter). The state association permits each team to have: (a) Two (2) 60-

second time-outs; (b) One (1) 60 and three (3) 30-second time-outs; (c) no 60 and four (4) 30-second time-outs; or (d) one (1) 60 and two (2) 30-second time-outs. **RULING:** State associations may reduce the number of charged timeouts, therefore, correct procedure in (a), (b), (c) and (d) (5-12-1 Note).

5.12.1 SITUATION B: The coach for Team A requests a 30-second time-out, but it is discovered that he/she does not have a 30-second time-out remaining, but does have one 60-second time-out remaining. The official grants the coach a 60-second time-out. **RULING:** The official was correct to grant the coach of Team A the last of his/her 60-second time-outs since the coach had already used two 60-second time-outs and two 30-second time-outs (5-11-2).

5.12.4 SITUATION B: Regulation play ends with a tied score. Even though Team A has used all its allowed time-outs. Team A requests a time-out before the overtime period begins. **RULING:** The time-out should not be granted. The additional 60-second time-out provided for each extra period(s) shall not be granted until after the ball has become live to start the extra period(s).

5.12.5 SITUATION: The state association has contractually arranged to have live telecasts of state semi-final and final games. One TV time-out each quarter will be permitted (at first dead ball closest to 3:30 remaining in quarter). The state association permits each team to have: (a) Two (2) 60 and two (2) 30-second time-outs; (b) one (1) 60 and three (3) 30-second time-outs; (c) no 60 and four (4) 30-second time-outs; or (d) one (1) 60 and two (2) 30-second time-outs. **RULING:** State associations may reduce the number of charged time-outs, therefore, correct procedure in (a), (b), (c) and (d).

When Time Expires

The ball becomes dead, or remains dead, when time expires for a quarter or extra period. However, the ball does not become dead until the try or tap ends, or until the airborne shooter returns to the floor, when time expires while a try or tap for a field goal is in flight (6-7-6; 6-7-6 Exc a).

Granting Time-outs

Time-out occurs and the clock, if running, shall be stopped when an official grants a player's/head coach's oral or visual request for a time-out. The request may be granted only when the ball is in control or at the disposal of a player of his/her team; the ball is dead, unless replacement of a disqualified, or injured player(s), or a player directed to leave the game is pending, and a substitute(s) is available and required (5-8-3a-b).

Rationale

A time-out can be used by a coach to confer with his/her players in a "cooling off" attempt when the game seems to be deteriorating and tempers are rising.

Granting Time-outs: Caseplays

5.8.3 SITUATION A: A1 fouls B1. The official who made the call moves toward the reporting area. A2 immediately signals the free official for a time-out. Momentarily thereafter, the scorer notifies the calling official that A1 has fouled out. **RULING:** A1 must be replaced before the time-out is granted.

COMMENT: The first responsibility the calling official has is to report the foul to the scorer. Officials should not be hasty in granting an immediate time-out after the game has reached a point that players may begin to foul out. Rather, they should take a second or two after reporting the foul to see if the scorer may report a disqualification (2-8-4; 10-5-3).

5.8.3 SITUATION B: Following a time-out, both teams are at the sideline with respective coaches after all signals have been given prior to a throw-in by Team A. Team A or Team B requests a time-out: (a) before; or (b) after, the official places the ball on the floor at the throw-in spot. **RULING:** In (a), either team may be granted a time-out. In (b), Team A may, but Team B may not be granted a time-out after the ball is at A's disposal.

> ## In Simple Terms
>
> A time-out can only be granted when the ball is in player control or the ball is dead.

5.8.3 SITUATION E: The official erroneously grants Team B a time-out in a situation when Team B cannot have one. What happens now? **RULING:** Team B is entitled to use the time-out since it was granted. The time-out once granted cannot be revoked and is charged to Team B. All privileges and rights permitted during a charged time-out are available to both teams.

> ## In Simple Terms
>
> A time-out may be granted until the conclusion of play. If a foul occurs at the end of regulation with no time remaining on the clock and free throws are forthcoming to decide the outcome, either coach may request a time-out until the outcome of the game has been decided.

5.12.4 SITUATION A: Team B requests a time-out following the first free throw for a technical foul which occurred prior to the start of the game. Should the official grant the request? **RULING:** The request should be granted. The ball became live when it was at the disposal of the free thrower.

Location

The 60-second time-out conference with team members shall be conducted within the confines of the time-out area. Players shall remain standing within the confines of the time-out area during a 30-second time-out (5-12-5).

Request Denied

A time-out shall not be granted until after the ball has become live to start the game. The additional 60-second time-out provided for each extra period(s) shall not be granted until after the ball has become live to start the extra period(s) (5-12-4).

Request Denied: Caseplays

*5.8.3 SITUATION C: A1 fouls B2. The scorer notifies the nearest official that this is A1's fifth foul. The official notifies the coach of Team A of the disqualification. The official then instructs the timer to begin the 20-second replacement period. The official then notifies A1. After 15 seconds have elapsed: (a) the captain of Team A; or (b) the captain of Team B requests a time-out. **RULING:** In (a) and (b), the time-out request is denied as disqualified A1 must be replaced prior to any time-out being granted to either team (2-8-4; 10-5-3).

5.8.3 SITUATION D: A1 or A2 requests a time-out: (a) while airborne A1 is holding the ball; (b) while A1's throw-in is in flight toward A2; or (c) when the ball is on the floor at A1's disposal for a throw-in. **RULING:** The request is granted in (a) and (c), but denied in (b), as there is no player control while the ball is loose between players.

5.8.3 SITUATION F: A1's dribble is "interrupted" when the ball deflects off his/her shoe. A1 or a teammate asks or signals for a time-out as the ball bounces toward: (a) the sideline; or (b) the division line. **RULING:** The request cannot be granted in (a) or (b), since A1's dribble has been "interrupted" and the ball is loose (4-15-6c).

5.12.4 SITUATION A: Team B requests a time-out: (a) as the teams position for the jump ball to start the game; or (b) just prior to the toss on the jump to start the game. Should the official grant the request?

RULING: The request should be denied in (a) and (b). The game must be started with the ball becoming live or by a violation or foul prior to this before a time-out request can be honored.

Time-outs: Scorer and Timer Duties

The scorer shall record the time-out information charged to each team (who and when) and notify a team and its coach, through an official, whenever that team is granted its final allotted charged time-out (2-11-6), and signal the nearer official each time a team is granted a time-out in excess of the allotted number (2-11-9).

The timer shall sound a warning signal 15 seconds before the expiration of a 60-second charged time-out and at 15 seconds of a 30-second time-out, immediately after which the players shall prepare to be ready to resume play, and signal again at the end of the time-out (2-12-4); sound a warning signal 15 seconds before the expiration of the 20 seconds (maximum) permitted for replacing a disqualified or injured player, or for a player directed to leave the game (2-12-5); stop the clock at the expiration of time for each quarter or extra period and when an official signals time-out; and, for an intermission or a charged time-out, start the stopwatch and signal the referee (2-12-6).

The official shall signal the timer to begin the 20-second interval for replacing an injured player after the injured player has been removed from the court and the coach has been notified that a replacement is required, except when the coach uses a time-out to keep the injured player in the game (2-12-5 Note).

 # Rationale

A warning signal was brought into the rules book in 1964 so that teams would break the time-out huddles at the appropriate time.

Time-outs: Scorer and Timer Duties: Caseplays

2.12.5 SITUATION: A4 commits his/her fifth foul. The official notifies the coach, then signals the timer to begin the 20-second interval for replacing the player and then notifies the player regarding the disqualification. In (a), the required substitute reports within 5 seconds; (b) no substitute has reported 10 seconds into the replacement interval; or (c) no substitute has reported by the end of the 20-second interval. **RULING:** In (a), the substitute is beckoned into the game by the officials and play resumes. In (b), the timer shall signal a warning horn when 5 seconds has elapsed. In (c), the timer shall signal a warning horn at 5 seconds and then sound another horn at 20 seconds if the required substitute has not reported to the scorer's table. A technical foul shall be assessed to the head coach (10-5-2 Penalty).

Successive Time-outs

A successive time-out is one which is granted to either team before the clock has started following the previous time-out (4-43-2).

Successive time-outs shall not be granted after expiration of playing time for the fourth quarter or any extra period (5-12-3).

Successive Time-outs: Caseplays

5.12.3 SITUATION A: A1 is fouled by B1 while in the act of shooting. While the try is in flight the horn sounds, ending the fourth quarter playing time. The ball continues its flight and goes through the basket to tie the score. Before A1 attempts the free throw as part of the fourth quarter, Team B captain requests and is granted a 60-second time-out. Team A or B captain then requests a 30-second time-out during the same dead-ball period. **RULING:** The second request is denied. At the end of playing time for the fourth quarter or any overtime period, successive time-outs shall not be granted. This means a time-out cannot be granted either team until the clock has run in the extra period – assuming the free throw is missed. Successive time-outs may be granted in all situations except after time has expired in the fourth quarter or any extra period.

5.12.3 SITUATION B: Following the expiration of time for the first extra period, the coach of Team B is charged with a technical foul. Team B requests a time-out before the free throws are administered to start the second extra period. The time-out request is granted. Thereafter, the official administers the first free throw to A1. Following the attempt: (a) Team B; or (b) Team A, then requests a time-out. **RULING:** The request cannot be granted in either (a) or (b), as it would be considered a successive time-out. The fact that the ball did become live between the two requests has no bearing on the ruling. Another time-out request by either team cannot be honored until after the clock has started in the second extra period.

Time-out Ends

A single 60-second time-out charged to a team shall not exceed one minute. A warning signal for the teams to prepare to be ready to resume play is sounded at 45 seconds. Such a time-out shall not be reduced in length unless both teams are ready to play before the time-out is over (5-11-1).

 Did You Know? In the original rules of basketball, the only player allowed to call time-out was the captain.

A single 30-second charged time-out shall not exceed 30 seconds. A warning signal for teams to prepare to be ready to resume play is sounded with 15 seconds remaining. No on-court entertainment should occur during this time (5-11-2).

Time-out Ends: Caseplay

5.11.1 SITUATION: Team A requests and is granted a 60-second time-out. After approximately 15 seconds of the time-out period has elapsed: (a) Team A comes back on the court ready to play while Team B players stay at their bench; (b) Team B is ready but Team A is not; or (c) both teams take positions and appear ready to resume play. **RULING:** In (a) and (b), the time-out period will continue as only one team is ready to play. In (c), the game will resume as soon as both teams are ready to play.

Topic:
Halftime

Duration

Games shall include an intermission of 10 minutes between halves. The halftime intermission may be extended to a maximum of 15 minutes for special activities, provided home management has properly notified the visiting team prior to the start of the game (5-5-1).

Referee's Duties

The referee shall confer with the official scorer at halftime to determine the possession arrow is pointed in the proper direction to begin play in the third quarter (2-5-6) and check and approve the score at the end of each half (2-5-7).

Halftime: Timer's Duties

The timer shall note when each half is to start and shall notify the referee more than three minutes before this time so the referee may notify the teams, or cause them to be notified, at least three minutes before the half is to start (2-12-1); sound a warning signal 15 seconds before the expiration of an intermission, immediately after which the players shall prepare to be ready to resume play; and signal again at the end of the intermission (2-12-4).

Topic:
Overtime

An extra period is the extension of playing time necessary to break a tie score. The length of each extra period is four minutes (4-17).

If the score is tied at the end of the fourth quarter, play shall continue without change of baskets for one or more extra periods with a one-minute intermission before each extra period (5-7-1). The game ends if, at the end of any extra period, the score is not tied (5-7-2).

The length of each extra period shall be four minutes (or half the time of a regulation quarter for non-varsity contests). As many periods as are necessary to break the tie shall be played. Extra periods are an extension of the fourth quarter (5-7-3).

Once the ball becomes live in the extra period, it will be played even though a correction in the fourth quarter score is made (5-7-4).

Overtime: Caseplays

5.7.1 SITUATION: The score is B-62, A-60 when A1 is fouled with no time on the clock in the fourth quarter. The horn sounds immediately after the foul is called. Team A is not in the bonus but erroneously A1 is awarded a bonus and makes both free throws to tie the score. Team B controls the jump to start the overtime and B1 scores to make it 64 to 62. Before the ball becomes live on the subsequent throw-in, the scorer alerts the officials regarding a correctable-error situation. **RULING:** The error is corrected by canceling the two erroneous free throws. However, once the overtime started with the ball becoming live, the extra period cannot be canceled even though the points were. The score is B-64, A-60 and the overtime continues with the throw-in by Team A (2-10-1b; 2-11-11; 5-7-4).

5.7.3 SITUATION: Following a violation in the first extra period, the timer beckons the referee to the table. The timer informs the referee that by mistake the period started with: (a) more; or (b) less than four minutes on the clock. **RULING:** In (a), if the mistake is discovered before the clock reaches four minutes, the clock shall be set at four minutes and play resumes. If discovered after reaching four minutes, no correction is allowed. In (b), the appropriate amount of time shall be added to reflect a four-minute period (2-5-5).

5.7.4 SITUATION: The score is tied at the end of regulation time. During the overtime period, the official scorer informs the referee that Team A had an additional point in the fourth quarter that was not counted. In (a), the referee reviews the scorebook and recognizes where a point was not properly credited to Team A; or (b) the referee does not have definite knowledge that a point was not credited to Team A. **RULING:** In (a), the referee adds a point to Team A's score. In (b), the referee does not add a point to Team A's score. In either case, the referee continues the overtime period to completion (2-11-11).

In 1961, the "sudden death" overtime was eliminated and changed to three-minute overtime periods.

Topic 17

Officials and Their Duties

PlayPic™

Key Terms

The game officials shall be a referee and an umpire or a referee and two umpires who shall be assisted by an official timer and scorer (2-1-2). The official's uniform shall be a black-and-white striped shirt, black pants, black shoes and black socks (2-1-1).

Topic:
Authority and Duties of the Referee

The referee shall make decisions on any points not specifically covered in the rules (2-3).

Prior to the game, the referee shall Inspect and approve all equipment, including court, baskets, ball, backboards, and timer's and scorer's signals (2-4-1). He or she should also designate the official timepiece and official timer prior to the scheduled starting time of the game (2-4-2) and the official scorebook and official scorer prior to the scheduled starting time of the game (2-4-3).

 COMMENT: A state association may authorize use of supplementary equipment to aid in game administration.

The referee shall be responsible for having each team notified three minutes before each half is to begin (2-4-4). Prior to each contest, the head coach shall verify that his/her team member's uniforms and equipment are legal and will be worn properly, and that all participants will exhibit proper sporting behavior throughout the contest (2-4-5).

During the game, the referee shall designate the official to toss the ball in the center-restraining circle for all jump-ball situations (2-5-1).

 COMMENT: If the referee feels one of the other officials is better suited to toss the ball to start the game, he or she shall designate that official to toss the ball as indicated in the 2007-09 Official's Manual.

The referee shall administer the alternating-possession throw-in to start the second, third and fourth quarters (2-5-2) and decide whether a goal shall count if the officials disagree (2-5-3). The referee may declare the game a forfeit when conditions warrant (2-5-4) and shall decide matters upon which the timer and scorer disagree and correct obvious timing errors (2-5-5).

In addition the referee shall confer with the official scorer at halftime to determine the possession arrow is pointed in the proper direction to begin play in the third quarter (2-5-6) and check and approve the score at the end of each half (2-5-7).

The referee shall not permit any team member to participate if in his/her judgment, any item constitutes a safety concern, such as, but not limited to, a player's fingernails or hairstyle (3-7).

Authority and Duties of the Referee: Caseplays

2.4.3 SITUATION: Prior to the game, the home team athletic director informs the officials that the school has purchased a new timing system whereby the game clock is controlled by the game officials via their whistle and a timing pack. **RULING:** The device shall not be used unless the state association has approved its use and the game officials have been properly instructed/trained on how to use the equipment (2-4-3 Note).

2.4.4 SITUATION: Following pregame warm-ups, Team A returns to its dressing room. The referee has each team notified three minutes before the game is scheduled to begin. Despite this notification, Team A delays the start of the game for nearly two minutes by not returning to the court. The referee determines there is no excusable reason for Team A's tardiness. **RULING:** Team A is charged with a technical foul for delaying the start of the game by a minute or more (10-1-5a).

2.4.5 SITUATION A: Before the contest both coaches verify that their teams are legally equipped. In the third quarter A1 is discovered wearing a ring. **RULING:** A1 must leave the game and remove the jewelry and may re-enter the game at the next substitution opportunity, but no penalty is assessed against A1 or the coach.

2.4.5 SITUATION B: To the referee's pregame inquiry of coaches regarding all team members being legally equipped and wearing the uniform properly, both coaches responded "yes." Three minutes into the first quarter, U1 observes A5 with a tongue stud. **RULING:** When the tongue stud is noticed, A5 must leave the game and may not return until the stud has been removed. There is no technical foul assessed (3-5-6).

Topic:
Officials Authority and
General Duties

The officials shall conduct the game in accordance with the rules. This includes:

• Notifying the captains when play is about to begin at the start of the game (2-7-1).

• Putting the ball in play (2-7-2).

• Determining when the ball becomes dead (2-7-3).

• Prohibiting practice during a dead ball, except between halves (2-7-4).

• Administering penalties (2-7-5).

• Granting time-out (2-7-6).

• Beckoning substitutes to enter the court (2-7-7).

• Signaling a three-point goal by raising two arms extended overhead (2-7-8).

• Silently and visibly counting seconds to administer the throw-in (7-6), free-throw (8-4; 9-1-3), backcourt (9-8) and closely-guarded (9-10) rules (2-7-9).

• Report a team warning for delay to the official scorer and then to the coach (2-7-10).

The officials shall penalize unsporting conduct by any player, coach, substitute, team attendant or follower (2-8-1). The officials shall penalize and disqualify the offender if flagrant misconduct occurs (2-8-2); remove a player from the game who commits his/her fifth foul (personal and technical) (2-8-3); notify the coach and request the timer to begin the replacement interval, and then notify the player on a disqualification (2-8-4); and determine when a player is apparently unconscious. The player may not return to play in the game without written authorization from a physician (MD/DO) (2-8-5).

COMMENT: Unsporting tactics, in general, involve relationships between opponents, between the players and officials, between the spectators and officials, between the players and spectators, between the coaches and spectators and between coaches and officials. In some situations, it can also apply to the relationship of a player to teammates and to the coach and members of the team. For example, profanity on the part of a participant, coach or member of the team is considered to be an unsporting act, whether or not the profanity is directed at any individual or is merely a means of "letting off steam" (10-1-8; 10-3-6; 10-4-1).

Officials Authority and General Duties: Caseplay

2.8.1 SITUATION: What guidelines should be exercised by the officials when spectators' actions are such that they interfere with the administration of the game? **RULING:** The rules book states "the official may call fouls on either team if its supporters act in such a way as to interfere with the proper conduct of the game." It is significant to note the word used is "may." This gives permission, but does not in any way imply that officials must call technical fouls on team followers or supporters for unsporting acts. Thus, while officials do have the authority to penalize a team whose spectators interfere with the proper conduct of the game, this authority must be used with extreme caution and discretion. While the authority is there, the official must rarely use it, because experience has demonstrated that calling hasty technical fouls on the crowd rarely solves the problem and may, in fact, result in penalizing the wrong team because the official may not have proper knowledge as to which team's supporters were responsible for the unsporting act.

COMMENT: The home management or game committee is responsible for spectator behavior, insofar as it can reasonably be expected to control the spectators. The officials may call fouls on either team if its supporters act in such a way as to interfere with the proper conduct of the game. Discretion must be used in calling such fouls, however, lest a team be unjustly penalized. When team supporters become unruly or interfere with the orderly progress of the game, the officials shall stop the game until the host management resolves the situation and the game can proceed in an orderly manner. In the absence of a designated school representative, the home coach shall serve as the host management.

Official's Signals

When a foul occurs, an official shall signal the timer to stop the clock. The official shall designate the offender to the scorer and indicate with finger(s) the number of free throws (2-9-1). When a team is entitled to a throw-in, an official shall signal the timer to stop the clock and clearly signal the act which caused the ball to become dead, the team entitled to the throw-in and the throw-in spot unless it follows a successful goal or an awarded goal (2-9-2 a through c).

Topic:
Official's Jurisdiction

No official has the authority to set aside or question decisions made by the other official(s) within the limits of their respective outlined duties (3-6).

The officials shall make decisions for infractions of the rules committed within or outside the boundary lines. The use of any replay or television monitoring equipment by the officials in making any decision relating to the game is prohibited (2-2-1).

NOTE: A state association may permit game or replay officials to use a replay monitor during state championship series contests to determine if a try for goal at the expiration of time in the fourth quarter or any overtime period (0:00 on the game clock) should be counted, and if so, determine if it is a two- or a three-point goal.

The officials' jurisdiction, prior to the game, begins when they arrive on the floor. The officials' arrival on the floor shall be at least 15 minutes before the scheduled starting time of the game (2-2-2). The officials' jurisdiction extends through periods when the game may be momentarily stopped for any reason (2-2-3).

The jurisdiction of the officials' is terminated and the final score has been approved when all officials leave the visual confines of the playing area (2-2-4).

◻ Rationale

A state association may now permit game or replay officials to utilize available replay equipment to determine the outcome of a state championship series game. Individual state associations will determine if the equipment will be used, at what tournament round(s) and by whom. This same technology is already being utilized after state contests by the media and being showcased on the internet. State administrators should also be permitted to use this same technology, if available and desired, to assist in making the correct call when the outcome of the game hangs in the balance and a team has no further opportunities to overcome a critical error.

Official's Jurisdiction: Caseplays

*2.2.1 SITUATION A: During a state championship series contest in which the state association has authorized the use of video replay, A4 releases a try as time expires in a tie game; the try is successful. The covering official rules that the attempt was still in A4's hands when time expired and waves off the basket, forcing overtime. **RULING:** Since the try occurred at the end of the game, with zeros on the game clock, a review is permissible. The replay official rules that the shot was released prior to the expiration of time. The game officials count the basket and declare Team A the winner.

*2.2.1 SITUATION B: Prior to the game, the home team athletic director informs the officials that the school has purchased a new state-of-the-art scoreboard with video replay capabilities to review end-of-game situations. **RULING:** The video replay equipment shall not be used. Video replay is only permitted by authorization of the state association at the conclusion of state association championship series contests (2-2-1 Note).

2.2.4 SITUATION A: The score is Team A-62 and Team B-61 when the horn sounds to end the fourth quarter. Prior to the referee's approval of the final score, the coach of Team A directs obscene gestures at the officials. **RULING:** A technical foul is charged and the result of the free throws will determine which team wins or whether an extra period is required (5-6-4; 10-4-1c).

2.2.4 SITUATION B: Time expires to end the game with a score of 64-61. Immediately following the signal to end the fourth quarter, the officials are moving off the court toward a door to their dressing room. The referee enters the door and is in the hallway to the locker room, but the umpire is still in the court area when he/she notices the scorer frantically trying to get the officials' attention due to a possible scorebook error. **RULING:** Since one of the officials has not left the visual confines of the playing area, the game jurisdiction has not ended. The officials may work with scorer's table personnel to rectify any errors.

2.2.4 SITUATION C: Team B leads by a point with seconds remaining in the fourth quarter. A1 releases the ball on a try, but the noise level makes it difficult for the covering official (umpire) to hear the horn. The umpire signals a successful goal. The referee definitely hears the horn before A1 releases the ball, but does not realize the umpire counted the goal. The officials leave the visual confines of the playing area and are not aware of the controversy until the scorer comes to the officials' dressing room. **RULING:** Even though the referee could have canceled the score if the officials had conferred before leaving, once the officials leave the visual confines of the playing area, the final score is official and no change can be made. In situations such as this, it is imperative that officials communicate with each other and that they do not leave until any problem regarding scoring or timing has been resolved.

2.6 SITUATION A: The umpire observes traveling, stepping out of bounds or another violation by A1. At approximately the same time, A1 tries for a field goal or the referee observes contact by B1 on A1. **RULING:** The officials must decide definitely which act occurred first. There is no rules coverage to administer the acts as occurring simultaneously. If the violation occurred first, the ball became dead. If the ball was in flight during the try before the touching of the boundary, there was no violation. If the contact occurred after a violation was observed, it is not a foul unless the contact is intentional or flagrant.

2.6 SITUATION B: A violation and personal contact occur at about the same time. Both are observed by the same official, or the violation is observed by one official and the contact by the other. What is the proper procedure? **RULING:** The officials shall decide which occurred first. If the violation was first, it caused the ball to become dead; hence, the contact which followed was not a foul unless intentional or flagrant. If the contact occurred first, it caused the ball to become dead and no violation occurred.

Start Clock

Stop Clock

**Stop Clock for
Jump/Held Ball**

Stop Clock for Foul

**Stop Clock for Foul
(Optional 'Bird Dog')**

Directional Signal

Designated Spot

Visible Count

Beckon Substitute

60-Second Time-out

30-Second Time-out

Not Closely Guarded

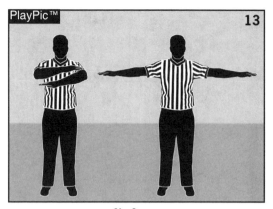

No Score

Goal Counts

Point(s) Scored: Use 1 or
2 fingers after signal 14

3-point Field Goal

Bonus Free Throw

Delayed Lane Violation

Traveling

Illegal Dribble

Over and Back or
Palming/Carrying Violation

Three-second Violation

5-second Violation

10-second Violation

**Free Throw, Designated
Spot or Other Violation**

**Excessive Swinging
of Arms or Elbows**

Kicking

Illegal Use of Hand

Hand-checking

Holding

Blocking

Pushing or Charging

Player Control

Team Control

Intentional Foul

Double Foul

Technical Foul

COACHES-OFFICIALS

MEMBERSHIP INFORMATION

NFHS Coaches Association
NFHS Officials Association

$30.00 ANNUAL DUES INCLUDES

ONE COACH AND ONE OFFICIAL SERVE ON EACH NFHS RULES COMMITTEE!

GENERAL LIABILITY INSURANCE

COACHES' OR OFFICIALS' QUARTERLY SUBSCRIPTION

AWARDS AND RECOGNITION!

———————— JOIN NOW ————————

NOTE: *DO NOT USE FOR CHEER/SPIRIT COACHES - REQUEST NFHS SPIRIT ASSOCIATION FORM FROM ADDRESS BELOW*

COACHES ASSOCIATION   OFFICIALS ASSOCIATION

Mr/Mrs/Ms: _____ First Name: _____ M.I. _____ Last Name: _____
(as it appears on your driver's license)

Home Address: _____ This is a new address ☐

City: _____ State/Province _____ Zip _____

Country: _____ Fax: ( ) _____

School/Organization Phone: ( ) _____ Home Phone: ( ) _____

For Insurance Purposes:
Social Security Number _____ Birthdate _____ ☐ Male ☐ Female

E-Mail Address: _____

Primary area of interest/expertise (sport) _____

First Year Officiating _____

First Year Coaching _____

CHECK TYPE OF MEMBERSHIP
☐ **COACH** $30.00
☐ **OFFICIAL** $30.00
(Residents of foreign countries add $9.00 mailing costs)
☐ Check ☐ VISA ☐ MasterCard ☐ American Express

Account No.: _____ - _____ - _____ - _____

Exp. Date: _____ Card Security Code: _____
(call your merchant card provider for location of code.)

Cardholder Name _____

No purchase orders accepted

I WORK PRIMARILY IN: *(Check only one)*

☐ High School Sports
☐ College Sports
☐ Youth League Sports

DO NOT MAIL FORM WITHOUT PAYMENT
One annual payment provides member benefits for one year from the date payment is received by the NFHS.

Mail Payment to: NFHS
PO Box 690
Indianapolis, IN 46206

Signature _____

TOTAL AMOUNT ENCLOSED $_____

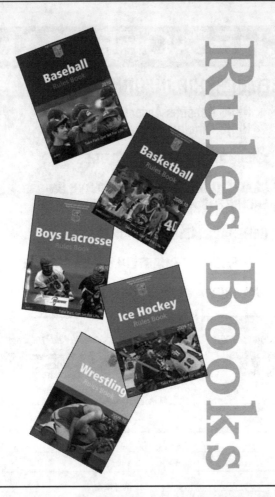

NFHS PUBLICATIONS
Prices effective April 1, 2009 — March 31, 2010

RULES PUBLICATIONS

Baseball Rules Book	$7.20
Baseball Case Book	$7.20
Baseball Umpires Manual (2009 & 2010)	$7.20
Baseball Simplified & Illustrated Rules	$7.95
Baseball Rules by Topic	$7.95
Basketball Rules Book	$7.20
Basketball Case Book	$7.20
Basketball Simplified & Illustrated Rules	$7.95
Basketball Officials Manual (2009-11)	$7.20
Basketball Handbook (2008-10)	$7.20
Basketball Rules by Topic	$7.95
Field Hockey Rules Book	$7.20
Football Rules Book	$7.20
Football Case Book	$7.20
Football Simplified & Illustrated Rules	$7.95
Football Handbook (2009 & 2010)	$7.20
Football Officials Manual (2008 & 2009)	$7.20
Football Rules by Topic	$7.95

Girls Gymnastics Rules Book & Manual (2008-10)	$7.20
Ice Hockey Rules Book	$7.20
Boys Lacrosse Rules Book	$7.20
Soccer Rules Book	$7.20
Softball Rules Book	$7.20
Softball Case Book	$7.20
Softball Umpires Manual (2010 & 2011)	$7.20
Spirit Rules Book	$7.20
Swimming, Diving & Water Polo Rules Book	$7.20
Track & Field Rules Book	$7.20
Track & Field Case Book	$7.20
Track & Field Manual (2009 & 2010)	$7.20
Volleyball Rules Book	$7.20
Volleyball Case Book & Manual	$7.20
Wrestling Rules Book	$7.20
Wrestling Case Book & Manual	$7.20

MISCELLANEOUS ITEMS

NFHS Statisticians' Manual	$6.75
Scorebooks: Baseball-Softball, Basketball, Swimming & Diving, Cross Country, Soccer, Track & Field, Gymnastics, Volleyball, Wrestling and Field Hockey	$11.20
Diving Scoresheets (pad of 100)	$7.25
Volleyball Team Rosters & Lineup Sheets (pads of 100)	$7.25
Libero Tracking Sheet (pads of 50)	$7.25
Baseball/Softball Lineup Sheets - 3-Part NCR (sets/100)	$8.75
Wrestling Tournament Match Cards (sets/100)	$7.25
Flipping Coin	$5.50
NFHS Pin	$4.00
Competitors Numbers (Track and Gymnastics – Waterproof, nontearable, black numbers and six colors of backgrounds	
Numbers are 1-1000 sold in sets of 100	$15.00/set
Lane Numbers (1-8), size 4" x 2 1/2"	$7.25/set

MISCELLANEOUS SPORTS ITEMS

High School Sports Record Book (2009)	$13.20
Court and Field Diagram Guide	$20.20
NFHS Handbook (2008-09)	$9.00
Let's Make It Official	$5.00

Sportsmanship. It's Up to You. Toolkit	19.95
High School Activities — A Community Investment in America	$39.95

2009-10 NFHS ORDER BLANK

Name_____ Phone _____

School and/or Organization _____

Address _____

_____

| City | State | Zip |

(No PO Boxes. If charging order to a credit card please use address on card.)
If address has changed in the last year please fill in old address.

_____

| Street | City | State | Zip |

Check one of the following: ☐ Visa   ☐ MasterCard

Account No. _____ - _____ - _____ Exp. Date_____

Signature _____

P.O. # _____ (Order totals $50 or more)
                    (attach P.O.)

Item#	Description	Quantity	Unit Price	Total

SHIPPING & HANDLING CHARGES: If your subtotal is:

$10.00 to $15.00 ....add **$7.95** $75.01 to $100.00 ...add **$15.95**
$15.01 to $25.00 ....add **$9.95** $100.01 to $250.00 .add **$18.95**
$25.01 to $50.00 .....add **$10.95** $250.01 to $500.00 .add **$21.95**
$50.01 to $75.00 .....add **$12.95**   Over $500.01 add 5% of subtotal

Second Day = Standard shipping charges plus **$15.00**
Overnight = Standard shipping charges plus **$25.00**
All shipments to Alaska, Hawaii, Virgin Islands and Canada – add **$10.00**
Call for charges outside continental U.S.
Minimum purchase on each order $10.00 before shipping charges

Subtotal _____

Shipping &
Handling Charge _____

TOTAL _____

Send to: **NFHS CUSTOMER SERVICE**
PO Box 361246, INDIANAPOLIS, IN 46236-5324
Phone 800-776-3462, Fax 317.899.7496 or online at www.nfhs.com

ORDERING INFORMATION

PURCHASE ORDERS are welcomed but all orders under $50 must be prepaid. Purchase orders may be **either faxed or mailed** to our Customer Service office. If you mail a purchase order after it has been faxed to our Customer Service office, please show it as a **confirming order**. All back-ordered items will be billed additional shipping charges. Terms net 30 days per invoice. All delinquent accounts are charged 1.5% finance charges. **PREPAID ORDERS** will be shipped upon receipt of completed order form accompanied by a check or money order. **All orders must include the proper amount for shipping and handling.**
*SHIPMENTS OUTSIDE UNITED STATES OR CANADA: Please write to NFHS headquarters for a quotation of total charges which will include a $2.00 surcharge and actual shipping charges. **Payment must be in U.S. dollars.** Please refer to www.nfhs.com to view our Return Policy.